published in 1989 to mark the 170th anniversary of Peterloo,
was his last book. He died in 1990.

## ALSO BY ROBERT REID

# The Peterloo Massacre

ROBERT REID

 WINDMILL BOOKS

1 3 5 7 9 10 8 6 4 2

Windmill Books
20 Vauxhall Bridge Road
London S W 1V 2S A

Windmill Books is part of the Penguin Random House group of companies
whose addresses can be found at global.penguinrandomhouse.com.

 Penguin
Random House
UK

First published in Great Britain by William Heinemann in 1989
Reissued in paperback by Windmill Books in 2018

www.penguin.co.uk

A C IP catalogue record for this book is available from the British Library.

ISBN 9781786090409

Typeset in 12/15 pt Fournier MT Std by Jouve (UK), Milton Keynes
Printed and bound in Great Britain by Clays Ltd, St Ives Plc

 MIX
Paper from
responsible sources
FSC
www.fsc.org  FSC® C018179

Penguin Random House is committed to a
sustainable future for our business, our readers
and our planet. This book is made from Forest
Stewardship Council® certified paper.

# CONTENTS

v

## Contents

# MAPS

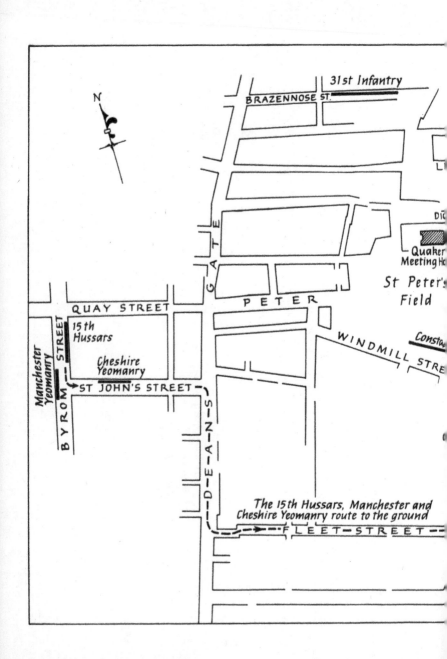

LOYD STREET

COOPER STREET

The Manchester Yeomanry route to the ground

NICHOLAS STREET

MOSLEY STREET

PORTLAND ST.

Manchester Yeomanry

DICKENSON STREET

88 Infantry

use

STREET

St Peter's Church

Magistrates assembled here

STREET

les

ET

Royal Horse Artillery
(two 6-pounders)

LOWER MOSLEY STREET

## ST PETER'S FIELD

showing the positions at about 1:30 p m on 16 August 1819

The Manchester Yeomanry (2 troops, Portland Street)
(1 troop, Byrom Street)

The Cheshire Yeomanry (St John's St.)

15th Hussars (Byrom St.)

31st Regiment (Brazennose St.)

88th Regiment (Dickenson St.)

Royal Horse Artillery (Lower Mosley St.)

Line of Constables (St Peter's Field)

0          100          200
Scale of Yards

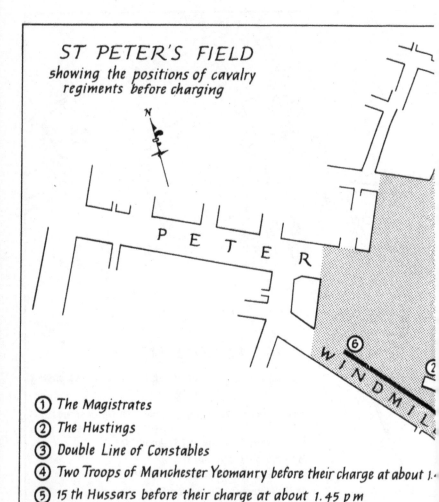

ST PETER'S FIELD

showing the positions of cavalry
regiments before charging

N

PETER

W
I
N
D
M
I
L
L

⑥

②

① The Magistrates
② The Hustings
③ Double Line of Constables
④ Two Troops of Manchester Yeomanry before their charge at about 1.
⑤ 15 th Hussars before their charge at about 1.45 pm
⑥ Cheshire Yeomanry before their charge at about 1.45 pm
⑦ 88 th Regiment before advancing to the Quakers' Meeting House

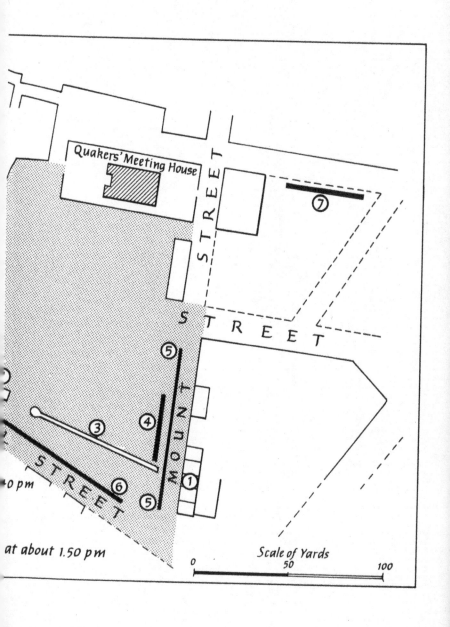

Quakers' Meeting House

STREET

S T R E E T

MOUNT

STREET

⑦

⑤

④

③

①

⑤

⑥

·0 pm

at about 1.50 pm

Scale of Yards
0          50          100

# INTRODUCTION

The conflict at the focal point of this book is a unique incident which stains the long path leading to the emancipation of the people of Britain. The name Peterloo is well-known, but what it involved is becoming less familiar to successive generations. The intermingling of characters involved in the Luddite Revolt with those intimately concerned with Peterloo provided a sure guide to the contemporary sources; these supply key evidence of the events leading to the Massacre. In chronicling these events I have laid emphasis on the critical role played by technological change. In parts, I have repeated some ideas concerning technology and its signal power from a previous book, *Land of Lost Content*, which dealt with the Luddite Revolt. I have done this because I believe these ideas are important to an understanding of the conditions leading to Peterloo, and the lessons to be learnt from it – and, no less, to an understanding of the problematical forces shaping our present civilisation.

I am deeply in the debt of J. E. Stanfield for his invaluable advice which helped shape my manuscript. Equally, I must thank Dr Robert Glen, not only for his informed comments, but also for the use I was able to make of his scholarly study, *Urban Workers in the Early Industrial Revolution*. Of books dealing with events leading to Peterloo, I have found Dr Donald Read's *Peterloo, the 'Massacre' and its Background* to be the most informative and the most reliable.

I am grateful to the librarians of the British Library, Chester Library, Chester Record Office, Chetham's Library, Manchester, Colindale Newspaper Library, Doncaster Borough Council Archives Department, Balby, Doncaster Central Library, Exeter Library, the John Rylands University Library of Manchester, the London Library, Manchester Central Library, the National Horseracing Museum, Newmarket, the Public Record Office, the RIBA, the Royal Institution and Stockport Public Library for the generous help they have all unfailingly given.

# I

# The Soldier's Return

In the autumn of 1816, the senior British officer who, the previous year, had commanded the second Guards division at
Waterloo, stood one day on a beautifully contoured patch of
ground above the Norman tower on the edge of an English
village and reconnoitred the unhindered view south. He took
particular note of the fields to his front leading down to
Campsall church, and to the rolling, long-settled countryside
beyond. Behind him was a substantial stone-built mansion.
From its windows, over its walled gardens, there was a view
in every direction as commanding as that which the soldier
contemplated. The historic name of the hill, Campsmount,
described adequately enough the site's military potential.

The general, Sir John Byng, had had a military career
which had not been short of either experience or incident.
He had many times served under Wellington, had been
wounded more than once in military encounters, had on one
occasion in the Peninsula in 1813 personally charged through
to plant the colours of the 31st Regiment behind enemy lines,

and had been knighted before he even reached the field of Waterloo.[1]

The modern visitor to Campsmount can still extract from the view – but with difficulty – what so engrossed Byng. The general's aspect to the south was one of unblemished rural beauty. But today, there is a striking addition. Some distance beyond the patchwork fields of corn and grass still descending to the Norman church tower, rises an incongruous hulk: a prominent red-brick Victorian scab to which, over many years, have been added vast asbestos-clad structures, warehouses, winding gear and coal shutes. This is the coal mine at Askern. The nineteenth-century South Yorkshire town of the same name which spread as the pit's productivity grew, stands alongside, its houses in the new smokeless age, no longer pushing out the coal fumes which for decades blackened their walls.

The panorama from Campsmount provides a vivid example of how the demands of nineteenth-century technology overwhelmed both the rural English landscape and its economy, enriching the nation and transforming forever the way of life of its inhabitants.

The purpose of General Byng's visit to this hillside, paradoxically, was to discover a place where he could be sure to be free of the sight which today assaults the visitor. He had just come from a district where the dominant image – that of the process of the transformation of Britain – was too evident and too brutal to his sensitivities. In 1816, from this South Yorkshire vantage point, any sign of the metamorphosis was invisible. And the fact was, that the indisputable military advantages and defensive capabilities of Campsmount were of no interest whatever to him. Still fully employed as a lieutenant general in an England no longer at war, he had come — temporarily at least — to seek his personal peace here.

The eighteenth-century mansion behind him was owned by the Yarborough family and was to be let, fully furnished, along with its Manor Garden, Pleasure Ground, farmyard and buildings for £150 per annum. The surrounding 400 acres of high quality farmland were also being offered for a further £400 and additional acreage could be made available when required.[2] Costly as these sums were, the farming prospects presented by such an estate with such excellent corn and root-crop potential were considerable. John Byng, who most certainly needed to augment his military pay, estimated the business possibilities of Campsmount very favourably.

There was, however, one further highly desirable quality of the site which made him look on it with an even keener eye. Byng was the owner of an expensive and obsessive habit. Scarcely a better place could be imagined in which to indulge it than here.

The Manor House had been mostly built by the Yorkshire mason Robert Carr. But part of its structure — and certainly that part in which John Byng was most interested — had been designed by Carr's talented, self-taught architect son John. It was later said of this young man, 'It was to Carr's good taste that so many families in the county of York are indebted for the comforts and elegancies of their dwelling.'[3] In Britain at this time, interest in horse racing and breeding were nowhere more fervent than here in Yorkshire. One piece of architecture at York Races had attracted the attention of the gentry. It was the product of the untutored John Carr's extraordinary gifts: his elegant design for the Knavesmire grandstand. Many important commissions for houses had followed. However, his skill at designing with stables had been well noted. Soon his work was to include the magnificent octagon at Buxton – with stabling for 300 horses – for the Duke of Devonshire, and the quadrangle at Wentworth Woodhouse which the Marquess of Rockingham had financed from the winnings of his beautiful and fabulously successful racehorse, Whistle Jacket.[4]

The double block which housed the stables at Campsmount and which Sir John Byng examined that day, had been one of young John Carr's first commissions for a north country grandee.[5] These were the buildings – more than adequate to house a personal string of racehorses in style and comfort – on which John Byng fixed his eye on his first visit.

For Byng's grand passion was his bloodstock. And like many of his contemporaries, he was caught up in the fashionable Regency obsession with gambling which was inseparable from the sport. He was more than ready to bet substantial sums of money in support of his judgement as owner and breeder.

There were other features supporting the attraction of Campsmount's location. It was within hacking distance of some of the great racing centres of northern England. Seven miles to the south was Doncaster, the home of one of the country's greatest classic races where, each season, phenomenal sums of money were placed in bets. To the north, at the same distance, lay Pontefract and its course. The fashionable York meetings were only another 20 miles beyond.

To Byng, after many years spent so faithfully and fearlessly serving his country abroad, this place can have seemed little short of an equine Eden.

Byng's move to northern England had not been of his own choice. That decision had been taken by the Home Secretary who, in the autumn of 1816, appointed him to the command of the Northern Forces. When Byng had appeared for his interview at the Home Office, Lord Sidmouth had discovered for the first time how distinguished, how active but also how circumscribed Byng's career had been. Since the age of 15, Byng readily admitted, he had known nothing but the army life. Almost the whole of his adulthood had been spent in military service on the European continent. And probably the most significant feature of Byng's *curriculum vitae*, as far as Sidmouth was concerned, was the experience he had gained as a young soldier suppressing rebellion – terrorism it would be called today – in Ireland, where again he had been wounded.

The ability to put down violent rebellion and to deal firmly with civil unrest were qualities the Home Secretary knew from vivid experience to be imperative for the Northern Commander if he were to succeed in his job. The previous appointee, General the Hon. Thomas Maitland had possessed these skills, and several more, which had made him ideal for the appointment.

In 1812, Maitland had effectively destroyed the Luddites. With the well-advertised and well-attended public hanging of 17 men, Maitland had ended their rebellion and taken the north country back from the edge of revolution.

But the technological forces which had unbalanced the emerging industrial nation four years earlier, now that Napoleon had been defeated, had not disappeared with the arrival of peace. Indeed, within a year of Waterloo, the Home Secretary – who had never visited the north of England – was being told by reliable magistrates in every manufacturing town of the north that the signs of discontent that had led to the Luddites' violence were as overt and worrying as they had ever been. And, just as it had been four years before, techno-logical change was fuelling the bubbling unrest.

This was the reason why Lord Sidmouth had chosen to interview Byng for his putative appointment on the active Military List. Sidmouth found the man he faced to be in extreme contrast to the extrovert, florid, prolix but politically astute General Thomas Maitland. Byng was precise, well ordered in his personal habits, as in other matters, to the point of obsession, and a man of few and direct words. At that first meeting, he at once gave Sidmouth a short summary of his position. He owned that, in addition to knowing no life what-ever but that of the army, he had had little time for politics. Nevertheless, if he were to go into Parliament it would be in opposition to Sidmouth's Tory Party.

Sidmouth perhaps thought he recognised in this trim, curt though courteous general a kindred spirit with a regi-mented accounting mentality; or perhaps he believed that Byng's undisciplined education would prevent any political or humanitarian concerns from interfering with the execution of orders from above. Whatever the reason, on the basis of this one interview, Sidmouth came to the decision that he had unquestionably found the right man for the right job. He told Byng, 'From this moment you have my entire confidence', and turning to his secretary gave instructions that every confidential letter on file concerning the Northern Districts was to be given to Byng to read.[6]

Byng had left for the north armed with all the knowledge he needed and an unusual amount of autonomy. What he found there was that part of the nation with which he was wholly unfamiliar – the new technologically driven England. Sidmouth had warned Byng that the reports of the worst unrest came no longer from where Thomas Maitland had found them, four years earlier, in the woollen districts of Yorkshire. They had shifted – and the reason was as obvious to Byng as to any other visitor to the north – as the technological advances had shifted. The organised violence and rowdiness of workers had now moved to the densely populated cotton spinning and weaving areas of Lancashire.

The Home Secretary, therefore, had directed Byng to the town which was already rising to be Britain's metropolitan industrial hub, Manchester. Byng had ridden into the place in mid-1816. There he had seen for the first time the embryonic city spawned by technological discoveries unknown a few years earlier. The great spinning sheds and weaving mills that created the wealth on which the town fed were visible on every approach road he chose to point his horse. So too, nearer the town's centre, were the counting houses and crowded office buildings where, as the cotton economy expanded, profits were collected and reinvested. Behind them were the shanty town buildings which housed the many thousands of cotton workers—not just Lancastrians sucked in from nearby villages, but agricultural labourers from southern counties, others from Wales and Scotland, and particularly noticeable, thousands of poverty stricken Irish immigrants, all come to benefit from the work the new machines provided: all come to live there and breed there.

Byng did not like what he saw. It was not the vision of the England he had left as a boy. Within a short time he was looking for some more congenial place to base the best part of both his working and his leisure hours. Within weeks he had made the journey across the county border to Campsmount.

## 2

## Manchester

Many people shortly before and shortly after Byng first rode into Manchester looked on the place with surprise. Friedrich Engels, himself the son of a wealthy Rhineland cotton manufacturer, used the cotton workers of the town much as a behaviourist uses the animals in a laboratory. He observed without much interfering. One of the earliest observations he made – and it surprised him – was that it was possible to live in early nineteenth-century Manchester, and travel in and out daily, without seeing any working people's quarter whatever.[1] The heart of the great town consisted almost entirely of offices and warehouses reached by busy thoroughfares lined with shops. These roads effectively insulated the traveller from the girdle of insanitary cellars, disordered shanties and stinking courtyards of the spinners and weavers. Byng, though not so diligent an observer as Engels, took the trouble to look closely at the new phenomenon of the industrial worker. He was awed by what he saw, particularly by the passivity of simple people living at high density in manifestly poor conditions. Theirs was, in any case, behaviour quite different from that of the European peasants among whom he had moved for most of his adult life.

Byng's dislike of Manchester was no different from that of other Northern District commanders who found no beauty in this cotton boomtown where, each day, or so it seemed, a new brick-built factory rose up beyond its neighbour. His predecessor, General Maitland, had disliked the people as much as the place. Sir Charles Napier, one of Byng's successors, left a clear unrestrained impression of both:

> Some duties are not to be done voluntarily, and to live in a chimney is one. Manchester is the chimney of the world. Rich rascals, poor rogues, drunken ragamuffins and prostitutes form the moral; soot made into paste by rain the physique, and the only view is a long chimney: what a place! The entrance to hell realized![2]

This was not just a soldier's blinkered view. Shortly after Byng visited Manchester, *The Times* sent one of its correspondents there to look at the condition of the poor manufacturing workers in the New Cross district. He wrote of it,

> It is occupied chiefly by spinners, weavers ... its present situation is truly heart-rending and over-powering. The streets are confined and dirty; the houses neglected, and the windows often without glass. Out of the windows the miserable rags of the family ... hung up to dry; the household

furniture, the bedding, the clothes of the children and the husband were seen at the pawnbrokers.[3]

To the new breed of sociological observer, seeing factory life for the first time, there was no doubt what it was that had driven the poor to such desperate straits. The technological revolution was the devil and the machines which gave it momentum his pronged fork. In the generation following Waterloo, in his *Moral and Physical Conditions of the Operatives employed in the Cotton Manufacture in Manchester*, the doctor John Kay wrote in horror,

> Whilst the engine runs the people must work – men, women and children are yoked together with iron and steam. The animal machine – breakable in the best case, subject to a thousand sources of suffering – chained fast to the iron machine, which knows no suffering and no weariness.[4]

But, as even Friedrich Engels was to note, it depended upon how you looked at Manchester as to what you saw. Dr Andrew Ure, writing after Byng arrived there, took an entirely different view of the factory system.

> In my recent tour, . . . through the manufacturing districts, I have seen tens of thousands of old, young and middle-aged of both sexes, many of them too feeble to get their daily bread by any of the former modes of industry, earning abundant food, raiment, and domestic accommodation, without perspiring at a single pore, screened meanwhile from the

summer's sun and the winter's frost, in apartments more airy and salubrious than those of the metropolis in which our legislative and fashionable aristocracies assemble. In those spacious halls the benignant power of steam summons around him his myriads of willing menials, and assigns to each the regulated task, substituting for painful muscular effort on their part, the energies of his own gigantic arm, and demanding in return only attention and dexterity to correct such little aberrations as casually occur in his workmanship.[5]

Byng saw in Manchester sights he could never have seen on any of the long journeys he had made around Europe. Neither the size of the mills, nor their concentration was to be found anywhere in the world. The town centre alone had 43 factories employing 12,940 workers. And they were growing in size to become vast emporiums. Already five of these buildings each housed between 400 and 700, three held between 800 and 1,020, while George and Adam Murray's monster mill enclosed 1,215 people.[6]

What most of these workers could expect from life was not, materially at least, good. A skilled spinner could earn up to 30s a week. However, for a six-day week of 12–16 hours per day, a weaver's maximum pay ranged from 10s–12s a week – about 2 pence an hour.[7] This was at a time when the wholesale price of wheat, after the most dreadful harvest of 1816, was rising rapidly to almost 4 pence a pound and the price of potatoes, the most common food of the poor, reached 1 penny a pound. The weavers' earnings were plainly inadequate even by the depressed standards of the times.

Children worked the same shifts. Their families lived in squalor. Peter Gaskell, another of those shocked by what he found in Manchester, described their existence as 'savage' and their houses as,

> Filthy, unfurnished, deprived of all accessories to decency or comfort . . . blankets and sheets in the strict meaning of the words unknown – their place often being made up of sacking, a heap of flocks, or a bundle of straw, supplying the want of a proper bedstead and leather bed, and all these cooped in a single room, which serves as a place for domestic household occupation.[8]

For those above the breadline there was one preponderant diversion for any spare pennies. Dr Kay counted 270 taverns, 216 gin shops and 188 beer houses.[9]

But irrespective of the effects of alcohol, there was no guarantee that length of life could be won by industry. Even for the rich in the early years of the nineteenth century, life was generally short. The average age of death of professional people and gentry and their families in Manchester, was 38. But for the poor – mechanics, labourers and their families – it was just 17.[10]

This was the nature of Manchester life and the condition of its people which Sir John Byng found on his arrival there. Although it was for Byng a new aspect of humanity, unlike his predecessor, he sent to London relatively few accounts of what he saw of the way people lived and worked. But what little he wrote shows he was sensitive to the hardships and suffering he encountered. His first detailed reports, written in his own impeccably neat hand, could not be in greater contrast to those of Maitland, whose writing in any case was almost illegible and who invariably used secretaries. Unlike Maitland, who dealt only with the Home Secretary himself, Byng modestly corresponded with either one of the two Under Secretaries. He replied in the same hand-written way to every letter written to him, including those of the pestering small-town magistrates whom Maitland had despised. Byng considered it 'a respect due to them to answer all myself'.[11]

Byng was to give meticulous attention to the most bureaucratic aspects of his job. It was perhaps not quite the strategy expected from one in command of the largest and potentially most explosive military districts of Britain. However, should the occasion ever arise when any of Byng's actions were questioned – and in the fulness of time that occasion would arise – he would have clear, impersonal documentation available to which to refer his superiors.

Having reviewed his Northern Districts, Byng announced to the Home Office where he intended to place his headquarters. The location can only have surprised Lord Sidmouth. Pontefract in Yorkshire was well to the east of even the most troublesome West Riding districts, besides being 50 miles distant over difficult, hilly Pennine roads from Manchester, now the most turbulent district of all.

It was true that four years earlier General Maitland had eventually based himself at Wakefield in West Yorkshire. But that had been at a time when the centre of gravity of rioting had temporarily moved away from Lancashire. Without demur, the Home Secretary, Lord Sidmouth, accepted Byng's decision to base his headquarters at Pontefract Barracks. Before long Byng had finalised the terms of his acceptance of the tenancy of Campsmount – so conveniently situated half an hour's gentle ride from Pontefract. By the following spring, he was sowing his first crop of wheat in the fields which led down to the Norman church, and moving his racehorses into John Carr's elegant stables.

# 3

# The Determinant of Change

A momentous change was overcoming Britain. Eventually the same process of change would overtake the whole of the Western world. Its effects would continue to the present day. The first place to experience this upheaval on a substantial scale had been Manchester. It was already en route to becoming the first city of the Industrial Revolution. Traumatic events in the months following Byng's arrival in the north of England were to be the consequence of this experience.

Even in the late twentieth century, history books still fail to emphasise sufficiently the power of technology in moulding man's culture. Wherever man lives, the shape and texture and colour of the civilisation he imposes on himself are determined overwhelmingly by the techniques he has invented or discovered. The sight, the touch, the sound and even the very smell of the environment are the consequences of his ability to manipulate these techniques. The more advanced the civilisation and the more densely man populates it, the more these qualities submerge those of the natural surroundings. The early civilisations of Assyria and Mesopotamia came into being because of man's ability to apply coded technique to agriculture. The Bronze Age and the Iron Age prospered as a result of his ability to raise the temperature of the substances he found in the ground. And the enduring monuments to Egypt, Greece and Rome's achievements were raised because of his technical ability to augment the power of his own muscles, then those of animals. The revolutionary, social and political changes which overtook northern Europe and America were equally due to technique – technique, however, which increasingly depended on a new, energetic intellectual base.

By the late seventeenth century, machines had been invented which did things other than extract food, or metals, or energy from the Earth's crust. These machines were apparently unproductive; they simply measured with great accuracy. Refined balances measured minute weight differences, ingenious artefacts calculated small distances, clocks of delicate mechanism determined time changes with previously unequalled accuracy, and these machines were used with new or newly refined instruments of observation – optical devices: the telescope and the microscope among others – to probe the visible limits of nature.

From these instruments and machines the ability to quantify – to measure nature with an exactitude not approached by previous civilisations – was realised. It was the facility which gave birth to technology's great achievement – to modern science itself. It cannot be too much emphasised that the enlightened age of Galileo and of Newton which produced this great civilised and civilising achievement, incomparably the most influential of man's cultural creations, owed its success to technological skill. Science grew from technology, and not the other way round. It was the Scientific Age that gave what became known as the Industrial Revolution its might.

The chance conjunction in English, Scottish and Welsh valleys and hills, of substantial quantities of running water, coal and steel helped locate the event in this particular plot of Europe. Less easily explicable is the flow of ideas, of inventions which, about the middle of the eighteenth century, began to pour out of the workshops of the Midlands and of northern Britain. Without the need to understand any of them in detail, a simple statement of only a few of the discoveries applied to the industries of the nation, paints a graphic picture of the mechanistic changes overtaking the once agricultural landscape. Significantly, most of these inventions were being applied in districts many miles from London – most in the Midlands and the north of England. In the few years after 1748, at Coalbrookdale, Abraham Darby perfected the coke smelting of iron; at Swansea, zinc smelting was established; at Birmingham, John Roebuck worked the first lead-chamber process for the production of sulphuric acid; in the north, too, crucible steel was established commercially, the Carron Iron Works were built, the Worsley–Manchester Canal was opened, the first iron nails were cast, Jesse Ramsden invented his screw-cutting lathe and John Wilkinson designed his boring machine. By 1776, James Watt's steam engine was in use and Britain was extracting and consuming five times more coal than any other nation in the world.

These few highlights from not much more than a single quarter of a century show how Britain's geographical source of wealth was undergoing its great change. At the beginning of the century that wealth had depended largely on the cloth got from the wool of home produced sheep and woven by hand on the wooden looms of country cottages in East Anglia, Hampshire, Wiltshire, Devon, Somerset and, to a lesser extent, the northern counties. By its end, the produce from the lengthening list of inventions is entirely different. It included chemicals capable of turning metal ores into the durable material for machines – steam driven machines fired by coal. And of the many end products being manufactured, the single most important commodity vital to Britain was no longer that which had dominated her economy for four centuries, home grown wool: it was imported cotton.

The success of cotton is a paradox. In its natural state it is a short fibre not much thicker than a human hair. After being picked and gathered in an unpromising matted bulk form it has strictly limited uses. The triumph of the technique of the cotton industry is the ability to manipulate it in such a way as to convert the intractable organic material into a strong, durable textile and supply it cheap to thousands of millions of people – to virtually the whole of the world's population.

There are three main steps in the production of cotton cloth. Carding is the process which cleans the fibres and separates them into parallel lengths. Spinning converts the prepared lengths into a continuous yarn of uniform cross section. And in weaving parallel strands of yarn are interlaced by more yarn placed at right angles over, then under, each parallel strand.

The basic process of weaving is no different from that of darning. Cloth continued to be produced in this slow, laborious fashion until a great Hindu innovation provided the first leap in production volume. The parallel warp yarns were divided and fixed to a harness so that half could be lifted, then lowered for the weft yarns to pass between.

This one device provided a phenomenal increase in a weaver's speed. In spite of the introduction of other techniques – for example, the use of a shuttle to carry the weft across the warp – the Hindu invention remained the single most influential in the hand craft. Still, long after the beginning of the eighteenth century, weaving was the quicker of the two key processes. Several spinners needed to be employed to supply each weaver. Around that date, with Liverpool as the port of entry for raw material, 30,000 spinners and weavers in the Manchester–Bolton area were producing cotton cloth by hand in their homes.

An invention by John Kay, around 1733, primed the technological pump that was to flood northern Britain with improvements in the technique of textile production. Kay designed what became known as a flying shuttle. By a sharp jerk on a cord with one hand, his mechanism sent a wooden shuttle, carrying the weft, at speed through the warp in either direction.

Again, this ushered in a new age of speed for the weaver. Spinners could no longer cope with the demands made on them. Yarn was in desperately short supply, unable to meet the requirements of a market hungry for the cloth.

The need for new technology for spinning was obvious. But the problem to be solved was not easy. From a matted mass, a spinner needs to draw individual fibres and get each of these to lie parallel. These adjacent fibres have then to be drawn out steadily into a fine yarn. In hand spinning, spinners developed skills to do this by turning a spindle which simultaneously gave the yarn a twist as it rotated.

By 1738 the idea had been conceived of spinning by drawing cotton or wool between pairs of rollers. In his patent of that year, Lewis Paul stated succinctly the germ of his idea and, so that nobody could mistake it, wrote his key words in capital letters. After the first pair of rollers came 'a succession of OTHER ROWLERS, Cillinders, or Cones, MOVEING PROPORTIONATELY FASTER THAN THE FIRST . . .' so as to draw the cotton into as fine a yarn as was required.

These two simple inventions, the flying shuttle in weaving and the pairs of rollers in spinning, were unmistakeable markers in the great encyclopaedia of nineteenth-century technological invention. Within a few more years, probably about 1764, James Hargreaves's Spinning Jenny, which turned out fine twisted yarn at a speed and of a quality no hand spinner could begin to match, was in production. His invention embodied the essential elements of the modern spinning machine.

In this cotton cloth-making area of the country – where production was still almost entirely a home-based industry – the stimulus for change was unequalled. Every decade for many to come was to introduce a fresh mechanical device which would not only quicken and refine the textile process, but would also make it possible for each of its distinct elements to be driven by harnessed power – that of horses, then water, then steam.

The social upheaval created by this dramatic change from an agricultural to an industrial culture, from a rural to an urban environment – the consequence of this essentially uncomplicated technology – was to be immense. The flow of thought of the nation's leaders in both politics and religion would veer markedly, the intellectual thrust of its thinkers would have new aim, the lives of the mass of people in the country would change pattern and – though this, unbelievably, was scarcely noticed at the time – the centre of gravity of the nation would shift from south to north.

At the hub of this change was Manchester. It would act as the template for the world in both its growth on technological foundations, and in the manifestation of the brutal social and cultural consequences which accompanied that unparalleled growth.

It would be foolish to try to attribute the momentous rise of cotton in the economy of Great Britain to the key invention or action of any single individual. But there is no doubt that, had it not been for one man, the growth of the industry, the manner in which it affected millions of people throughout the world could not have been so extraordinary as eventually it was to become. He was described by Thomas Carlyle, perfectly fairly, as 'that bag-cheeked, pot-bellied, much enduring much inventing barber . . . and it was this man that had to give England the power of cotton.'[1] He was Richard Ark-wright. His phenomenal contribution to the industrialisation of the nation lay not so much in his inventions, but in how he manipulated human beings in relation to his own, and to others' inventions.

Arkwright was essentially uneducated; once a lather boy in a Preston barber's shop, his spelling was bad and his grammar, like his manners, rudimentary. His powers of observation, however, were acute. As he matured he looked at a number of locations in the north of England, several of which had been particularly noted earlier that century by another with the same singular ability to extract and retain in his mind key details of what he had seen. Daniel Defoe differed from Richard Arkwright in that he could record with a clarity and brilliance equal to that with which he observed.

Defoe had visited, and looked with admiration, at an Italian silk mill built to make use of the water power of the river Derwent in Derbyshire. Arkwright had followed him to the same spot years later. Each had looked with wide eyes and had quantified the effects of organised mechanisation on both production and – indirectly – on human beings. Defoe described the type of machine in the mill. It was such that,

One hand will twist as much silk, as before could be done by fifty, and that in much truer and better manner. This engine contains 26,586 wheels, and 94,746 movements, which work 73,726 yards of silk thread, every time the water-wheel goes round, which is three times in one minute, and 318,504,960 yards in one day and night.[2]

The simple sum was not just a fifty-fold increase in product-ivity per man hour, but additionally the machine, provided it was manned twenty-four hours a day, could be made to produce twenty-four hours a day. The implication for the working man was profound: if his workday was not deter-mined by the number of daylight hours, the advantages – in terms of output at least – were prodigious.

The word of neither Daniel Defoe nor Richard Arkwright could, or can, be trusted. Both, however, had exceptional insight into the ways of their fellow men. Defoe translated his into brilliant text, admirable in spite of its doubtful accuracy; Arkwright his into brilliant invention, the functionality of which, however, cannot be doubted.

It was in 1771 on the river at Cromford that Arkwright, well possessed of the necessary qualities of drive to get others to do his will, and ruthlessness in persisting with his aim once he had done so, set up his first cotton spinning factory. It was powered by a constant stream from a dam on the river Derwent driving a single water-wheel. It was out of sight of the prying eyes of rivals, and it was also some distance from the large population centres where workshops were easier prey to machine wreckers.

The principle involved in Arkwright's cotton spinning machine of thirty years earlier, was essentially that described in Lewis Paul's patent. The cleaned and combed raw cotton was drawn through two pairs of rollers. The second of these turned faster than the first and so stretched the cotton before it passed to a spindle mechanism which automatically twisted the thread before it was wound on to a bobbin. This first spinning machine of Arkwright was powered by water, and was therefore called a water frame.

In 1769 Arkwright had taken out his first patent. More followed. One patent spoke of 'employing a great number of poor people in working the said machinery'. In other words, Arkwright had soon introduced human beings, not only into his invention, the factory, but he had also introduced them into his patent specification.

It would fit well within the character of Arkwright for him, without blinking, to have filched the ideas of other men. But the perfectly valid historical claims to priority of John Wyatt, Lewis Paul, James Hargreaves and others pale when faced with the human applications Arkwright subsequently foresaw for his technology.

As Arkwright already knew to his cost, this technology was not only revolutionary, it was also unprecedently controversial. When cloth production was a hand craft, a skilled weaver could weave in a day as much yarn as twenty spinners could spin by hand in a day. Now, the situation was reversed. Alone, one of the machines in Arkwright's factory was capable of supplying far more spun yarn than a single hand weaver could begin to cope with. Already spinners who correctly foretold that this new technique's first effects would be to reduce the numbers of available jobs, were trying to preserve their livelihoods by the most obvious violent means.

By 1776 Arkwright & Co. were employing 5,000 men, women and children in several factories; his business was valued at £200,000, and it was growing. The uneducated Arkwright would later boast that, if need be, he could pay off the National Debt. He was the first great cotton-spinning capitalist.

But on June 25th, 1785 Arkwright's patent was challenged in the court of the King's Bench. Thomas Highs gave evidence there that, working with John Kay in Leigh, Lancashire, he had made rollers for spinning cotton two years before Arkwright's first patent. Kay gave evidence that he had communicated these plans to the Preston barber. Arkwright lost his case. The floodgates for spun cotton were wide open for others to pour through. Within two years of the annulment of Arkwright's letters patent, 143 cotton mills were in operation in Great Britain, 41 of them in Lancashire.[3]

As Arkwright imitated, so he was imitated. His demonstration that the cloth manufacturing trade was ripe for exploitation inspired many others to apply whatever new technology was available to other processes of the industry, and, if it was not available, to invent it.

In 1784, the somewhat unworldly member of a gentle, middle-class family, Dr Edmund Cartwright, while on a brief holiday at Matlock in Derbyshire had overheard a group of Manchester businessmen discussing how the weaving of cotton remained a hand operation, even though spinning the fibre was now fully mechanised. Within a year, though he knew little of the business and was not particularly mechanically minded, he had patented a power-driven weaving loom. In the same year, the first cotton mill, worked by James Watt's steam engine, had started to turn at Papplewick, Nottinghamshire. Five years later, Drinkwater's spinning factory, driven by steam, was operating in Piccadilly, Manchester, and plans were afoot for a 500-loom steam-powered weaving mill nearby.

And so, well before the end of the century, both the most time-consuming processes in the manufacture of cotton cloth were not only mechanised, they could be powered by steam.

With its nucleus of a home cotton industry, its port of Liverpool well placed to receive vast shipments of raw fibre from the United States, and with its easy access to the coal to drive the steam engines and the iron from which to make them, South Lancashire was poised for change. And change it did.

The steam engine meant that factories no longer needed to be built on rivers at the best point for their flowing waters to give power to the machinery. Now the steam power could be taken to the towns where a working population already existed. As the industry burgeoned, so did the town. There is no better example than Manchester. In 1774 it was still essentially what Daniel Defoe had seen as 'the greatest mere village in England',[4] with a population of 41,032. But by the time Lieutenant General Sir John Byng first set foot in the town 42 years later, that population had experienced a historically unmatched rise, approaching 200,000. In the same period the surrounding towns had shown similar inexplicable population explosions. Ashton and Bolton, in the 1770s villages of 5,000 or so, now each held numbers approaching 30,000 or more, while Oldham was near 50,000.[5]

Lancashire as a whole during the same period had quadrupled its population to more than a million. Except for Middlesex, it now had the largest number of inhabitants of any county in England. Together with the West Yorkshire towns lying close alongside over the Pennine hills, the area had the greatest and the most dense population of people working in manufacturing industries in the world.

The sources of the wealth generated for the nation had undergone equally momentous changes. Wool was a fading industry. Woollen exports in 1785 had stood at £4 million. The trade was shortly to become almost stagnant. Now, almost 35 years later, it had scarcely reached £6 million. Cotton exports, on the other hand, before the challenge to Arkwright's patent in 1780, had an official value of a mere £355,060, by 1800 they stood at £5,406,501.[6] Nineteen years later it was already five times even this amount.[7] The consequences inside and outside Britain were substantial and in some cases catastrophic. In 1813 £2 million of cotton cloth had passed out of Calcutta to England. Before the 1820s ended, India was importing £1.5 million worth of British machine-made cotton, emptying whole Indian towns of both industry and people.[8]

Here then was the birthplace of technologically based capitalism on a previously inconceivable scale. Engels, then Karl Marx, when later they saw the conditions under which the industry was growing, were to believe it could only be the soil for unprecedented social upheaval. Engels was quite explicit about the cause: it was technological. To him it was extraordinary and unmistakeable. He wrote,

> The history of South Lancashire contains some of the greatest marvels of modern times, yet no one ever mentions them, and all are the product of the cotton industry.[9]

# 4

## Land of Liberty

In 1817, the British Cabinet was still blind to the reality that the factors which had already totally changed the nature of the land it governed were the consequences of technology. Why was it then, that by the criteria of the day at least, its administration was considered so successful? Lord Liverpool, in spite of his obvious lack of qualities of leadership, was on the road to becoming the longest serving nineteenth-century British Prime Minister. Disraeli's judgement of him was succinct; he called him 'the Arch Mediocrity'. The fact that posterity remembers so little of him supports that view.

But the powerful stimulus which helped Lord Liverpool's Tory government stay in office – and the modern era is not without its parallel – was success in war. For 22 years Britain had been almost perpetually fighting France. The cost to Britain of that enterprise had been £800 million – until that date an inconceivable sum, far outstripping any other investment the nation had ever made. In the last year of the war alone, 1815, it had been £81 million of which £27 million were raised by loan. The nation was now bled white of the wealth it had earned by both the old established industries and the new technology.

But the spectacular victory at Waterloo was, it seemed, manifestly adequate justification for the expense. That year, a grateful Parliament voted the Duke of Wellington, on his triumphant return to London, additional remuneration of £200,000. Other veterans of the same battle returning to the cloth towns of northern England were to find remuneration, additional or otherwise, flowed far less freely. With the war successfully concluded, and the demand for woollen and cotton cloth for soldiers' uniforms and blankets suddenly removed, the industry to which they now returned was in one of the worst of its cyclical depressions. In large numbers they found themselves either unemployed or in short-time work.

To the British citizen, the prosecution of the nation's wars was the most obvious return given by the State in exchange for the tax he was forced to pay. It was true that the adminis-tration of justice and of the rudimentary postal service also were the responsibilities of the State. Otherwise there was little immediate benefit for those who paid their tax. Central government did nothing to provide for the young and weak; it supported no schools; it gave relief neither to the poor nor to the old; nor, most importantly when, as during the past half dozen years order had been endangered by violent riots, did it secure the safety of the citizen. There was no police force as we know it today.

In general throughout England law and order were the responsibility of the appropriate local authority. In

Manchester, for example, the Police Commissioners were responsible for the night-watch, but in addition they directed road building, street cleaning, street lighting and the maintenance of fire-engines. The area's justice was administered by local resident magistrates with day-to-day affairs controlled by a stipendiary, that is to say a paid magistrate.

The overall coordination of these local peace-keeping groups was, however, the task of a central government minister. In 1819 that minister was one who left his mark on a crucial period of British history in a way his Prime Minister never could. Lord Liverpool's Home Secretary was Lord Sidmouth. This 60-year-old lawyer with the mentality of an accountant, though unquestionably well-meaning, left a cold thumbprint on every aspect of government policy he touched. Even the brilliant, enduring invention he bequeathed to the people of Britain – the deduction of income tax at source – still today warms few hearts.

Sidmouth was born Henry Addington, the son of a doctor who had opened a profitable lunatic asylum for the rich of Berkshire. Henry, after reading for the Bar, had made a parliamentary career for himself in the face of what others saw as enormous disadvantages. He was an abysmal speaker, had a stammer and was made fun of by the fashionable society in which he so enjoyed moving. The patrician Lord Holland described the reason for the mockery: 'The hostility he met with from the upper classes of society proceeded, I fear, more from his want of birth than his other manifold deficiencies.'[1]

But in spite of these deficiencies, Addington's career had

included being Speaker of the House of Commons, Chancellor of the Exchequer (when he introduced income tax at source), a brief and unhappy spell as Prime Minister, elevation to the peerage and now, as Lord Sidmouth, Home Secretary. It was in this role that in 1812 he had combined his cold administrative talents with those of the tough, coarse and quixotic Lieutenant General the Hon. Thomas Maitland to contain the Luddite Revolt in the Midlands and the north country. At the Special Commission set up at York to deal with the rebellion in January, 1813 – not the first Sidmouth had authorised – 64 men had been arraigned and 17 hanged for their part in the rebellion.

Partly from his cramped office in Whitehall, and partly from his home in Richmond Park, Sidmouth administered the law and order of Great Britain. The staff he maintained to carry out this task on behalf of the nation was laughably small: 2 Under Secretaries of State, 14 clerks, 1 secretary, 1 precis writer, 1 librarian, 2 chamber keepers, 2 porters and the housekeeper, Mrs Moss. The number of staff, in the face of any lessons which might have been learned in 1812, the year of the most severe and worrying Luddite violence, remained unchanged from seven years earlier when it also stood at 24 – including Mrs Moss, still occupying her comforting position.[2]

The number appears even more derisory when the business for any one day, excluding matters of law and order, is considered. For example, it could – and did – include an application for the extension of the licence of the Haymarket Theatre, a personal request from a baronet to become a peer, a request from a sea captain to become a Poor Knight of Windsor Castle, a request from the Dean of Connor, Northern Ireland, for royal dispensation for two years in consequence of the state of health of the female part of his family, with whom the air of that part of the United Kingdom so much disagreed, a question relating to the costs of the prison hulks off Dover, a request from the Phoenix Fire Office seeking free pardons for informants in cases of suspected arson – and so on, in infinite variety.

The two Under Secretaries in the years leading up to 1819 were crucial to Sidmouth's continuing ability to deal with the internal political problems of the country. Their function should have been to relieve the Home Secretary of key administrative tasks. One of these men, the Permanent Under Secretary, John Beckett, a member of a Leeds woollen manufacturing family, continued as he had during the troubled times of 1812, to work diligently under the constant pressure of the little office.

The other, the Parliamentary Under Secretary, was neither so reliable nor so diligent, but certainly as clever. He was Sidmouth's younger brother, Hiley. Any suspicion that this appointment by the Home Secretary was tainted with nepotism would be entirely justifiable. It was a practice Sidmouth had stuck faithfully by for many years. In 1810, for example, he gave his 15-year-old son, Henry, one of the most lucrative sinecures in England – the Clerk of the Pells – worth £3,000 a year. At another time he simultaneously made Hiley Paymaster of the Forces and his brother-in-law, Charles Bragge, Treasurer of the Navy.

Hiley and his eldest brother were very different characters. Where Henry was cold, self-controlled and ascetic in his habits, Hiley was unpredictable and self-indulgent. Over-fond of wine and food, he was said to have 'the stomach of an ostrich'. Earlier in his career Bragge had convincingly described for Sidmouth his brother's eating habits:

> If I had wanted any additional proof our last supper would have convinced me, when he ordered a couple of woodcock to succeed half a barrel of oysters, and then quarrelled with the waiter because there were no sausages to succeed, so that he was obliged to finish with nothing higher than ragou'd lobster which he washed down with two tumblers of mixed punch.[3]

Sadly for the gluttonous Hiley, he was not physically strong – a characteristic which, combined with a frequently displayed hypochondria, led to problems. Sidmouth often needed to send sympathy to his brother, who was resting his afflicted body at some distant holiday spot rather than on his Home Office desk.

Yet, in spite of, or because of their different characters, there remained an unusual closeness between the two brothers. Sidmouth was never more comfortable nor more confident than when Hiley was alongside him. He had good reason. In the years since Sidmouth had achieved high office, Hiley, acting as a most astute public relations man, had served him well.

Some years earlier Hiley had used his considerable charm

to persuade the owner of *The Times*, William Walter, to support the administration of Addington (as Sidmouth still was). Within a short time a generous *quid pro quo* resulted: Walter's eldest son entered government service with a place in the Audit Department worth £600 per annum. Not long after that, Hiley was contributing sometimes three or four leaders to *The Times* each week in support of the Addington government. And when his brother resigned his Prime Ministership, Hiley, with an aplomb which can only be admired, wrote an anonymous article published without any accompanying murmur by the same paper, saying, 'We have heard, and hope it is true, that the King insists on Mr. Addington retaining the house at Richmond Park.'[4] He did retain it.

Above this quagmire of nepotism and intrigue Sidmouth's head rises clear, apparently unsullied by the unseemly mess he straddled. It has to be said that the decisions which, in the year he occupied his great office of state, deeply affected tens of thousands of men and women, appear to be influenced only by his studied logical accounting thought processes. He never intended personal gain and he believed deeply that what he did was for the rights and the good of others.

For many of these decisions he frequently relied on the advice and support of his brother. Hiley it was who sent north most of the instructions to magistrates when the first serious signs of unrest appeared in Manchester in late 1816.

Hiley, therefore, at a crucial period in Sidmouth's career, helped shape his brother's views, frequently those relating to the policing of his fellow men – in particular to his poorer fellow men. These views were faithfully transmitted to and reflected by the government which then ruled the country. In particular they were shared by the key members of the Cabinet, Lord Liverpool, the Prime Minister, Lord Eldon, the Lord Chancellor, Lord Castlereagh, the Foreign Secretary and Lord Sidmouth himself. It would not be unfair to say that the resulting collective attitude these men held towards home affairs was that the art of good government lay solely in the maintenance of discipline. The law of the land existed for few purposes other than the control by punishment of the working classes. Sidmouth, with his unbending reverence for law and order, oiled the mechanism which put this policy into effect. The product was to be a nation in which most citizens experienced taxation without representation, where there was severe restriction on the freedom of the press, and where trade unions were forbidden by law. The Habeas Corpus Act would soon be suspended and imprisonment without trial became widespread. In truth, there was no justification for the Englishman's predilection, as common then as now, to burst into song rejoicing in his freedom.

One other creeping and insidious infringement of civil liberties, to which Lord Sidmouth and his brother were turning with more and more conviction of its value, was the use of paid spies. The Home Office had a special fund which it distributed to magistrates to maintain the system. Magistrates in the Manchester area used it freely. Since the spectacular successes in which Yorkshire Luddites had been arrested in 1812 and convicted on the evidence of spies, it was now being put to good use again in the north country. When, in December, 1816 large bands of working men began to gather for meetings

on the fields and moors near the cotton towns of South Lancashire, Hiley Addington was ready to reassure any magistrate
that the system of having one Englishman spy on another
should be furthered whenever it was believed it might be useful. He wrote in delicate but clear terms in December, 1816 to
the Manchester magistrate, the Reverend Mr Ethelston, to
bolster his confidence in the use of two of his spies:

> As it appears to be your decided opinion that Fleming and
> Campbell might be usefully employed as secret agents to
> obtain further intelligence of plans and movements of the
> disaffected, there can be no objection to make such weekly
> remuneration to them, on a modest scale, as you may con-
> sider sufficient for their trouble.[5]

During this period Hiley was making regular payments to
Colonel Ralph Fletcher, the Bolton magistrate whose spies 'B'
and 'A B' were supplying reams of paper reports on working
men's meetings, forcing Home Office clerks into hours of
work transcribing page after page of crabbed handwriting
and feeble grammar.

Another magistrate, the Reverend Mr Hay too was using
the system discreditably but well. Two of the spies he relied
on, 'no. 1' and 'no. 2', were beginning to bring in disturbing
reports. The town's Deputy Constable, Joseph Nadin, was
properly financed for the small group of spies he personally
operated – not just in Manchester, but as far afield as Halifax
in Yorkshire.

One other freely used, and free, source of information was

the postal service. At the whim of the Home Secretary or one of his close advisers, any postmaster could be, and frequently was, asked to intercept letters from named individuals. Letters from the politically suspect, particularly members of the middle class who were involved in parliamentary reform movements, workers attempting to organise union activities, and certainly letters from prisoners gaoled for political offences, would be directed to the Home Office, copied and sent on their way, or permanently retained. The delay in delivery of the envelope – sometimes days or weeks – was a sure indication to the recipient that its contents had been carefully noted for use, if necessary, as evidence against whomever the Home Office chose.

The result of this web of reportage was to engender fear and hatred in the working people it was meant to control. Where civil liberties were already reduced to an unacceptable level and where by far the larger proportion of men and women had no proper representation in Parliament, the nation, by 1817, had come closer in spirit to that of the early years of the Third Reich than at any other time in modern history.

# 5

# The Major

Before his death by hanging in 1813, George Mellor, the 23-year-old West Yorkshire Luddite leader, wrote his last letter from his cell in York Castle. It was intercepted and sent to the Home Office. There, it was copied and its slightly faulty grammar corrected. The main purpose of the letter was to persuade those who had given alibis on his behalf not to change their story when tempted by government rewards or bribes.

But Mellor ended his letter, which was addressed to his cousin, 'I have heard you are pettitionary for a parliamentary reform and I wish these names to be given as follows . . .'.[1] He then listed 39 of his fellow prisoners, most of whom had been involved with him in his machine-wrecking activities in the woollen districts of Yorkshire.

Mellor had gone to extremes in a society he considered fundamentally inequitable and one in which the social problems were becoming more complex as each piece of new technology introduced into the cloth industry reduced the number of available jobs. He had committed murder by shooting a manufacturer who was introducing the new technology, and he had paid the price for his violence.

In 1813 parliamentary reform was the afterthought trailing behind violence as the means to the end of an unfair society. But in the years since then much had happened. A great war had come to an end, and as is so often the case in history, that event had triggered new attitudes and new behaviour. New patterns of the spoken and written idiom can be observed. Before 1815, for example, letters in the Home Office files look curiously anachronistic compared with those of a later date; their abbreviations and their phraseology are those of a bygone age. After that date the idiom of the modern age arrives. Equally noticeable, the letters in that repository written by working men surge in number. No longer are those, such as George Mellor's last written page, a rarity. The Sunday schools of the turn of the century had worked marvels. The literate cobbler and the poet-weaver now add to the figures on the canvas to give a far more representative picture from which to scrutinise the lives, beliefs and attitudes of the mass of the people of a nation. The autobiography of a young hand-loom weaver, Samuel Bamford, who lived and worked near Manchester, gives a colourful – coloured might be a better adjective – working-class view of this violent period in the internal history of Britain.

Working men, literate or not, had no difficulty in understanding the inequities of the political system ranged against them. In the then House of Commons, a majority of the sitting members was actually elected by only 154 voters, and some of these voters were themselves members of the House of Lords. In each of three Rotten Boroughs, Midhurst in Sussex, Newton in Hampshire and most famous of all, Old Sarum in Wiltshire (a hill without a single building on it), one man sent two members to Parliament while another twelve members of the Commons were returned by eleven electors. On the other hand Manchester, Salford, Bolton, Blackburn, Rochdale, Ashton, Oldham and Stockport had between them not one Member of Parliament. The best part of a million people of Lancashire were being represented by only two elected county MPs and two members for Liverpool. Parliament meanwhile voted a Civil List of sinecurists who received sums of money which, to the working man, were of incomprehensible, astronomical proportion. Each year, for example, Lord Arden received £39,000 and Earl Bathurst £33,000. These were but two out of dozens. Ecclesiastical salaries were just as munificent; the Bishop of Durham yearly drew £24,000. To reach an equivalent purchasing power in today's currency it is necessary to multiply these figures by up to a hundred.

By contrast, the token money set aside by government for the alleviation of distressed areas was £42,000. It was calculated that this sum would have provided every poor individual in the country with about 2 pennyworth of soup.[2]

The nation was a perilously laden see-saw. The Luddite Revolt had been the shifting weight which had almost brought the plank of State crashing disastrously to the ground. Not since the Civil War had the country been so close to national rebellion as in 1812. Many, not without reason, had believed that the outcome of that Revolt must end with the bloodshed seen in the French Revolution. Only the icy grip of the Home Office policy with its hangings of errant workers followed by the equilibrating effect of the war against France had returned the delicately poised State temporarily back to its balance.

But the demands for change, for reform, for self-determination and for truly representative parliamentary government, so uncertain in 1812, had begun to rise substantially in volume. As before, the only articulate voices to be listened to with a degree of tolerance by government were those of the upper and middle classes. Chief among these was that of a man who had been heard much – too much – in the past. He was the aristocrat George Mellor had believed might lead the working classes to their rightful democratic vote.

Sir Francis Burdett, in 1817, was a slim, 47-year-old patrician. He should have been far from passing the peak of the prime of life. He was still as verbose as ever he had been in the past in Parliament, his love affairs still entertained the higher strata of society and his annoying gout interfered only minimally with his hunting. But as middle age crept on, he was becoming more and more unsympathetic to those whose cause he so frequently, and at such inordinate length, proclaimed in the House of Commons – the poor and the unrepresented people of England.

Several others were eager to point the path their less fortunate countrymen should tread. Two were landowners, though neither sought to pretend they ranked in the same stratum of society as Sir Francis Burdett.

William Cobbett, the self-educated pamphleteer was one.

The *Political Register*, which he established to advocate reform, was a publishing sensation. In 1816 he began publishing a cheap version of the *Register* at a price working men could afford. The 'Twopenny Trash', as it was known, sold by the thousand, particularly in the manufacturing districts of northern England.

Henry Hunt was another. He had first come to the fore in public life in 1812 when he fought and lost the Bristol election as a radical. Even then it had been observed how Hunt, like Burdett, loved an audience and drank in its adulation. But four years further in to his picaresque career, he had still not appeared in front of a crowd of northern manufacturing workers, and would have gone unrecognised had he done so.

Other than their common belief in the necessity for a reform of Parliament, there was little to join these three leaders of radical reform. Cobbett, a vacillating supporter of Burdett, was approaching a final period in which he would despise him. Hunt had despised the baronet since the time when it had become obvious that the latter had lost his popular appeal. And Burdett, for his part, despised them both as vulgar upstarts.

In one opinion, however, they were united. That was in their assessment of the fourth leading English reformer. Major John Cartwright was the oldest of the pack. Approaching 80, he was now, to them as to most others, a historical figure – a spent force. Though even that description would seem an overstatement of the past history of such a mild-mannered elderly gentleman.

Cartwright had originally seen service in the navy but

later joined the Nottinghamshire Militia. Even though he had lost his commission as long ago as 1792 he still used his rank as his title. His life seemed to be a fragment forgetfully left behind by another age. He rose at six o'clock every day and worked until three in the afternoon. He still wore small clothes and a brown wig – both of which fashions had disappeared with the French Revolution. Unlike Burdett, Cobbett and Hunt he was almost devoid of charisma. Most of those who knew him recall him as a sufferable bore, but nevertheless, unmistakeably, a bore, particularly when dealing with his favourite subject, the reform of Parliament.

Cartwright had now been advocating reform for more than 40 years. His chief work on the subject, *Take Your Choice*, had been published in 1776. It is true that this is an extremely dull book. Nevertheless, it is also noteworthy in that it laid down the principles of parliamentary reform which many others had since adopted. His package included manhood suffrage – that is, one man, one vote – voting by ballot, annual elections, equal electoral districts, the abolition of property qualifications for membership of the House of Commons and the payment of salaries to MPs.

So many of the tenets of Cartwright's political philosophy seem such natural constituents of modern democracy that it is sobering to realise what little response the venerable Major had to his ideas after advocating them for nearly half a century.

Cartwright would have lived most of his life like most of the gentry of which he was part, effectively insulated from the revolutionary changes in technology on which the new wealth of the nation was being built, but for one event. His younger brother, Edmund, was the parson who, hearing of Richard Arkwright's success with his cotton spinning machine, had returned home and, within a few months, invented a weaving machine.

By 1812, Cartwright had made little impression on the world in which he lived other than on the metropolitan group of radical reformers who tolerated the fastidiousness and tediousness of this old-world gentleman. But in that year events connected with the Luddite Revolt and its effects on the fears of the nation triggered an astonishing rejuvenating process in the elderly campaigner.

In August, with the rebellion drawing to its close, Major Cartwright had his bags packed and set off for the north country to see some of the consequences of the machines invented by Arkwright and by his own brother, Edmund. He had heard that 38 men had been arrested in Manchester by the Deputy Constable, Joseph Nadin. They had been found in an upstairs room of the Prince Regent's Arms in Ancoats Lane discussing a petition for parliamentary reform. Cartwright arrived in court ready to finance their defence. He found the men being acquitted. Nadin, unusually careless on this occasion, had failed to arrest one man hidden under the stairs, who gave evidence in their favour.

But with the main purpose of his visit having evaporated, Cartwright decided to discover more of the background to the lives of the men he had seen sitting in the Manchester courtroom. He set off, for the first time in his life, to visit the cities and towns of the new Industrial Revolution. From

Manchester he went to Liverpool, Halifax, Sheffield and Nottingham. The tour simply whetted his appetite. A few months later in early 1813, he launched himself on towns in Leicestershire, Yorkshire, Lancashire, Cheshire and Northumberland as well as taking in places in Gloucestershire, Hampshire and Berkshire – all in the space of 29 days. He returned to London bearing petitions advocating parliamentary reform carrying 130,000 signatures which he had collected in town squares, village markets, pubs and houses. The tour appears all the more remarkable when it is remembered that it was carried out by a septuagenarian in an unheated horse-drawn carriage in mid-winter.

The result was a political landmark. Cartwright had discovered the north. Britain, he found, was two nations. One was centred on London, where men of government lived and made decisions as to how the wealth of the nation was to be distributed. The other was centred on Lancashire and Yorkshire where underprivileged manufacturing workers produced a substantial proportion of that wealth. Others more famous than he were to make the same discovery and Disraeli was to coin the phrase which accurately described England's schism as 'two nations'. But Cartwright was to stake his just claim for priority by translating the ideas he formed as a result of his tours into actions which would not only make workers of the north conscious of their disadvantaged northern nation, he would suggest to those same workers means by which they could diminish the disadvantages.

In 1812, along with Sir Francis Burdett, Cartwright had founded in London the Hampden Club. Its members were to be dedicated to furthering parliamentary reform. The qualification for membership typified Burdett's view of the citizen of England. It was open to any man who could show an income of £300 per annum rental from landed property – the same qualification as for membership of the House of Commons. The Club, not surprisingly, failed to prosper. At one meeting in 1815 the always reliable Cartwright found himself a lonely, and to others a sad, figure – the only person to attend.

But, with a new-found energy added to his persistence, he was not to be put off. He had seen the north and seen the fertile ground in which the seeds of reform could be planted. He now conceived the idea of provincial Hampden Clubs in manufacturing and country districts, with workers paying penny subscriptions. And the workers responded unpredictably well. On offer were organised groups which mimicked those of the middle and upper classes and were therefore legal – vitally important in an age where unions formed by working men were outlawed by government. The first of these, formed in 1816, was at Royton, Lancashire. Other towns in the Midlands and the north, particularly in the densely populated area surrounding Manchester followed suit. By late 1816 Cartwright could see that his conception was working so well that he could begin to plan a great London rally of delegates from all the provincial Hampden Clubs.

But Cartwright was not the only reformer now organising on an increasing scale. Henry Hunt, in keeping with his flamboyant character was planning a monster meeting, also in London, at which he would be chief speaker. On

November 15th, 1816 Hunt stood in front of the huge and excitable crowd which had gathered at Spa Fields in Southwark.

The numbers there, particularly of working men, probably surprised Hunt. The importance of this gathering lay not only in the unusual size of the crowds, but also in the presence of one or two north country workers, who were able to take news of it, and of this flashily good-looking man, back to Lancashire.

Hunt, no less than anybody else present that day, had been alerted to the potential of the response to his own impressive performance as a crowd gatherer. It fuelled his enormous energies and he immediately planned a second meeting, again at Spa Fields, for December 2nd.

The crowd on this occasion was equally immense and even more excitable. Contrary to Hunt's wishes, one portion of it went on the rampage.

The news of rioting crowds of reformers in the capital city, several of whom had been arrested was, on its own account, serious enough for the Home Secretary, Lord Sidmouth. The news from the north of England of the effect the activities of middle-class reformers was having on the working class there, was now just as worrying.

One Manchester government spy, 'no. 2', prepared a detailed report of what was happening. Soon, his report was on the desks both of Lord Sidmouth and of his Northern Commander, Sir John Byng. 'No. 2' told how explosively the working class of Lancashire had responded to the news from Henry Hunt's second Spa Fields meeting. Public houses in the Manchester area had that night been crowded to the doors with workers waiting for the Bridgewater mail coach to bring reports of the happenings in London. As its horses pulled into Manchester, the crowds led by a worker named Josiah Booth, rushed towards it. The coach's guard, thinking it was about to be attacked, levelled his pistol at Booth and threatened that, unless he stood back, he would blow out his brains.

Quickly, irrespective of the real dialogue between Booth and the guard, word spread that the Tower of London had been attacked by the Spa Fields crowd and, like the Bastille in Paris before it, had fallen to the people. In delight, the Manchester crowd celebrated by going on their own rampage through the town.

'No. 2's' full report of what else he had heard, was also passed on to Lord Sidmouth's office and to Sir John Byng's headquarters. The spy had, he claimed, talked to the mob's leaders who were preparing to arm their followers. The message, irrespective of the fact that it was based on no firm evidence whatsoever, was clear: an armed insurrection centred on Manchester was being planned.[3]

# 6

## Orators

These were not the first exaggerated reports Lord Sidmouth had heard by tapping the Home Office network. He had long since learnt to discount the more extreme conclusions of paid informers. But he could not discount the most unusual frequency with which reports were now pouring in of workers' gatherings; that of 'no. 2' was only one example of many. In addition to the news of strikes and of rowdy workers' meetings in Manchester, in the first week of 1817 alone Sidmouth's office was told of well-attended Hampden Club meetings at Preston, Rochdale, Radcliffe, Blackburn, Macclesfield, Middleton, Oldham, Stalybridge and Denton.[1]

From his knowledge of the Hampden Club gatherings at least, the Home Secretary had the reassurance that these were reasonably well-ordered groups, run in a quiet, law-abiding fashion, as their founder, Major Cartwright wished. The Middleton club, for example, whose secretary was the young weaver-poet, Samuel Bamford, levied a penny a week subscription on its members and discussed its issues to a carefully drawn-up agenda, in grave imitation of similar middle-class gatherings.

Of much greater concern to Lord Sidmouth, to General Byng and to the magistrates and manufacturers of the Manchester area, however, was the sudden increase in meetings of significant numbers of workers which were not only well organised, but which also took little trouble to hide the commitment of their leadership to violence.

By the last weeks of 1816 the name of one worker in particular had begun to feature strongly in the reports of spies sent via magistrates to the Home Office. He was clearly extraordinary, since his methods of attracting vast numbers of working men were both unusual and unusually successful. He was also reported to be barely 18 years old. His name was John Bagguley.

It is not easy to understand why those eager to erect a pantheon of heroes of the working class's struggle have neglected a memorial to this young man. His achievements were significant.

Physically, John Bagguley was not particularly well-endowed. A slight, thin boy, he was probably no more undernourished as a child than others raised in the back streets of the cotton town. Nevertheless, he did have the unusual advantage of having parents who could both read and write reasonably fluently and who set out to teach him to do the same. At this they seem to have been most successful. His command of the language was outstanding. He wrote copiously, and, although documents describe him as a 'Turner and Tiler' (a machine toolmaker),[2] he had already established himself as a teacher of cotton workers' children, and of cotton workers themselves. But in addition, even by this age, he clearly recognised that he had a singular ability to attract and harangue a crowd and grip it with his oratory.

In the era of television the power of the public orator has waned to become of unrecognisably small consequence. Historical black-and-white film gives a poor two-dimensional representation of the force it could exert on large crowds. In this early nineteenth-century period of history the skill of directly moving masses of people by word of mouth was reaching its zenith. John Bagguley had acquired it.

During late 1816 and early 1817, Bagguley went from town to town in the district surrounding Manchester, to wherever unemployed, striking or reformist workers were meeting. He frequently travelled with his friend, the hot-headed son of immigrant Irish parents, Samuel Drummond. On some journeys they were accompanied by a third young man who, discharged from the navy, was now a Salford tailor, John Johnston. Like both his companions Johnston had a sharp persuasive tongue.

In each town they visited, Bagguley saw the poverty and despair of the Lancashire manufacturing worker. He also saw how, when gathered in crowds away from the sobering atmosphere of the Hampden Clubs, the dull distress in the eyes of poor people could be turned to flashing hope. Oratory – crowd stirring would be a better description of what Bagguley put into practice – could be used to phenomenal effect on underfed, underprivileged people who had few other opportunities for emotional release than that of taking part in mass assemblies of people like themselves.

By December, 1816, Bagguley, sometimes alone, and

sometimes with Drummond and Johnston was attracting substantial crowds. Soon, with great ease, he could gather round him in Manchester groups of 2,000. And he had no more difficulty in operating in towns such as Blackburn, Bolton and Stockport. Quickly, he discovered the advantages of addressing these people in the language of violence and revolution, rather than in the peaceful phraseology of lawful change heard at Cartwright's Hampden Clubs. The result was that by the beginning of 1817 he was drawing in to his meetings ever greater numbers of working and out-of-work men, as well as substantial numbers of government spies.

One spy, encouraged by Hiley Addington, struck up a specially close relationship with Bagguley. He attended one of the young teacher's mass meetings held at Eccles, which had been called with the idea of directly petitioning the government for reform. As the crowds drifted home that night, after the speeches had ended, the spy succeeded in latching himself on to Bagguley. This man described how, arm-in-arm, they had walked the dark streets back to Bagguley's home discussing the outcome of the meeting.

Gradually the spy turned the conversation to the likely response to the meeting's topic – the planned petition to Parliament. The government, the spy told Bagguley, was bound to reject the petition. Bagguley readily agreed, but said the masses were not to know that. In any case, he added, an organisation was already in place to take direct action. Ready trained bands of militiamen, volunteer corps members and army veterans were available when needed. Arms caches were also in place. Three of these were in Manchester.[3]

All this could have been the wishful thinking of the spy or of Bagguley. Nevertheless, it was also closer to the language which, as the weeks passed, Bagguley and his friends, Drummond and Johnston, were increasingly using at meetings, as many reports verified. Frequently the older men at these gatherings, such as John Knight, a small-time cotton manufacturer and a much revered reformer, were seen to tug in a worried fashion at the younger men's sleeves as they roused a crowd of workers. Seditious language, as some of these older men well knew from experience, could be rewarded with imprisonment.

Just as spies' reports of these encounters were being passed to the Home Office, so too were those of more openly identified sources. Joseph Nadin, Manchester's Deputy Constable, was, for such a tough and experienced policeman, surprisingly worried by what he could see beginning to happen in his district. 'The lower orders,' he said with the image of the Luddite Revolt clear in his mind, 'are everywhere meeting in large bodies, and are very clamorous. Delegates from all quarters are moving about amongst them, as they were before the last disturbance, and they talk of a general union of lower orders throughout the kingdom . . .'[4]

Nadin's report and his warning that a working-class revolt on a considerable scale was in the offing, were added to the pile of sobering letters Hiley placed in front of his brother, the Home Secretary. As a result, Lord Sidmouth was beginning to note what was happening inside the Hampden Clubs with apprehension. In particular he had been alerted to a meeting planned by Major Cartwright, to be held in January, 1817 in the great hall of the Star and Garter Inn in Westminster, to which invitations had been sent to worker delegates of Clubs in all parts of England. The majority was expected to travel from the manufacturing north country.

The delegate from Middleton, in Lancashire, was the tall, bearded and articulate young weaver, Samuel Bamford. When he arrived in the hall of the Westminster public house, he closely observed the figures of the leading advocates of the nation's reform. They were in sharp contrast to those of the poverty-stricken young advocates of violence he had recently watched operating in the Manchester area – those such as John Bagguley and Samuel Drummond.

In the chair at the Star and Garter was Major Cartwright: thin and pale and, at 75, still wearing a surtout, hose and a brown wig; William Cobbett: more than six feet tall, portly, round cheeked, with twinkling small grey eyes, wearing fine linen and looking 'the perfect representation of what he always wished to be – an English gentleman-farmer'. Most closely of all Bamford took in the tall, well-formed figure of Henry Hunt with its blue-lapelled coat and top boots:

His features were regular, and there was a kind of youthful blandness about them which, in amicable discussion, gave his face a most agreeable expression. His lips were delicately thin and receding; but there was a dumb utterance about them which in all the portraits I have seen of him was never truly copied. His eyes were blue or light grey – not very clear nor quick, but rather heavy; except as I afterwards had opportunities for observing, when he was excited in

speaking; at which times they seemed to distend and pro-
trude; and if he worked himself furious as he sometimes
would, they became blood-streaked, and almost started from
their sockets.[5]

Bamford's picture of Hunt, drawn retrospectively, was
made by a pen dipped in acid. As yet there was no reason for
the vitriol. The reason would develop as the motives and the
methods of men such as Bamford, Hunt, Cartwright, Cobbett
and Burdett – all authors, orators and duennas – interacted.

Burdett was not present at that meeting. He manifestly
preferred hunting in Leicestershire to associating with Henry
Hunt's schemes. Nevertheless, the quarrelsome collection
which gathered at the Star and Garter that January day was
divided by an issue of some importance: whether the plank on
which they should step towards parliamentary reform should
be one of household, or of universal suffrage. The absent
Burdett, supported by Cartwright and Cobbett, was happy to
see the vote given to householders only. Hunt strongly advocated
one man, one vote. Neither party considered offering the
franchise to women. Bamford and the remainder of the worker
delegates from the north, few of whom had the slightest
chance of ever owning their homes, supported Hunt. In the
end, Hunt triumphed. The decision was one of considerable
significance; it welded the aspirations of the north country
manufacturing workers to those of this unusual man, Hunt.
Many of those present were seeing him for the first time. From
this meeting descriptions of Henry Hunt would soon be carried back to Manchester and its surrounding districts.

Important as the outcome was, it paled in national interest and excitement alongside another event of that week. January 28th had been chosen for the opening of Parliament. Henry Hunt, having won a groundswell of support for the universal suffrage he believed to be vital to the reformers' cause, decided to use the crowd the opening would attract, for his own advantage. He resolved to present the massive petition he had raised, demanding parliamentary reform, to one of the two Members of Parliament for Westminster. In Sir Francis Burdett's unfortunate absence, this meant that Lord Cochrane, Burdett's fellow Member of Parliament for Westminster, was asked to accept it at the Palace of Westminster. Before the day was out, Hunt was having the compliant young Cochrane carried head-high in an armchair through a vast crowd towards the doors of Westminster Hall.

But, a short distance away, much else was happening. The highly significant detail varies with the teller. The Prince Regent, fat and well past 50, had just delivered his speech to the new Parliament in which he had spoken of 'the attempts which have been made to take advantage of the distress of the country for the purpose of exciting a spirit of sedition and violence'. He had gone on to express confidence in the British system of law and government since, he said, 'it is acknowledged by other nations to be the most perfect that has ever fallen to the lot of any people.'[6] Apparently oblivious to the fact that vast numbers of his own nation would not have agreed with that assessment, he settled his body in his carriage, and began the journey back from Westminster through huge crowds which had been tuned to high levels of excitement not by his own royal presence, but by the charismatic star oratorical qualities of Henry Hunt.

There were, as the Prince had come to expect those days, few cheers raised by the royal coach as it reached the dense crowds. As it passed Marlborough House there was even considerable hissing and booing.

What happened after that was, it was said, sensational. So much so that, later that afternoon, Lord Sidmouth himself reconvened the House of Lords to describe in his own words to the assembled, hushed peers what had occurred.

He spoke with enormous gravity. He had to make, he said, one of the most important communications ever to have been laid before Parliament. Strangers in the House were asked to withdraw. Then, to the freshly silent galleries, the Home Secretary disclosed that, as the Prince Regent, returning home, had passed behind the garden of Carlton House, the glass of his carriage had been shattered by the bullets of a gun – or perhaps it was a stone – aimed at his Royal Highness.

What Sidmouth did not reveal, however, was that there were substantially varying views as to both the nature of the missile and the seriousness of the intent with which it had been propelled. Henry Hunt insisted that what had been launched at the royal presence was nothing more sinister, nor more solid, than a potato.

Irrespective of differing opinions, Lord Sidmouth saw only one purpose behind the attack. He believed, and he told their Lordships, that an attempt – and the disturbed nerves of the shaken and affronted Prince confirmed his belief – had been made on the life of the Regent. Moreover, it had been made at a time when crowds of reformers, many of them working class, had been gathering in Westminster. It had also been perpetrated when many of the Home Office's best and most sober informers were reporting that a serious revolt of the lower orders was in the offing. It called for as draconian a response as circumstances would permit.

In truth, the act of aggression against the Prince Regent was unfortunate. Little else could be said of it. When evidence was later collected, Mr Charles Burke, a gentleman of Camden Town testified that, as he strode out of Bird Cage Walk towards Marlborough House, he had seen a man 10 yards away pull something from his pocket and take aim with a raised arm. However, the owner of the hand that held the stone – or vegetable – that was launched at the royal carriage, had melted back into a protective and sympathetic crowd, and nothing further amiss had occurred.[7] Nobody had died, and only pride had been injured.

But these facts were irrelevant to Lord Sidmouth, incapable as he was of deviating from the parallel lines of thought which typified his rigid accounting mentality. He had been at the centre of government when the Luddite Revolt had brought the nation to the edge of revolution. He was prepared now to use the same strong-arm methods he had used then.

He was convinced – despatches from Manchester continuously reminded him of the fact – that the Hampden Clubs were a real threat to peace. The numbers of these societies in the manufacturing towns of the north were growing rapidly. The crowds attracted by the reforming aims of their well-known leaders were swelling ominously. Crowds of two or three thousand workers, such as those raised by the young John Bagguley, were becoming commonplace. Sidmouth needed to be able to give his magistrates and his military commanders more effective powers to control these situations than they now possessed, and to insist that they demonstrate these powers.

In the absence of a culprit for the attack on the Prince Regent, the worst of all draconian punishments available to Lord Sidmouth and that which he had liberally used during the Luddite Revolt – hanging by the neck – could not be invoked. This incident, nevertheless, was what Sidmouth needed: a powerful lever. He could use it to introduce legislation to control the communication between organised groups he believed the nation should fear.

His immediate action on hearing the news of what was now referred to as an assassination attempt on the Prince Regent, was to instruct the Lord Mayor of London to double the guard on the Bank of England and be prepared to call out the military in aid of the Civil Power if need be.[8] More to the point, he had Hiley sift evidence from the letters and despatches collected from Manchester and its surrounding towns into an impressive dossier. This was used as the basis of reports by Secret Committees of the Houses of Lords and Commons which Sidmouth quickly set up.

As a result, parliamentary bills were introduced on February 18th and 19th, 1817 seriously curtailing the right of public meeting. It was proposed that no public gathering of any kind could be held without the sanction of magistrates, who were empowered to arrest anyone speaking sedition.

Then, tightening the grip on the Hampden Clubs, all societies which formed links with 'fraternised branches', and societies which sent delegates as their representatives to any other societies were to be made illegal. It was all tailor-made to prevent Cartwright's clubs from gathering together their working-class delegates and uniting them in nation-wide action.

At the second reading of the first of the bills in the House of Lords on February 24th, Sidmouth rose to make sure nobody had misunderstood the reasons that had brought it into being: 'An organised system,' he said, 'has been established in every quarter, under the semblance of demanding parliamentary reform, but many of them, I am convinced, have that specious pretext in their mouths only, but revolution and rebellion in their hearts.'

He ended his speech with the stunning appeal to the House to suspend the Habeas Corpus Act – that is, to suspend the Act which prevented arrest and detention without trial – the Englishman's best-established defence against violation of his civil liberties.

Before the following month was out, his proposal having been rapidly pushed through Parliament, Sidmouth had the internal affairs of the nation in a grip no Home Secretary in peace time, before or since, has ever matched.

# 7

## Local Law

General Sir John Byng was the most senior and most powerful arm of the forces of law and order which could be called in
to act if and when there was a failure of the local measures
normally used to preserve the peace of Manchester. The men
who administered this law, in these troubled times, the magistrates of the town and its district, needed therefore to be
constantly in touch with the officer commanding the armed
forces. Their relationship with Byng, after the attack on the
Prince Regent, and the suspension of the Habeas Corpus Act,
was to become crucial. It was inevitable that in the present
climate imprisonment without trial would provoke some sort
of working-class demonstration.

Surprisingly, the most senior of these Manchester magistrates, and the man in whom the Home Office had learnt to
put great trust after the Luddite Revolt, lived many miles
from the district for which he was responsible. The Reverend
William Hay actually had his parish at Ackworth in
Yorkshire. Byng, when he moved into his Pontefract

headquarters, found that he and Hay were near neighbours. It was a remarkable fact, therefore, that the two officials on whom the peace of Manchester most depended both lived a day's ride from it over the Pennine hills.

Hay was a most stern administrator of the law. His no-nonsense style of magistracy was much admired at the Home Office. Those who watched him at work on the judicial bench quickly learnt to respect him. 'When he winks, heaven blinks, when he speaks, hell quakes,' wrote one.[1] And much of Hay's time on the bench was spent in keeping a firm rein on the behaviour of the ever-growing population which the innovatory technology of Manchester and its district had created: the workers of the cotton mills. Hay was the son of the Earl of Kinnoull, and of the daughter of the Earl of Oxford. The social gulf between him and those who so frequently stood before him, therefore, could scarcely have been greater.

However, unlike many of his brother magistrates, Hay was not without experience of the law. After leaving his Oxford college, he had practised as a barrister and had then taken holy orders before becoming Chairman of Salford Quarter Sessions.

Salford was already an urban extension of Manchester, separated from it only by the river Irwell. Friedrich Engels, when he saw Salford, took a particular dislike to its 'old and therefore very unwholesome, dirty and ruinous locality'.[2] Essentially one large working-class quarter, it was penetrated by a single broad avenue off which ran closely packed streets and courts. Engels claimed that many of its side roads had not been cleaned since the day they were built.

Hay had responsibilities which extended far beyond Salford and much of Manchester's criminal business passed through his hands in the Quarter Sessions Court. He had been instrumental in sending for trial several workers who were subsequently hanged for their part in violent Luddite incidents.

Dozens of Hay's letters in a precise, never corrected nor revised hand, made their way to the Home Office in the years that followed, and particularly in 1817. They appear to reflect the personality of an acutely efficient administrator with not much tolerance for human frailty. It is not difficult to understand why the Home Secretary had by now learned to place so much reliance on Hay's word. Indeed, there is a frightening collection of common characteristics in the impersonal, well-ordered, meticulously documented habits of the Establishment trio: Sidmouth, Byng and Hay. It was a formidable group that now had such power over the lives of so many citizens of the swelling cotton metropolis.

Hay, however, was only one of a dozen or more magistrates operating in and around Manchester. Another in close touch with the Home Secretary, and with his brother, Hiley, was the Rector of St Mark's, Cheetham Hill, the Reverend C.W. Ethelston. Pompous, and with a loud voice to match, Ethelston was the very model of the Establishment conservative Anglican magistrate. He also tried his hand at being a writer and poet. One of his works bore the arresting title, *A Pindaric Ode to the Genius of Great Britain*. The style of his long-winded reports to Lord Sidmouth is such that they could well have been written in the previous century. They frequently included quotations from Horace, name dropping and useful homilies. In one letter he assured Sidmouth that, 'Till ye virtues of ye land owner like ye family oak over-shadow ye estate of inferior ranks of society will never but made sensible that the first link in the chain of social order is fastened to ye throne of God.'[3]

Ethelston's archaic style and interminable mixed metaphors can only have given the Home Office clerks reason to chuckle. Equally, they can only have made Sidmouth wary of acting on any of the information sent in by the melodramatic parson. Nevertheless, Lord Sidmouth's brother, Hiley, had no scruples when it came to making full use of Ethelston's compliant manner. He encouraged the parson to employ spies and, at every opportunity, Ethelston reverentially sent in their reports of workers' meetings in the Manchester area. Ethelston called his spies 'the wheels of my political machine'. Hiley periodically sent cash to keep them, in Ethelston's metaphor, adequately 'oiled'.[4]

Several of the other leading magistrates were, like Hay and Ethelston, either high Anglican or high Tory or both. None had won Hay's reputation for steadiness under pressure.

A few were newcomers to the bench. W. D. Evans, a nervous, insecure man, was one. Another who had not long gone down from Brasenose College, Oxford, was – though it would not last – a figure of considerable fun. William Hulton, the 29-year-old heir to a local landed fortune, had effeminate airs and expensive clothes to match. He was known to the locals as 'Miss Hulton'.[5] Whatever his qualities under difficult circumstances, they were as yet too untried to be familiar to central government.

One individual – quite uneducated – whose name and fame in connection with the magistrates had spread far beyond Lancashire, and certainly as far as London and Lord Sidmouth, was that of Joseph Nadin. This bull of a man, the town Deputy Constable, held the day-to-day policing of the town in his manifestly powerful grip. His Neanderthal forehead under his black hat, along with his immense brown coat had made Nadin the most easily recognised figure in early nineteenth-century Manchester. For 30 years he had been an official fixture there. Once a master spinner, he applied the law to the working class with unmatched severity. As a result, he was hated by most of the community in which he lived. According to one of his contemporaries, Archibald Prentice, 'this coarse man was the real ruler of Manchester.'[6]

His physical methods were notorious. One respectable townsman, John Royles, a joiner, told how late one night in August, 1816 Nadin had approached him and accused him of theft. Before he could respond, Nadin struck him viciously between the eyes with a truncheon, breaking his nose. It took Royles some time to recover. When he had done so and was at last able to speak, he told Nadin he would make him pay for his brutality. Hearing this, Nadin immediately rushed him, covered in blood as he was, down to the Police Office. Once there, Royles continued to protest. Nadin now instructed one of his beadles to, 'Put the bridle on this fellow and stop his tongue.' The metal 'bridle' or gag was forced into Royles's mouth and cruelly buckled fast. He was made to stand in this state, with blood pouring down his face from his broken nose for 15 minutes. It was two o'clock in the morning before Royles was given medical attention.[7]

When it came to money matters, Nadin used somewhat more subtle methods of manipulating his powerful office to his own advantage. There was already evidence that he was registering many petty offences as felonies, each of which entitled him to a reward. The more serious the offence, the greater the monies due to him. In addition, he could qualify for a 'Tyburn ticket' – the right of exemption from service in parish affairs. Nadin was reputed to be able to sell these tickets for £300 a piece. Already it was said he had made as much as £20,000 from these dealings – in 1817 a huge fortune for this autonomous policeman.

Just as the Home Office regularly supplied magistrates with funds to operate spies, so the Reverend Mr Hay in his turn supplied cash to Nadin to operate his own special secret service. Not that it was wholly secret. By early 1817 when John Bagguley and Samuel Drummond were organising workers' meetings they were permanently on their guard against Nadin's disguised special constables. And in the same manner that the Reverend Mr Hay had his special relationship with Nadin, so too magistrates in the towns lying outside Manchester formed other links with particularly useful citizens. At Bolton, for example, the resident magistrate was the fiercely patriotic Colonel Ralph Fletcher. In order to feed the Home Secretary with as much information as he could cull from workers' meetings, Fletcher had formed an unusually fruitful relationship with an Oldham resident, William Chippindale. This manufacturer was clearly fascinated by secret service assignments. In modern times he would have figured large in newspaper revelations of MI5 activities.

Chippindale was never happier than when he himself was attending secret meetings in disguise. His detailed reports in late 1816, signed 'XY', hinting at plans for uprising and rebellion among workers, had made Fletcher rush into communication with the Home Office. There, Addington quickly recognised the authenticity of at least some of Chippindale's descriptions, and was soon instructing him to write direct to his brother, Lord Sidmouth.[8]

Sir John Byng too received direct reportage from 'XY', making Chippindale one of the government's most highly regarded sources of sensitive information. In addition to his own activities, Chippindale ran a small school of spies which provided a daily account of covert working-class activities. One member of this school was the spy who had the ear and friendship of the unsuspecting young John Bagguley.

There remained one other whose information to government, in spite of his humble origins and his lowly office, was listened to with extraordinary attention. John Lloyd, the Clerk to Stockport magistrates, had now been regularly consulted by the Home Office on northern affairs for five years. In 1812, when all else had failed, Lloyd's unusual energy in trailing suspects, and his tough mental and physical treatment of the prisoners he took, had been instrumental in unlocking the Luddite wall of silence. He it had been who extracted the confessions which had sent the first of a stream of north country workers to trial and eventual execution.

Whatever else can be said of Lloyd, he did little he was

not prepared to display to the world. Unlike Chippindale, he never operated as a spy nor left any record of having used any spies. His profile at meetings of Stockport and Manchester spinners and weavers during this time was high and he appears to have taken a perverse pleasure in knowing that, not only did his presence electrify a workers' meeting, it engendered hatred.

Lloyd's ambition was as naked as much of his behaviour. As a boy, he had been sent by his widowed mother from Shropshire to Cheshire. There he had become an articled clerk in the office of the successful Stockport attorney, Holland Watson. No young man can have had a surer eye for his future career than the young Lloyd. Not only did he become an ensign in the Stockport Volunteers, the militia regiment commanded by his employer, he also married Watson's sister and took over the clerkship of Stockport magistrates from him. In addition Lloyd adopted some of Watson's high Tory attitudes and genteel values.

Of the towns surrounding Manchester, Stockport was one of the most attractive and certainly the most interesting. It lies on a group of hills alongside the river Mersey from which its steep streets climb. First the silk industry, then the hat-making industry had blossomed on its water-powered streams. Finally cotton had brought the steam engines and the factories. When Lloyd arrived there as a boy its transition from a market to a cotton town was far from complete. The defacing side-effects of the Industrial Revolution that were eventually to make it notorious as a smoke-filled hole in the Cheshire hills had not yet overtaken Stockport.

Lloyd, on his arrival there, was attracted to and excited by this place made vibrant and profitable as a result of its new technologically based industries. Its dynamism suited his. The first steam engine was installed there in 1791. Fifteen years later it had 26 engines driving factories that were beginning to rival Manchester's in size and output.[9]

Lloyd was proud of the town. He went to extraordinary lengths to ensure that its inhabitants maintained the same loyalty to King and country as his own – recently minted, as it was, by his acceptance both by occupation and marriage into the Establishment. As clerk to two elderly magistrates – the Reverend John Philips was well past 80 and infirm, and the Reverend Charles Prescot, only a few years younger and more than glad to delegate – Lloyd was able to administer much of the law of Stockport according to his own wishes. He had enough energies left over to act as a policeman to the district. His efforts in suppressing Luddite risings in 1812 had earned him glowing testimonials from his fellow townsmen.

The Luddite episode naturally brought Lloyd to the notice of Lord Sidmouth, the Home Secretary. Lloyd's unequalled success in squeezing information out of captured Luddites had not gone unpraised. In spite of this his ambition-driven hints to the Home Office that he be found employment in government service had been ignored. Nevertheless, for five years now he had kept up an intimate correspondence with the Under Secretaries in Whitehall, reporting in detail the resurgent, rebellious mood of the cotton spinners and weavers when the depression following the end of the war with France again hit the industry.

Frequently Lloyd was unsure that his work on behalf of government was appreciated. He sought reassurance. It was freely given. Early in 1816, for example, John Beckett patted him on the back after his latest communication and told him that Lord Sidmouth returned 'his thanks for your communication, and to express his approbation of your zeal and activity'.[10]

Sidmouth's brother, Hiley, always alert to the dangers of covert communication among the supporters of parliamentary reform, was ever ready to urge Lloyd on. Lloyd had been one of the first to report his concerns about the revived worker interest in reform. Hiley told him in December, 1816, 'It would be of great importance if a correspondence could be traced between the leaders of the disaffected of Stockport and persons of a similar description in London, from whence there seems to be strong reason to believe that all the mischief emanates.'[11]

Lloyd need have had no doubt as to how seriously his reports of the meetings of cotton workers in and around Stockport were being taken. When, after the 'attempt on the life' of the Prince Regent, Lord Sidmouth had Hiley prepare the impressive and frightening documents to be put before the Secret Committees of the Houses of Parliament, one of Lloyd's clearly written and well-organised letters was to be the first in the folder. It told of a new upsurge of unrest in the district and of how workers in Stockport were trying to organise a meeting to petition the House of Commons for parliamentary reform. But Lloyd wanted to make clear that, in his view, the reforming activity was nothing more than a front for a much more serious purpose. He had heard seditious language used at these meetings making comparisons between France, whose Revolution was well within living memory, and England. He had listened to one speaker draw parallels between the King of France and the Prince Regent. The Speaker, John Knight, described what happened when the French King had been faced with reform: 'The *King* refused gentlemen – and what was the consequence? Why – *he lost his head*!!' 'The inference' of this speech, Lloyd wrote, 'was obvious – the Prince refuses and he is to be impeached by his *subjects*! Such I believe to be within their sapient speculations.'

Lloyd was already beginning to identify the ringleaders. 'I wish very much to have the names of those who dare step forward to support revolutionary principles,' he wrote, 'for there no longer remains a doubt as to the ultimate object.'[12]

# 8

## A Leader

Throughout January and February of 1817 the size and frequency of meetings of workers in and around Manchester increased at a phenomenal pace. By the month's end there was scarcely a day or a night without the report of a gathering on the open spaces near several of Manchester's churches. Other groups met in fields near Salford, Stockport, Oldham, Eccles and similar towns.

Lloyd, with unmatchable energy, would ride his horse from town to town, stand at the edge of the crowd and carefully take note. Often, late into the same night, he would write at great speed to be in time for the mail coach so that his report could be on the desk of Hiley Addington or John Beckett at the Home Office within 48 hours. Post horses were capable of getting urgent messages to London within 24 hours.

Frequently several government agents reported on the same meeting. More than once Lloyd stood alongside a disguised William Chippindale, collecting information for General Byng or Mr Ethelston. Unrecognised by either of them, at least one magistrate's spy was customarily among the crowd of workers, listening both to shouted speeches and to the more intimate conversations of those standing nearby.

Lloyd needed little time to learn to identify the crowd's leaders. At meeting after meeting the same men spelling out the same message emerged. Most impressive of all was the badly dressed, thin figure of young John Bagguley daily polishing his oratorical performance as the crowds round him grew. By early 1817 he was attracting more than 3,000 workers to Bibby's Rooms, the huge empty spinning shed in the New Islington back streets of Manchester. As the days passed the imagery Bagguley used grew more colourful. One spy reported how he was making comparisons which still today would not be found unfamiliar. At Bibby's he called to the crowd 'of the blood which had been spilt in Ireland' and of how ready the people there were to spill more blood to win their freedom.[1] Englishmen, by implication, should be prepared to do the same.

Two days later he was yelling at those massed round him to petition the Prince Regent for their rights. If that failed, he said, they would petition the King. And if, after 40 days, they still had no response, then the people had a right to imprison the King and his family. On this occasion, as on others, the chairman, George Bradbury, sitting alongside him on the wooden platform, and knowing that this brazen and seditious talk was courting arrest for both of them, tried to hiss him into silence. But also on this occasion, as on others, the crowd rose to shout Bradbury down.[2] They adored Bagguley and the more they showed their adoration, the closer his speeches moved towards blood and revolution.

Bagguley's acolytes, Samuel Drummond and John Johnston, had by now acquired their own oratorical skills. On some occasions they would stand alongside Bagguley, on others they would travel to the outlying cotton towns and harangue their own meetings. Always in attendance on the speakers' platforms at these gatherings, not always sitting comfortably at what they heard, were the politically more mature. George Bradbury was one. Old John Knight, 'the Manchester Cartwright', Joseph Mitchell and William Haigh were others. They had spent years in the quieter by-ways they had hoped would lead to parliamentary reform, sitting in at Major Cartwright's Hampden Club meetings and taking what resolute, but passive action they could. Both Knight and Haigh had been among the 38 arrested by Joseph Nadin at the Prince Regent's Arms reform meeting in Ancoats Lane in 1812.

Lord Sidmouth, now that he had successfully seen the Act of Suspension of Habeas Corpus through both Houses of Parliament was carefully preparing a list of Manchester reformers for whom arrest warrants were being considered. It was gathered from information supplied daily by Lloyd, Chippindale and others. The names of Bagguley, Drummond, Johnston, as well as Bradbury, Knight, Mitchell and Haigh were already on that list. He was by now ready to encourage his Commander of the Northern District, Sir John Byng, to take direct action.

But despite the fact that he too, like the Home Office, was hearing still more shrill information describing how Manchester workers were organising for some kind of ill-defined action, Byng remained motionless. In a few short, crisp and neatly penned sentences he told the Home Secretary that he preferred to observe the situation from a suitable distance, and to control the north from where he sat – this despite the fact that Sidmouth had expected him to take up his command in Manchester.

At about this time Byng had concerns about his 'business' – either his farmland or his bloodstock – but he did not mention them in this correspondence. Hiley Addington responded on behalf of his brother,

> Lord Sidmouth is abundantly satisfied with the reasons that you assign for having decided to remain at Pontefract and begs me to assure you that it will always be his wish that you should exercise your own discretion where local intelligence [which] cannot have been received here, may dispose you to doubt the expediency of acting under the directions or suggestions that you may have received from this office.[3]

Byng, therefore, had confirmed the principle that he was his own master as far as military activities in the north were concerned, and that the principle included minimal activity.

But neither Byng nor anyone else could have been under the illusion that the worrying activities of the manufacturing working class were beginning to subside. It was at a meeting in Stockport on February 10th, 1817 that the suggestion appears to have been made by Bradbury that workers should organise themselves in groups of ten to carry petitions for parliamentary reform to London. Some worker had discovered an archaic law made during the petitioning which preceded the beheading of Charles I. Ten people, it seemed, could carry a petition; an eleventh would turn it into a 'tumultuous assembly'.[4]

John Bagguley's were among the first pairs of ears to be wide open to the possibilities this law offered – if it existed. Within a few days he was incorporating the idea into his speeches to crowds of workers. A few days more and he had a plan. By Monday, March 3rd it was a firm proposal.

John Livesey, the magistrate's spy, was one of a tightly packed crowd who that night assembled in Manchester's Bibby's Rooms to hear speeches from every leading reformer in the district. Livesey reported that not only were Drummond and Bradbury intoxicated by the heady atmosphere of the cheering mass of men crammed into the great shed, they appeared to be actually drunk.[5]

Bagguley, however, was sober and at his rabble-rousing best. In his piercing, clear voice he described his plan to his listeners, all of them poor, most of them unemployed, and many hungry. They would, he told them, in a week's time, on March 10th, march in groups of ten, each carrying a petition for the Prince Regent in London. What the petition would say, however, was not at this point disclosed to them. Each man would carry a blanket on his back. Although it was still the depth of winter, no detailed logistical arrangements were necessary. The march to London would take nine days there and nine days back.[6] People in villages on the road would provide shelter in houses, barns and schoolrooms. They would be joined by other poor people of a similar political persuasion from different towns and distant counties. All those in work were to give half their earnings to the families of men out of work so that they could join the march. Nevertheless, both the march itself and the meeting on St Peter's Field were to be peaceful. At no time were those to be involved encouraged to carry arms of any kind – nor was there later any suggestion that they did.

Bagguley delivered his speech with his now skilled rhetoric. It was well noted by John Livesey.[7] Here for the first time Bagguley used the phrases he was to develop and expand during the next few days, asking the crowd for the first time of many, 'Will you turn back when you get to Stockport and face those high and cold hills in Derbyshire?' And from all sides the crowd yelled, 'No, no!'

'I am a Reformer, a Republican and a Leveller,' he went on, 'and will never give up the course till we have established a Republican Government.'[8]

Again the meeting's chairman tugged at the foolhardy though fearless young man's sleeve trying to silence his words, so obviously seditious to any government agent in the crowd. Again it was too late to stop the flow. The crowd yelled its support and its delight. Bagguley was again forced to push his way through the throng to address the many hundreds gathered outside the doors. They stood to hear him repeat his great scheme.

Nobody, certainly not Bagguley, had any doubt that his words were being recorded by both government observers and paid spies. John Lloyd was the first of several to relay to London the plans for what was to become known as the Blanketeers' March.[9]

Others too, whose information the Home Office had learnt to respect, were sending messages insisting that the trouble now brewing had a much more frightening purpose than that of winning the vote for the working man. Joseph Nadin sent an urgent report to the Reverend Mr Hay. The parson thought his Deputy Constable exaggerated somewhat; nevertheless, he sent copies of Nadin's alarmed letter to both Lord Sidmouth and General Byng. Nadin had clearly spelt out his concerns:

> There cannot be a doubt that they intend next Monday to be the Grand Field Day with them – they will go by tens and as they go thro the country they will breed a commotion in the towns as they go along and by that they will have a heavy body together and try at a Revolution. I never saw people so dissatisfied and determined in my life – shure there will be something ordered before that time to prevent any meeting. I assure you there is something more amongst them than reform of Parliament.[10]

Reports to the Home Office were still being rushed in by every post horse and mail coach. Several of the magistrates' spies in and around Manchester were coming to identical conclusions after listening to the speeches of Bagguley, Drummond and Johnston. Colonel Fletcher, the Bolton magistrate, told Hiley Addington how delegates at meetings represented vast numbers of people, all of whom were ripe for insurrection.[11] One of his spies, 'A B', in spite of the march's proclaimed peaceful purpose, assured him that

> There is not soldiers in the Kingdom fit to cope with 3 millions of people . . ., there is Manchester, Huddersfield,

Sheffield, Derby, Nottingham, and Birmingham all within the compass of two days march from each other and nothing would stop the people if they were to go to London.[12]

Yet another workers' meeting was held on the Wednesday of that week at Bibby's Rooms. Outside the building Johnston worked on the crowd of 2,000 who had not been able to push their way into the great shed to hear the chief speakers. Johnston's view of the manner in which the St Peter's Field gathering should be conducted had a somewhat different emphasis from that of Bagguley. Cynically he told the cheering mob of workers he would advise them in preparation for next Monday's meeting, *not* to take pistols with them, nor to 'make different articles into warlike implements nor to fix their carving knives to the ends of sticks', but this he would say, 'that if they assembled together in large bodies and were *not* armed they would certainly fall into the hands of the Civil and Military Powers'. His meaning was crystal clear to those who heard him, in particular the spy who nervously noted every word.[13]

Inside Bibby's, Bagguley, excusing the fact that he and Drummond had not yet drafted the petition, assured his audience that 3,000 copies would be in print by next day. And outside, the crowd, tiring of Johnston, began to yell for, 'Our leader! Our leader! Bagguley!' The roars drowned what was being said outside. 'Bagguley!' they yelled, 'Bagguley forever!'[14]

In contrast with the elation of the crowd and the bombast of the orators, the slip of paper eventually produced for marchers to wear strapped to their arms on the road to London bore words which were markedly humble and reasoned.

Its main purpose was to draw attention to the abject poverty, the everywhere visible hunger, and the widespread general distress of those workers and their families living in the manufacturing towns of the north of England – the conditions which had enabled Bagguley to gather so many people around him with such ease. It begged,

> Your Royal Father, your Royal Highness, and the House of Commons, for redress, which applications, we are sorry to say, have in our humble but firm belief, not received that attention which their importance merited so that now, when the waste of war is over, our sufferings are become more general and deeper than ever.

The petition drew attention to the quadrupling of taxes and the doubling of rents during the war. It pointed out the injustices of the Corn Laws and of the suspension of Habeas Corpus. Its strongest words were to call for the dismissal of ministers who had devised such repressive measures. It asked for parliamentary reform. It promised, if these wishes were granted, that the Prince Regent could then rely on the petitioners' support and gratitude. Its only meek threat was to add in bold print, 'WITHOUT THIS WE CAN NEITHER SUPPORT YOU NOR OURSELVES.'[15]

On both the Friday and the Saturday of that week more giant meetings were held at New Islington. At each one Bagguley shouted to those massed in front of him to 'come on Monday morning with your knapsacks on your backs.' At one of the gatherings there was some discussion as to whether one blanket or two would be sufficient to keep out the many nights of cold on the road to London. Doubters were assured that friendly assistance and shelter would willingly be given by like-minded friends en route. A Scottish contingent, it was said, had already set out for the south. Many Yorkshire towns-folk were preparing to join the march. There were Yorkshire men in the crowd that night as proof.

Every word of Bagguley, Drummond and Johnston was by now being reported to the Manchester magistrates. But they had already heard enough. Early the following day, 24 hours before the march on London was due to begin, Nadin was ordered first to arrest Johnston. His increasingly violent phrases from the New Islington hustings made the magis-trates certain that, in his case, they could take immediate action without awaiting further instructions from London.

Also arrested was the septuagenarian printer, William Ogden, who had been responsible for producing the handbill, his name in bold type at its foot, announcing the next day's meeting in St Peter's Field. That night Nadin burst into his room, pulled the old man from his bed, and without allowing him to wear proper shoes, dragged him before a magistrate. Nadin then clamped a 30 lb manacle on Ogden which, not surprisingly, ruptured him.

But even before taking direct action against the identifiable leaders of the planned march, at least some of the Manchester magistrates had come to the conclusion that the situation was developing into one they could no longer handle. On Thursday, March 6th, the frightened W. D. Evans had sent a messenger to Sir John Byng in Pontefract requesting his personal attendance in Manchester and the assistance of as large a military force as he could supply.[16]

Byng felt there was still insufficient reason for military involvement. But there was little else he could do but click his tongue in annoyance and set off with his horse over the Pennines, gathering troops on the way. It was the first formal request of this kind that had been made of him. Little as he approved of panicky magistrates, he could not refuse a direct magisterial request. At nine o'clock on the following Saturday night, only a few hours before the Blanketeers began to gather on St Peter's Field, he was in Manchester's Police Office listening to the mostly elderly magistrates gathered round the table in front of him who now openly expressed fears of a major working-class uprising.

When they had had their say Byng crisply described how he intended to distribute his forces and how he intended to deal with the situation when the workers gathered on the Field in a few hours' time. He then retired to his bed – but not before he had written a meticulously neat note to John Beckett at the Home Office, leaving him in no doubt as to what he thought of the quality of the magistrates, adding '*My private opinion* is that you need not take any alarm for tomorrow's proceedings here.'[17]

Some of the workers involved were less sanguine than Byng about the next day's outcome. They had already made plain their doubts concerning the adequacy of the preparations for a march of thousands of men over 200 miles in the depths of an English winter. One important workers' leader, Samuel Bamford, flatly refused to have anything to do with the affair. One of the reasons why the articulate weaver-poet did not take part, and dissuaded the whole of his Middleton contingent from so doing, was undoubtedly jealousy. The dynamism and success of young Bagguley, not yet out of his teens, had generated a scale of enthusiasm and support never seen before by Bamford or anybody else in Lancashire. Nevertheless, Bamford's stated reasons for not cooperating were not without foundation. He believed that the cold and the wet could kill great numbers of those foolish enough to set out for London. He also argued that, since the march was illegal, the authorities would prevent it.

At heart, the working-class Bamford was a man of the Establishment. As secretary of the Middleton Hampden Club, he revered Cartwright's maxim, 'Hold fast by the law.' He would stick by it for the rest of his life – and live very well by its observance.

The question was, however, what lay ahead for the less talented – the teeming masses of working-class Manchester whose condition had been determined by technological change. Was there any chance that they too would prosper if they demonstrated their plight strictly within the confines of Britain's laws?

# 9

## Blanketeers

On March 10th, 1817, the date on which John Bagguley planned to lead his march of workers from St Peter's Field in Manchester to present their petitions to the Prince Regent in London, the Prince had other activities in hand. Coming to the end of his State Visit was the Grand Duke Nicholas of Russia, accompanied by Prince Esterhazy and General Kutosoff. They had just passed a most pleasing few days in Brighton. There, 'a numerous cavalcade from the Pavilion had enjoyed the diversion of hunting with the subscription pack of harriers, which threw off from the racecourse.'[1] These days the Prince's girth prevented his covering more than a few yards on horseback in pursuit of the fortunate hare; his mounted appearances were token only.

But in other physical activities he could take a less passive part. That day, a brilliant evening party had been prepared as a farewell for his Imperial Highness. The State Apartments were to be thrown open for a ball of 150 invited guests. The Grand Duke, *The Times* was to tell its readers, would partner

Miss Floyd, and the Duke of Devonshire the Countess of Morley.[2] More importantly, the only dance planned for the evening, other than the quadrille, was to be the new waltz, introduced to the English Court during the previous summer. On that occasion *The Times* had not equivocated, it had said,

> This is a circumstance which ought not to be passed over in silence. National morals depend on national habits; and it is quite sufficient to cast one's eyes on the voluptuous inter-twining of the limbs, and close compression of the bodies, in this dance, to see that it is far indeed removed from the modest reserve which has hitherto been considered distinctive of English females. So long as this obscene display was confined to prostitutes and adultresses we did not think it deserving of notice; but now that it is attempted to be forced on the respectable classes of society by the evil example of their superiors, we feel it a duty to warn every parent against exposing his daughter to so fatal a contagion.[3]

For his ball of March 10th, therefore, the Prince Regent had elected to waltz and be damned.

The Home Secretary, on the visit he had some days earlier made to Brighton, had raised the topic of the worrying situation in Manchester, and what was planned for the day. But it is certain that the Prince's interest was engaged much more by the anticipated movements in the State Apartments than any that might involve hot-headed young men in the north country town.

The morning was recorded as unusually bright and warm

for the time of year. Bagguley and Drummond, now that Johnston was under arrest, can only have watched the first stirrings of activity on the streets with considerable apprehension. What was happening, however, was both surprising and reassuring. From dawn, workers from outlying districts had been seen arriving at the outskirts of Manchester. By the time the streets were lit by a clear sun, thousands of these badly dressed, underfed, but nevertheless determined people were on the march. Many carried bundles strapped to their backs. For the most part these packages consisted of nothing more than one or two tightly rolled blankets. Many had fastened to their arms a folded sheet of white paper – the petition.

The characteristic which appeared so threatening to the citizens of Manchester, anxiously watching from their windows, was the aggressive single-mindedness with which each group – many members of which carried walking sticks along with their bundles – strode towards the centre of the town. Each hour brought in a fresh mass of people from a different direction: Oldham, Blackburn, Bolton, Stockport, Rochdale and even as far as the Yorkshire border.

As the numbers swelled so did the confidence and the aggression of those who marched. They jeered at those townsfolk bold enough to stand on street corners and stare, and shook their fists at the cotton merchants angrily gazing out from behind the window panes of the Manchester Exchange's reading room. And as the numbers swelled so did the fears rise of all those who watched. Neither the marchers nor the observers could know that this occasion and the emotions it was now provoking were to be merely a rehearsal for a much greater event.

As the morning moved on towards ten o'clock, to those responsible for maintaining law and order the influx had begun to reach worrying proportions. The Reverend William Hay estimated that already, by that time, there were 12,000 marchers on the streets.[4] At about the same time, a yeomanry cavalry officer, riding out of Manchester, estimated that he passed at least 10,000 workers marching down the Stockport road.[5]

Hay and several other key people with different degrees of responsibility and in varying states of apprehension now began to move towards the great open space near St Peter's Church to which the marchers were so purposefully heading. By agreement, the magistrates made their way to a cottage belonging to a Mr Brown on the edge of St Peter's Field. They felt that this little house, with its garden adjoining the Field, would be a suitable place from which to observe the morning's proceedings. Besides Hay were the talkative Reverend Mr Ethelston and the nervous W. D. Evans, both of whom had shown signs of over-reaction in the weeks leading up to this day's events. Another magistrate, Holland Watson, though not prone to lose his head, had neither sympathy with, nor much tolerance of the working class *en masse*. They were joined by Joseph Green, the town's boroughreeve and his two constables. Outside, in the crowd, easily distinguishable by his brown cloak and his bullneck was the more active arm of the law: Joseph Nadin. He had already spread throughout the crowd a number of his spies and special constables in plain clothes, while near him was gathered a substantial group of constables, identifiable by their badges of office, and armed with thick staves or truncheons.

The local newspapers' editors had arranged for their reporters to be present. London papers had engaged local correspondents for what promised to be a very newsworthy event. William Cowdroy's man, for the *Manchester Gazette*, estimated that by eleven o'clock that day there were already 40,000 men, women and children on the roughly square enclosure. *The Times* put the figure at 60,000 – others guessed even higher.[6]

One other most important figure of the Establishment was already in position within close range of Mr Brown's cottage. Lieutenant General Sir John Byng sat astride his horse in front of a squadron of cavalry in a street alongside St Peter's Field.

At various points in the town, either near the Field or within easy reach of it, though out of sight, was the body of a substantial military force. It included the rest of the cavalry regiment, the King's Dragoon Guards under Colonel Teesdale, five mounted troops of the Cheshire Yeomanry under Colonel Townshend, a detachment of the 85th Infantry Regiment under Colonel Thornton and a company of the 54th under Captain Birley with a second company of the same regiment near the gaol.

But there was no doubt among the senior officers as to who was to be unmistakably in active command should the forces move on to the Field. Byng himself would ride at the head of one of the squadrons. In his own words, he did so 'To present the best order among the troops, to prevent any wanton or improper use of them . . . I am therefore answerable for their appearance there,' he said.[7]

Byng himself was an excellent as well as a knowledgeable horseman. He could speak with the confidence of experience of cavalrymen's ability to act without panic when riding through a potentially violent mob of people.

It is a remarkable fact, as Charles Darwin was later to point out, that even a skilled child sitting on the back of a horse weighing more than half a ton, using no more than the hands and the legs, can comfortably restrain and guide this deceptively powerful creature. This control is made possible by one simple piece of technology, whilst a second device enormously enhances the rider's potential for violent activity. The first is the metal bit (attached to the bridle) which passes through the horse's mouth. If, as happens only very rarely, this metal fractures, so uncontrollable is the bitless horse that the rider is powerless to stop or even turn the animal.

The second is the stirrup. Unknown to the Romans, it was introduced into Europe about the seventh century AD. Its invention made it possible, not only for the cavalryman to exert better leg control over his mount, but it made the animal more easily manoeuvrable by reins held in one hand. More important, the stirrups added the horse's weight to that of the rider's body, thus powerfully increasing the momentum of the weapon held in the other hand – the sword or the lance. This enhancement of the power and control of the cavalryman's arm both revolutionised cavalry practice and vastly elevated the importance of cavalry in warfare.

The horse and its rider carrying a broadsword, therefore, unite to form a phenomenal weapon, many times more powerful than is required to kill a human being. Only when the restraining technological devices are abandoned in bad horsemanship, or removed by accident or design, can the horse itself become a maverick and potentially lethal force. This was the armament, with its restraints, which General Byng had assembled in large numbers to discourage civil violence on St Peter's Field. In the considered knowledge of its power, therefore, Byng had taken care to emphasise the necessity 'to present the best order among the troops'.

It was at some time just before ten o'clock in the morning, with the crowd already showing liveliness, that a horse-drawn chaise put into the square. Its appearance signalled the release of a great cheer from the crowd. Inside the carriage were John Bagguley and Samuel Drummond, seeing for the first time the vast numbers they had succeeded in attracting.

The chaise forced its way to the centre of the Field. There, makeshift hustings had been built from a table roped to a cart. Already at the table was a small group: a properly constituted committee with chairman and secretary.

To another great roar from the crowd, Drummond was first to be lifted bodily to the hustings. His task, as on so many previous occasions in weeks past, was to massage the audience for Bagguley to use: to raise it to a peak of expectation and preparedness for the leader. Much of what was to come had already been heard on several previous occasions by excited gatherings of workers at meetings in Stockport, Oldham and Ashton and all the other districts from which they had marched that day. They were delighted to have it repeated and, as then, they greeted and punctuated Bagguley's oratory with great yells of approval.

'Can you leave your wives and children and tear yourselves from all friends to go and claim these rights your ancestors got for you?' he shouted to them. 'Will you turn back when you get to Stockport, or when you come to face those high and cold hills of Derbyshire?'

And the crowd had screamed back, 'No, no, no!'[8]

'Will you be like the Egyptians in the wilderness under Moses and not turn back when after a few miles rain and hail falls?' he yelled.

'No, we will not!' they roared in response.

'I will go with you,' he shouted, as he stretched high his arm, 'and stick while a drop of blood shall circulate in these veins.'[9]

Drummond had already called those with blankets on their backs and petitions on their arms to move closer to the hustings and arrange themselves in files of ten in front of him. Bagguley – perhaps trying to make doubly sure that they were operating within the law – had the tens rearrange themselves in fives. There was much confusion, but order was soon restored with good humour and the first groups moved towards the Field's exits.

Bagguley and Drummond now had hats and kerchiefs passed round the crowd. From all sides copper coins poured in. To the surprise of the spies in the crowd silver too was generously given and some notes were even thrust up to Bagguley and Drummond.

It was at this point that a man pushed through the crowd. He shouted up to Bagguley that Nadin and a great many constables were arranging themselves ominously in the street outside the ground.

'Never mind,' Bagguley shouted back, 'he only means to alarm the meeting.'

As Drummond dispatched the first of the marchers off the Field in, so they believed, the direction of London, Bagguley continued to rouse the spirits with his unstoppable flow of words. One spy noted that in his speech he hinted that he knew he was likely to be arrested,[10] but the thought did not interrupt his torrent as he urged the marchers on.

It was the first concerted movement of the crowd towards the exits which General Byng took as his signal for action. At some time earlier he had made clear to the civil officials his view of which course he would prefer them to follow. The magistrate, Mr Holland Watson, and the boroughreeve, Mr Green, were to prepare themselves to accompany him and his lead troop of cavalry into the crowd. Once there, Holland Watson would read the Riot Act demanding that the workers disperse. Nadin was to organise parties of his constables to accompany each troop. They would move on Byng's command.

Apparently with no haste, and unfussed by the observation that large numbers were already marching out of the square, Byng, at a leisurely pace, sent a messenger to the magistrates in Brown's cottage. Did they, he asked, wish him to arrest the persons then addressing the meeting and using such violent language?[11]

Quietly, Byng waited for the answer. When it came – not that he doubted it would be otherwise – it was in the affirmative.

Byng spurred his horse in the direction of the Field and of the young man standing on the cart. Between them were several tens of thousands of men, women and children.

# 10

# A Neat Movement

It was over in a few minutes. Byng, strictly according to his plan, had Holland Watson and Joseph Green ride ahead of him to the edge of, and then into the crowd. Watson's refined voice, attempting to read the Riot Act, was soon drowned in a sea of jeers and cheers.

Byng now signalled Joseph Nadin and his special constables to move in on the hustings. Cantering on to the square behind them came Colonel Teesdale's regiment of King's Dragoon Guards.

Fearlessly, Nadin – he knew his own unpopularity – pushed his way into the throng. For an instant it seemed as though he and his constables were in real danger: not from the crowd's anger, but from being trampled by the hooves of the excited horses pounding behind them. Drummond, seeing the force now coming at them, called on the crowd to move closer round the cart to protect it.[1] But his cries went unheeded. One observer noticed how Bagguley, though shouting encouragement to his Blanketeers, was showing too plainly the signs of his extreme youth. He was trembling violently.[2]

Any fear that the cavalry would get out of control was unfounded. Teesdale, with what the *Manchester Chronicle* called a 'neat' movement, had his highly professional and experienced cavalrymen, some of them Waterloo veterans, wheel and turn, quickly surrounding and isolating the hustings.[3] In seconds Nadin had Bagguley and Drummond in irons. Mr Hay and his fellow magistrates, well positioned at Brown's cottage, had a clear, if distant view of the success of the operation.[4]

But for the last hour or more, long before Byng composedly put his troops into action, considerable numbers of workers had been leaving St Peter's Field. In groups of five and ten, unaware of the arrest of their leaders, many hundreds were now far down the Stockport road, heading for London. By the time the chaos in the square had subsided, many hundreds more were following in the same direction.

Waiting at Stockport on the bridge where the old southbound Roman road crossed the river Mersey, was John Lloyd astride his horse. Next to him was William Birch, a tough young constable, once Sir John Byng's orderly, who had recently become Lloyd's right-hand man. Behind him was a mounted troop of Cheshire Yeomanry. Lloyd had put himself in command.

As soon as he saw the first pathetically vulnerable group of marchers come down the hill in front of him, Lloyd swept into action. Both he and William Birch had a well-founded reputation for the rough handling of any worker incautious enough to break the law. 'I personally took the first man,' he told John Beckett later. Within minutes he had arrested another twenty.[5]

Galloping after the main body of marchers heading for Stockport were two posses of mounted horsemen. One was a second troop of Cheshire Yeomanry; the other was a group led by the clerical cavalryman Mr Ethelston. Some disorder occurred on the road near Stockport. In spite of Lloyd's resolve, crowds of workers moved downstream and managed to bypass his troops and pour across the river. The Cheshire Yeomanry quickly rounded up those who reached the town. One hundred and sixty-three prisoners were pushed into Stockport Castle yard. Lloyd, meanwhile, raced on to Macclesfield, the next town on the London road. In the darkness later that evening, 180 Blanketeers were apprehended there.

In the confusion in Stockport's town centre, the mounted yeomanry used some force. The day ended with reports of a considerable number of serious injuries. Some, running from the military, had been trampled by horses' hooves, some had suffered sword wounds. There was one ghastly fatality. An old man, John James, a cabinet-maker, hearing the noise of the crowd ran into his garden and was promptly sabred by a panicking trooper. He was to die two days later after great suffering.[6]

From several towns south of Stockport there came reports of the arrival of groups of dispirited bands of marchers, most of whom were persuaded without difficulty to turn their backs on London and head home. There were no reports yet from anywhere of a single member of the forces of law and order having been injured, nor even threatened. Nevertheless, there were many who convinced themselves otherwise. One Derbyshire magistrate who came across a tired, though still marching group, told Lord Sidmouth, '*I could not*, on conversing with them, *doubt that they were engaged in a conspiracy against the government.*'[7] His words, rather than the workers' actions, confirmed all the Home Secretary's preconceptions.

John Lloyd's night had not ended with his gallop to Macclesfield. In the darkness he rode on to Chester where his prisoners had been thrown into the gaol of the redstone castle, so forbidding in contrast to the black-and-white toytown it guarded. He was still interrogating them at three o'clock next morning. No doubt mindful of the psychological and physical methods Lloyd had used to extract information from Luddite prisoners, the Home Secretary sent a curt message suggesting he dealt leniently with them since they had 'been misled by others more artful than they'.[8]

It is unlikely that Lloyd used anything harsher than words on the dishevelled group he found in Chester Castle. Several were mere boys; most were in their twenties. The first Blanketeer he singled out for examination had the surname Mellor – the same as that of the Luddite convicted and hanged in 1812 at York Castle on evidence extracted by Lloyd himself. What this young man had to say, however, was, for Lloyd at least, disappointingly unsensational.

Benjamin Mellor was far from being the firebrand of his namesake. He confessed that he had set off for London with no idea whatever of how he was to get subsistence on his way, nor what he would do when he got there. He had heard he would be getting orders at Stockport. In his own laborious hand he had copied out the Blanketeers' petition asking for 'Parlimentary Reform', had it signed by 17 of his friends and, full of hope, had set off from St Peter's Field.[9]

Of the dozens of prisoners interrogated by magistrates that night and next day, not one produced a more self-incriminating reply than that of young Mellor.

Edmund Pickup, a 24-year-old weaver, when asked what he expected to gain from the march to London said, 'For my part I don't understand it properly . . . but they reckon a large part of these taxes would be taken off and that would ease us a great deal.'

Samuel Whitmore, a fustian cutter, said, 'I was going with a petition to the Prince Regent for the Habeas Corpus Act – I cannot say what the Habeas Corpus Act related to. I do not know its purpose . . . I had neither means nor money – except a little bread.'

John Shaw said, 'The most miserable looking of us was to kneel down and the others to take the petition and the Prince would then tell us why trade was so slack.'

Robert McMillan, a 17-year-old weaver, said, 'My shoes are not fit to carry me to London, it is plain to be seen.' He intended to go no further than Stockport.

William Bailey, an 18-year-old turner, said, 'I went for the sake of my godfather and godmother as much as anything. They live in London.'

And so the interviews were recorded for page after page: the testimony of naive, uneducated, underfed, badly clothed, unarmed and, for the most part, unemployed men.[10]

Byng compiled a full report of the affair for the Home

Secretary.[11] There had been, it transpired, one casualty among the soldiers. A trooper in the King's Dragoon Guards had suffered a head wound from a brick thrown in St Peter's Field which had shattered his helmet. Byng also told the Home Office how well his troops had behaved on the field: 'they were forced to use their swords, but they only licked with them, only one man was cut, a desperate character.'[12]

Even though Byng had ordered his troops to use only the flats of their swords, the sabre 'lick' suffered by old John James had cost him his life. Byng, in spite of his explanation to the Home Office, knew better than most the damage which could be done by an unsheathed sword, used from the back of a fast-moving horse, irrespective of the intentions of its bearer. It was, to say the least, fortuitous that on St Peter's Field on the morning of March 10th, so little blood had been spilt by the sword.

Equally, Byng said nothing to Sidmouth of the several workers trampled by cavalry horses in Stockport. It was again a small wonder that so little damage had been done to the human body by the thrashing of animal limbs. As many had seen, disaster came to within an ace of one group: that of Joseph Nadin and his constables walking into the crowd ahead of the cavalry advance.

Several observers that day recorded their awareness of the dangers. Some sensed that great tragedy on St Peter's Field had been averted only by luck and not by design. There was both spoken and newspaper criticism of the whole military operation against an orderly gathering of unarmed workers.

Byng heard the criticism and responded to it in his precise

fashion. His lengthy report to the Home Secretary, written five days after the affair, was a carefully documented piece of self-defence. It ended, 'I should not have trespassed on your valuable time with so long a statement had I not heard that the propriety of the proceedings at Manchester on the 10th. Inst. had been questioned by some persons, and even the legality of them doubted by others.'[13]

However, any fear Byng might have had that he was due for a reprimand for his military methods of controlling a peaceful crowd had evaporated within hours. Already by then the Home Secretary had made it plain to Byng that he looked on the day's events with enormous satisfaction.[14] A revolution had been prevented. The nation owed Byng its thanks. More gratifying still, the Prince Regent, having successfully waltzed through the evening of that noteworthy day, wanted to share in those thanks. With pleasure, Sidmouth commanded Byng to deliver 'H. R. H.'s gracious approbation' personally to the officers and privates of both regular and volunteer forces who had taken part on that great day 'with as little delay as possible'.[15]

For the workers, the failure could not have been more complete. From the mass of people which had gathered that morning in St Peter's Field, several hundred were now shivering in gaols in Manchester, Stockport and Cheshire. Humiliated, most hoped to be released in a short time with nothing worse than a caution. A few, however, knew the likelihood was that they would, in due course, spend a far longer, and far from comfortable period in more distant prisons. Bagguley and Drummond were two of these.

Not for the first time, workers' leaders had failed to sustain the movement they had nurtured. So miserably inadequate had been their plans to capitalise on the crowd they had persuaded to gather in front of St Peter's Church, they perhaps deserved no better fate. The inability of the working class to produce from its own ranks leaders who were effective as well as charismatic was a weakness which would persist well beyond the beginning of the twentieth century.

Of the 40,000 and more who had gathered on the morning of March 10th, 1817, one man, Abel Couldwell, reached London and, eight days after setting out, deposited his petition at the Home Office.[16] Lord Sidmouth had already read its contents; several spies had supplied him with copies.

The worst feature of the day of chaos – and it was the most damning indictment of the organisers – was that from this disorganisation and humiliation, not one iota of benefit could be salvaged for the advantage of the north country worker. The ordered forces of the Establishment had totally overwhelmed those of his leaders. He was still desperately poor, the laws which repressed him were still unchanged and he was still unemancipated.

However, there was one consequence from which the government could take a substantial measure of satisfaction. The day had shown that the people *en masse* could ultimately be controlled with ease by a well-ordered military force. Lord Sidmouth registered the fact in the orderly file of his mind, storing it carefully among those others he could use for guidance should his future experience as Home Secretary require it.

# 11

# Moscow out of Manchester

The middle class of southern England, no less than the workers of the north, now recognised the realities behind the restriction of civil liberties which Lord Sidmouth had imposed on the nation. Several prominent citizens had reason for fear. Major Cartwright, William Cobbett and Henry Hunt all knew that their mail was being intercepted by government agents. The suspension of Habeas Corpus raised the real possibility that they too could find themselves without warning in the same gaols as the imprisoned organisers of the Blanketeers' March. Cobbett had already taken the precaution of moving himself closer to a westerly port whence, if the worst came to the worst, he could flee the country. William Benbow, a supporter of Bagguley, also saw his freedom in jeopardy; he was preparing to set off for Ireland en route to America.

Meantime, the members of the middle classes of northern England were still decidedly nervous. They had been considerably shaken by the size alone of the crowd gathered with such seeming ease by the Blanketeers' leaders. In the week following the meeting, government spies, now thick on the ground in Manchester, continued to see every small workers' gathering as a prelude to a national threat. A few more days and they had discovered a plot to set fire to 40 or 50 factories and so 'make a Moscow out of Manchester'.[1] This, the theory went, would lead to a general uprising and the overthrow of the government.

The consequence was that Mr Hay yet again sprang into action. Again General Byng was persuaded to make the journey back from Pontefract to Manchester. Arrests of the supposed ringleaders were made. Adding belt to braces, Hay instructed Joseph Nadin to move quickly and take several other workers' leaders into custody on suspicion of high treason. These included Samuel Bamford, who had not only flatly refused to be drawn into any of the recent spy-stirred plots, but had declined even to support the Blanketeers and had steered well clear of St Peter's Field on March 10th. Also arrested was 'Doctor' Healey, the entirely self-educated, hearty Middleton surgeon who had become Bamford's constant companion. Hay quickly arranged for these men, eight in all, to be sent to London by 'The Tribulatory' stage coach, closely guarded and in irons. Hay described them to Sidmouth as 'miserable objects but I fear desperate incendiaries'.[2]

Nadin was present at six o'clock on the morning of March 30th to oversee the departure of the coach. Before it left, he insisted that, in addition to their leg irons, his prisoners should be placed in metal armlets and in body and neck collars. It is scarcely surprising that one prisoner's legs were dangerously swollen before the party reached London.[3]

William Cobbett, meanwhile, had taken the decision not

to wait to see whether the arrests would spread to the landed middle classes. He was now three days out from Liverpool on a merchantman bound for America. The day before he fled England, he wrote,

> I make an enormous sacrifice of property and of feeling; but when my heart feels the tug of friendship, and of all the interesting objects in Hampshire, it is reconciled to the loss by the thought that I can enjoy them only during the pleasure of the Secretary of State.[4]

Surprisingly, the Secretary of State had elected to become personally involved in the monitoring of the latest threatened uprising.

It was April 1st. Sidmouth had already had several April Fool's letters in his Home Office mail. The gathering in Whitehall that day must surely have seemed to at least a few of those present, if not foolish, then at least incongruous. For Sidmouth had arranged, not simply for himself but for the Privy Council, no less, to interview the suspected revolutionaries. Among others sitting alongside Sidmouth were the Foreign Secretary, Lord Castlereagh, and the Attorney General, Sir Samuel Shepherd, armed with his ear trumpet.

Opposite them was a group of Lancashire rustics. Bamford, somewhat precious, eager to show off his poetic use of the English language, was full of charm and good humour. 'Doctor' Joseph Healey, when his turn came, presented himself as a music-hall character ahead of his time. Asked to spell his surname, the 'Doctor' – who had learned his surgeon's trade from his cowman father – did so, according to Bamford, in his Lancashire accent: 'Haitch, hay, haa, ell, hay, wye.' The Council's secretary being unable to differentiate between the north country 'e' and 'a', asked Healey to write the word. Instead, Healey passed across the table one of his prescription labels on which was printed, 'Joseph Healey, Surgeon, Middleton. Plase take – table-spoonfuls of this mixture each – hours.' The Privy Council was reduced to guffawing at what it read and even Lord Sidmouth was reported to have smiled.[5]

After several such odd interviews, half the Lancashire prisoners, including Bamford, were released. The others, in spite of the Privy Council's good humour, were less fortunate and were each marked for imprisonment for unspecified periods. Healey, when he arrived at Dorchester gaol, found the young Blanketeers, Samuel Drummond and John Johnston, already incarcerated there. Another of Bamford's companions, John Roberts, when thrown into Gloucester gaol, discovered John Bagguley, the workers' leader, in solitary confinement.

With the young orators safely removed from their exposed roles as working-class leaders, it took only a few days for peace and quiet to return to the streets of Manchester. The Reverend Mr Hay had privately to confess that the reasons for panic measures had passed. He phrased his announcement telling Lord Sidmouth of the end of the emergency somewhat more dramatically: 'The proposed attack on Manchester,' he proudly said, 'has been averted.'[6] Byng can only have been one of many who suspected that the proposition had never existed.

# 12

## Oliver

The role of spies in history has always been, as it continues to be, one which attracts the agonised conjecture of both those who suffer from, and those who benefit from their activities. By the nature of their work, what they report has to be taken on trust. Yet, equally, by the nature of their work, they can only be successful if they are deceitful.

The paradox had not evaded Hiley Addington, who over-saw most of the spying activities which were controlled from the Home Office. Hiley, like his brother, had learned to sift government agents' reports with care, fully aware that the paid spy, in order to ensure a steady flow of remuneration, tends to tell what he believes the hearer wants to hear.

The problem now for Hiley, however, was twofold. First, the intensity of secret government activities had grown such that they were becoming difficult to control. It is unlikely that this latest suspected conspiracy would have generated such a high-level response had government spies not been so thick on the ground in the Manchester area. The very number of the reports they filed magnified the dangers out of all reasonable proportion. Second, the scale of activity was now so great that it was difficult to hide. When a spy's workings became public knowledge there was danger then, as there is today, of unfortunate press, or worse, parliamentary exposure.

Hiley began to take steps to cloak his operations more securely. On April 14th, 1817, he was writing firmly to the Reverend Mr Ethelston in Manchester telling him that when paying spies, he should exert 'extreme caution and secrecy'. Under no circumstances did he want provincial agents to know that the source of their funding was central government.[1]

But the secrecy of the operations was daily in increasing jeopardy as more and more citizens were affected by them. John Knight, the respected reformer who had supported John Bagguley at his meetings, had been taken into custody and put in solitary confinement in Reading gaol. He soon realised that letters from his wife were being intercepted. And whether he knew it or not, letters he sent to friends from the gaol invariably met a similar fate. Opening one of these, addressed by Knight to a fellow cotton manufacturer in Halifax, Hiley discovered Knight's detailed description of how State tentacles had now spread to all levels of society.

Knight told his friend of his midnight arrest by Nadin and of his journey by guarded mail coach to London where he was lodged overnight in a Bow Street public house. The landlord there had generously offered to let his son carry any letter Knight might wish to write to any friend in London. Knight therefore wrote two, one of which was to H. G. Bennet MP, describing his plight. Knight offered the landlord's son six-pence for his trouble. The boy politely refused saying his 'father did not allow him to take money of gentlemen.'[2]

A few hours later Knight was taken to be interviewed by Hiley's brother, Lord Sidmouth. To his mortification, as he stood in front of the Home Secretary, Knight saw the letters he had entrusted to the boy – clasped in the hands of Sidmouth.

However, this kind of incident was only the visible tip of the bulk of Home Office espionage activity. With the full knowledge of Hiley Addington and Lord Sidmouth, there were other substantial movements below the surface of Whitehall. In spite of all Hiley's attempts to keep them hidden, it was inevitable that eventually somebody must glimpse this activity and realise its purpose. The revelations of the involvement of the Home Office in this particular episode of espionage would soon touch a raw nerve at the centre of the nation.

The affair had begun when another of Bagguley's supporters, the nervous Liverpool reformer, Joseph Mitchell, fearing arrest before the Blanketeer's March even began, fled to London.

There he was introduced to a sympathetic stranger. This man, who introduced himself as Oliver, was later described as 'of genteel appearance and good address' with a lightly pitted, small-poxed complexion. He described himself as a carpenter and builder by trade, turned surveyor and accountant who had fallen on hard times.[3] But there was much more of interest in his *curriculum vitae* than these few facts and his alternative name of W. J. Richards. Subsequent investigations would show evidence of bigamy and fraud – both experiences of calculated deceit which would better qualify him for the activity he now had in mind.

Learning of Mitchell's background, Oliver told him that he too was a reformer, also in danger of arrest. He persuaded Mitchell to leave London and accompany him on a tour of northern towns.

Unknown to Mitchell, however, his new friend had already seen a means to a most rewarding end. Oliver succeeded in quickly making contact with the Home Office and, because of the fresh relationship he now had with northern reformers, in being interviewed by Lord Sidmouth and Hiley. This acceptance of Oliver at extraordinarily high governmental level, was all he needed to launch himself on a spectacular new career.

Under the guise of raising petitions for parliamentary reform, he set off with Mitchell on April 23rd on a tour of Yorkshire, Lancashire and Midland towns.

Soon, Oliver had been introduced by Mitchell to many working-class reform groups. Before the tour had ended Mitchell found himself under arrest. Totally unsuspecting, so he claimed, of any part played by Oliver in his downfall, he was returned to London and imprisoned.

Eventually Oliver too returned to London with much useful information gathered from this northern tour, ready to put it into the hands of Hiley Addington. So impressed was Hiley with his new protégé that on April 22nd, he wrote to several people in the Midlands and in northern England introducing Oliver and his services. One of those to receive Hiley's circular letter was Sir John Byng.

A curious interchange took place at this point. It has little to do with Oliver, but is very revealing of Byng, the man on whose shoulders the stability of so much of the north depended.

Almost by return of the post which told him of the existence of Oliver, Byng sent a letter on an entirely different subject: his own health. It points to an alarming and recurring trait in his character.

The letter is almost illegible, scrawled in a desperate, dramatically shaking hand. In it Byng asks for two weeks' leave. He has been far from well that winter, he says, and has not yet recovered – though the writing of no previous letter has varied in any way from the meticulous, steady hand Byng consistently used for all correspondence. It goes on to say that his illness, involving internal bleeding, is 'chiefly occasioned by a severe hurt I received at Waterloo'. He needs leave, he says, to consult the surgeon who attended him after the great battle.[4]

Byng undoubtedly had suffered severe wounds on more than one occasion in battles past, and did have physical problems. It is quite possible that his behaviour on some occasions was the result of the psychological stress caused by severe pain. Nevertheless, when, for whatever pressing reason, Byng felt that he needed to absent himself from military duties, he was capable of using extraordinarily dramatic, even devious means to achieve a simple, though passionately desired end.

Only conjecture can be used to divine the cause of Byng's peculiar state of mind during those few days. It might be just coincidence that that period was also the week of Manchester races, and it is possible that this did not in any way influence Byng's belief that he needed a respite. However, on a later occasion, the date of a race meeting most certainly would influence a crucial decision he needed to make.

Whatever the reason, it is astonishing how quickly Byng's apparently almost totally debilitating ailment disappeared. In reply to his letter, Hiley, whilst offering sympathy, passed back the news that his brother, Lord Sidmouth, desperately wanted Byng to remain in command: Oliver's reports had convinced the Home Office that an uprising was still imminent.[5]

Byng's handwriting on hearing this news next day remarkably recovers its copper-plate quality. He accepts, now that his indispensability has been pointed out to him, that his duty must be his first consideration.[6]

Oliver, meanwhile, was on the road to Yorkshire and to the neighbourhood of Byng's headquarters. Near Mirfield, Oliver met, not for the first time, two advocates of parliamentary reform who had been introduced to him on his first northern tour by Mitchell. Their names were John Dickenson, a linen draper, and a Mr Willans, a bookseller.

At their first meeting Oliver had argued that the cause of parliamentary reform would not be helped by petitions. Force, he said, would be necessary to impose reform, and that could come by organising the manufacturing towns. Oliver had calculated, Willans said, that Leeds could raise 40,000 men,

Wakefield 20,000, Birmingham 60,000 or 70,000, and Lancashire 'sufficient to carry the business into effect'.

On several occasions Oliver attempted to persuade Willans to be a delegate at a meeting to discuss the 'business'. It was to be held near Mirfield on June 6th. Willans was deeply suspicious of Oliver, and neither he nor Dickenson went to the meeting at Thornhill Edge. Ten others, however, did. There they were immediately swooped on by a party of soldiers. At their head was an officer: General Sir John Byng. Apparently fit and well, and certainly active enough to be astride a horse, Byng arrested the ten – and Oliver. He took them off to Wakefield under arrest.

Later that day, quite by chance, Dickenson himself travelled to Wakefield. To his surprise he saw, walking freely in front of the Stafford Arms Inn, a figure he was convinced he recognised. He had no doubt it was Oliver. But when Dickenson shouted Oliver's name, Oliver appeared not to recognise him. He began to walk off quickly until Dickenson insistently called him back. Oliver at last acknowledged Dickenson. He explained his behaviour by saying that strange things had been happening since last they met.

That day, he said, he had been arrested by Byng at Thornhill Edge, but released when nothing could be found on him. Oliver then said, 'I must clear this ground. I am not safe here. The coach is ready for Leeds. My luggage is there.' He was, he said, intending to leave the country that evening.

Suddenly, a waiter from the inn called Oliver's name and said the coach could wait no longer. As Oliver mounted the carriage, Dickenson hid in a nearby shop with a view of the inn's door. He then saw Oliver beckon to a servant and speak to him. Immediately the coach had left, Dickenson intercepted the servant and asked if he knew Oliver.

'You mean the gentleman I was speaking to in the coach?' the servant replied.

'Yes,' said Dickenson.

The servant then readily told how he had driven Oliver in a tandem from his Master's house near Pontefract.

'What is your master's name?' asked Dickenson.

'Sir John Byng,' the servant replied.[7]

Dickenson instantly recognised that he had in his hand a highly sensitive piece of information. It was nothing less than sensational. The commander of Britain's Northern Forces was involved in espionage activity, and in particular with a spy acting against working-class reformers as an *agent provocateur*.

Like many others since in similar circumstances, Dickenson now looked round for what he should do with his unexpected revelatory windfall. And like others, he concluded that perhaps his best confidante should be a newspaper reporter looking for a scoop.

# 13

## Scoop

Watched by the astounded John Dickenson, the night coach of June 6th, 1817 had pulled out of Wakefield. With Oliver aboard, it was heading for Nottingham. It was to be the spy's third visit to the town in three weeks. And as before, Oliver had arranged a secret meeting there with an out-of-work frame-work knitter, Jeremiah Brandreth.

Oliver left no recorded impressions of this poverty-stricken worker. Others did, however, and the image has passed firmly into history. Short and swarthy with black tousled hair and a cast in one eye, his gypsy looks gave him a wild, even romantic appeal. Such as it was, it undoubtedly succeeded in attracting a small band of Nottingham followers much dissatisfied with the conditions of poverty and unemployment in which they had to live.

Soon after Oliver's first visit to the town a plan was hatched whereby Brandreth would lead a Nottingham contingent in a general strike which would take place simultaneously in major cities – London, Manchester, Derby, Nottingham and Leicester were named. The different districts would be organised to seize military arms and police offices. The Leicester and Yorkshire groups would meet up in Nottingham and then the grand force would march on London 'to contend for a change in government'.[1]

It is not possible to know how much of this naive plan originated in the mind of Brandreth and how much in that of Oliver. Before it was put into operation, however, Oliver was back in London, reporting his travels to Hiley Addington.

When it occurred, the uprising – if a gathering of a hundred or so workers deserves the name – was led from Pentridge in Derbyshire on the night of June 8th, 1817, by Jeremiah Brandreth.

It was far from being the inspirational affair to fulfil the dreams of suppressed workers. Rain poured down on the badly clothed, ill-assorted and disorganised group carrying little more than a few sticks between them. They raided houses on the 14-mile trek to Nottingham and demanded arms. At one house there was tragedy. Brandreth, waving a gun, fired it through a window. The ball from it shattered the glass and passed through to kill a manservant.

By six o'clock next morning most of the sodden gang had been arrested by a lightly armed troop of 20 cavalrymen of the 15th Dragoons. Brandreth escaped, but was captured several weeks later.

Signs of uprising in other parts of the country were minimal. A mob had appeared in Huddersfield but, after facing a few soldiers of the local yeomanry, its members considered discretion to be the better part of valour, and melted away. A few of the workers who had appeared in the streets were later arrested.

This incident, like those at Pentridge and at Thornhill Edge, was a substantial anticlimax. What was not an anticlimax was the revelation that the three events were linked by the influence of one man: Oliver. For it was at this point, on June 14th, that the *Leeds Mercury* had become involved. Hints that there was an extraordinary tale to tell had been passed to the paper's editor, Edward Baines, by the bookseller friend of John Dickenson, Mr Willans of Dewsbury.

As soon as he got wind that Dickenson and Willans had something important to say, Baines – well known for his nose for a good story – quickly hired a chaise. With his 17-year-old son Edward, he set off for Dewsbury at top speed to collect information firsthand. Within hours, in the *Leeds Mercury* of June 14th, his copy was in print.

Baines's journalistic scoop had an electrifying effect on the country. Quickly, all over England, even those who had no sympathy with the reformers were able to reconstruct not only how Oliver had operated in different communities, but how insidious and dangerous governmental methods of control of its citizens had become. Other newspapers took up the affair and enlarged upon it.

Every activist north country worker was well aware of the government's use of paid agents to report on the behaviour of fellow citizens, and accepted it almost as a matter of course. But the middle class, particularly that in southern England, was almost wholly ignorant of the practice. Many were dumbfounded to hear of behaviour so contrary to what they held to be the spirit of English law and government which, the Prince Regent had assured them in Parliament only weeks before, was 'the most perfect that has ever fallen to the lot of any people'.

The sessions of Parliament immediately following the *Leeds Mercury* publication were turbulent. In the Commons, Sir Francis Burdett, and in the Lords, Earl Grey, each quoted long extracts from the *Mercury*. Scandalised Members from both sides of both Houses reflected the reaction from many parts of the country.

But as on other occasions when the ethical behaviour of the Home Office had been called into question, Lord Sidmouth stood cold and unflinching, singularly untouched by this explicit criticism. His insistence was – and he repeated it on subsequent occasions – that he had ordered Oliver not to encourage seditious behaviour. As he later told Byng, 'I am not conscious of having taken any step . . . which, under similar circumstances, I would not take again.'[2]

Hiley, meanwhile, organised a Home Office inquiry into the affair. He told Parliament that it exonerated Oliver from the charge of having been an *agent provocateur*. But – as many of his cynical contemporaries noted – had Hiley shown Oliver to be guilty, both he and his brother, the Home Secretary, would have had to share the guilt by association.[3]

General Byng's response to criticism of his relationship with Oliver subsequently sought to ensure, as on other occasions, that his correct and innocent behaviour was well documented. He wrote, 'In disclaiming for myself any employment of spyes . . . I never had the sanction of Government to do so – that while it appears to me not alone proper, but *necessary* for the *Magistracy* to have that power, it was not required by me . . .'

He also said that he believed the government to have been calumniated by spies. If he had held a different opinion, he insisted, he would not have hesitated to hand in his resignation. He added that in his present state of health, 'nothing but a sense of duty, would have induced me to remain, when a proper regard for myself and for my family, pointed out the prudence of retiring.'[4] Thus Byng left it to posterity to judge in the strict sense of this explanation whether or not he 'employed' spies.

Jeremiah Brandreth and 34 others taken in the Pentridge uprising came to trial at a Special Commission sitting at Derby on October 16th, 1817. On the wall of the court building had been scrawled 'JURYMEN REMEMBER OLIVER'. Whatever memory Oliver left in the minds of the jurymen, they condemned to death not only Brandreth, but two other of his simple-minded accomplices.

He was hanged outside Derby Castle gaol and his head severed. The incompetent axe-man failed to part the head from the body with one stroke. An assistant had to run in quickly and finish his work with a knife.

Cowdroy's *Manchester Gazette* described the spectacle for its northern readers in some detail. The paper also reported a simultaneous fall of 1 per cent in the Stock Exchange. This unusual fall, however, was in no way determined by fears of revolution. The causal factor turned out to be the simultaneous news of the loss of the heir to the throne: the 22-year-old daughter of the Prince Regent, Princess Charlotte Augusta, had died in childbirth. Her husband, Prince Leopold, was reported not only to be distracted and inconsolable, but to have been granted an annuity of £50,000.[5]

# 14

## Yeomanry Cavalrymen

England, those who ruled it believed, as a result of unequivo-cal, firm government had entered a period of unparalleled tranquillity. In mid-1817, the Prime Minister, Lord Liverpool, had privately told his Home Secretary, 'Whatever may be our internal difficulties, there never was a moment when we were so free from all external danger.'[1]

The drenching rains which had soaked Jeremiah Brandreth and his doomed followers, had very satisfactorily watered the spring-sown crops. Throughout the summer that followed, the sun shone and it was soon forecast that there would be a record harvest. Expectations were more than fulfilled. The price of wheat dropped from 111s. 6d. to 75s. a quarter.

At the opening of Parliament in January, 1818 the Prince Regent confirmed that the nation's internal problems also, were now resolved. His speech rang with optimism:

The improvement which has taken place in almost every branch of our domestic industry, and the present state of public credit, afford abundant proof that the difficulties under which the country was labouring were chiefly to be ascribed to temporary causes.[2]

As a sign of this return to confidence, John Bagguley was released from his solitary confinement and Samuel Drummond, as well as several other imprisoned radicals, was let out of his prison cell before the new year began. And shortly after Parliament was opened, Lord Sidmouth demonstrated to the public that he too apparently subscribed to the mood of optimism by introducing a bill repealing the suspension of the Habeas Corpus Act. His private letters, however, show that he was far from sanguine about the prospects for continuing quiet in the manufacturing districts.

It was also far from the truth that the whole of the nation shared the spirit which permeated most of the upper echelons of society. Elizabeth Knight, wife of the imprisoned but surprisingly unbowed old reformer, John Knight, unaware that he was to be released the next day, wrote a touching and dignified letter to him on December 28th, 1817. In his last letter he had told her to think less about him – he was in a damp, badly ventilated cell – in order that she could more easily bear the burden of his imprisonment. She replied:

I request however that you will not again repeat these commands, for you might as well lay claim to the powers of Joshua at once and command the 'Sun to stand still,' as to forbid me to think about you.

Tellingly, she goes on to speak of the worsening conditions of the poor. Provisions, she says, are 'advancing in price while there is no increase in the means of purchasing them.'[3] Whatever the Prince Regent believed to be the success of British industry compared with its competitors, and whatever the size of the harvest and the fall in the price of wheat, still none of the accrued advantages were being passed on to those who stood in the cotton mills or walked the corn fields.

Only a citizen utterly devoid of contact with the manufacturing workers of the north could believe that the tranquil period following the execution of Jeremiah Brandreth was other than a lull in a continuing storm. Lord Sidmouth, through Hiley's network of secret agents, was both well informed of the dangerous undercurrents of activity which a prudent Home Secretary could not neglect, and further, of what few resources he had at his disposal should these disturbances again break the surface.

The system of keeping civil order, through the Lords Lieutenant, the magistrates, their special constables and their secret agents, was as active as it had ever been. The force available to support it should violence erupt, however, was weaker than in living memory. In the whole of England there were now only 16,000 regular soldiers. Twice this number had been sent to India, and also twice the number to France where an army of occupation was still in position.[4] What was left on British soil was not large enough, nor sufficiently mobile, effectively to police the nation, and Sidmouth knew it.

Sidmouth had therefore continued to support enthusiastically the system of raising citizens' regiments particularly of cavalry, throughout the country. He himself had always enjoyed playing soldiers. Once when he had appeared in the House of Commons in the full dress uniform of the Woodley Volunteers, the day's proceedings had to be temporarily halted whilst Members of Parliament hooted with laughter.[5]

Nevertheless, the Yeomanry Cavalry regiments had played a critical part in supporting regular troops during riots of earlier years and when government economies were being sought, Sidmouth had on several occasions defended them from disbandment.

In any case, they cost the tax-payer very little. Some regiments of yeomanry were well endowed by rich patrons who, like the Home Secretary, enjoyed dressing up in uniform and riding out astride a well-groomed horse at the head of their very own regiment.

One such grandee, strategically placed near the most volatile of the north country manufacturing districts, was Sir John Fleming Leicester. Even discounting his enthusiasm for amateur soldiery, this Cheshire baronet was an extraordinary personage. He was an intimate friend of the Prince Regent. His country seat was one of John Carr's architectural masterpieces, the magnificent Tabley House at Knutsford. Here at Tabley, as at Sir John Byng's Campsmount mansion, Carr had designed the stables.

Leicester's interests were catholic. He had taken up music and natural history, had been a Member of Parliament, and was an excellent marksman. Like Byng he indulged in gambling on a not insubstantial scale. He once shot with £1,000 bet on him by the Prince Regent that he would perforate twice with a pistol ball the centre of the ace of clubs at 12 paces – the duelling distance.[6] He did.

With such an insouciant attitude to cash, therefore, Leicester was the ideal Colonel of the Earl of Chester's Yeomanry Cavalry, and had been for 20 years.

The government paid for and provided all yeomen's arms and ammunition, but horse, saddlery, bridlery and uniforms had to be provided by the volunteer with only an annual capitation grant, which stood at £1.3s. in 1817.[7] Any shortfall – and it was considerable – had to be found elsewhere. As in other industrial districts, Sir John Leicester's regiment consisted of officers who were factory owners and landowners, with other ranks made up of innkeepers, saddlers, smiths and similar tradesmen with access to a horse. In some rich counties a committee of gentlemen raised any necessary additional funds. But in Cheshire, John Leicester took on the deficit more than willingly. He now commanded six troops, each of more than 50 men. He had financed the whole of the most recently raised troop and additionally, again at his own expense, had completely reclothed the regiment in magnificent order: blue jackets were richly ornamented with silver braid, scarlet cuffs and collar, pantaloons were of French grey cloth, a black felt hussar cap was beautifully decorated with a silver lace band, plaited ear loops and a rosette, sword belts and pouch were of buff leather. Trumpeters were unmistakeable in bearskin caps and scarlet cloth bags.[8]

This, then, was the regiment which had chased Luddites across the Pennines in 1812 and which had supported General

Byng's regular troops on March 10th, 1817. On that occasion John Lloyd had stood his horse with theirs at the entrance to Stockport as the Blanketeers descended on the town. With them, he had chased those who had slipped his net as far as Macclesfield and they had together rounded up as many of the remnants as they could find.

It is scarcely surprising that this group in peacock dress, each man's arrogance augmented by the power of his horse, and with practically every member drawn from the employer or self-employed class, should attract the dislike of the working class they were meant to police. In the country villages of Cheshire where many of the men lived, the problem was not severe. But in the manufacturing towns of Lancashire into which they galloped when called on to suppress rioting, the loathing was intense. Some incipient trades unions and Friendly Societies went as far as to expel members who joined militia regiments. It took an Act of Parliament to put a stop to the practice.

The success of Leicester's regiment on the day of the Blanketeers' March only served to increase the odium in which the yeomanry was held in towns such as Manchester and Stockport. By the same token it visibly raised the value of territorial forces in the eyes of government and others. That day, the remarkable number of 397 men out of a total of 400, excluding officers, had voluntarily turned out.[9]

Such a performance could not be discounted. Already, through Leicester's close personal ties, his private army boasted the title 'His Royal Highness the Prince Regent's Regiment of Cheshire Yeomanry'. After the Blanketeers' day, the personal congratulations of the Regent, the Home Secretary and General Byng were publicly poured on to the regiment. There was now no question, as Leicester established from Lord Sidmouth, that the yeomanry would suffer cuts as a consequence of further government economies.

Manchester itself, with a population many times greater than that of any surrounding town, had no yeomanry regiment. The omission was a source of disquiet to the local magistrates, who had no readily available local force of cavalry at their disposal in cases of emergency. Equally, it was a source of annoyance and envy to many of the burghers of Manchester that their town could display nothing so brilliantly successful, nor so colourful and rich with pomp as the Cheshire Yeomanry. More annoyingly, Manchester's newspapers reported in full the regiment's triumphs and the royal honours and congratulations which had been heaped upon it.

It is no surprise to discover that on the day following the Blanketeers' uprising, Anthony Molyneux, a Manchester manufacturer, wrote to the Home Secretary suggesting the formation of a Lancashire Yeomanry. He proposed there should be ten troops of 60 men each. The government, he suggested, should encourage the less wealthy to join by loaning arms or selling them to yeomen at reduced prices.[10]

The Reverend Mr Hay quickly picked up the idea for himself and, at the next Salford Quarter Sessions, reported how the Grand Jury had come 'to a unanimous declaration of their opinion as to the necessity of having Corps of Yeomanry

Cavalry in the County'. On the spot, they had appointed a committee to confer with local magistrates 'as to the best mode of carrying this measure into effect'.[11]

With the encouragement of Hiley Addington and an enthusiastic General Byng, plans soon turned to substance. By September, 1817 the Manchester and Salford Regiment of Yeomanry Cavalry was, on paper at least, in being. From the start it had aspirations to outshine its Cheshire rivals. Its rules and regulations were published in an elegantly bound blue and gold leather book. The regiment would be composed 'of mercantile men . . . raised for the defence of the towns and neighbourhood of Manchester and Salford'. Initially, there would be three troops commanded by a major, each with 1 captain, 1 lieutenant, 1 cornet and 50 men. Commissioned officers would be chosen by ballot at a general meeting convened for that purpose.

It was expected that each member of the regiment would equip himself with a gelding or a mare – stallions were inadmissible. He would provide his horse at his own expense, as he would his saddle, bridle and uniforms – full dress and drill dress.

Recruitment to the new force was not a problem. Thomas Trafford, a respected manufacturer, was elected commanding officer, and Hugh Hornby Birley, also a manufacturer and a former boroughreeve of Manchester became second-in-command. Other officers would be chosen from several cotton manufacturers and merchants. Rank and file came from several trades and professions. The most numerous of these were publicans; it was said that the renewal of their licences by the magistrates was helped by their being seen to be supporters of the forces of law and order.

As 1818 approached, only the final design of a suitable uniform remained an open question before the regiment could muster on parade. For the rest, the Manchester and Salford Yeomanry Cavalry was, bar the shouting, a properly constituted regiment.

# 15

## This Intelligent Person

Lord Sidmouth's high hopes for the internal stability of the nation crumbled before even the first few weeks of 1818 had passed. It was by then clear that the calculated decision he had taken to release the young Manchester orators from their prison cells had been disastrous.

John Bagguley, once having enjoyed the heady sensation of moving the masses, now that he was released from gaol, had no intention of letting his skills go to waste. Within hours, he was once again actively organising; within days he was planning more large-scale reform meetings. But there was now a marked difference in emphasis in the way in which Bagguley viewed the expression of worker protest.

The Blanketeers' March had been entirely peaceful and entirely unsuccessful. Embittered at having seen the punishment meted out to so many of those who had put their trust in him, and hardened by so many months in solitary confinement, Bagguley now disposed of his self-restraint. The uncompromising attitude of the Establishment had pushed him towards Johnston's view that no material change to the condition of the workers of the north could be brought about other than by violent protest. And now Johnston too had been released from prison and had rejoined him and Drummond.

Like others before him, Bagguley had seen that Manchester was the natural focus for the industrial workers of the whole of the north. The focus within Manchester itself was self-evidently the great open space of St Peter's Field. Workers from scores of miles around appeared to accept it as the main stage on which to air their grievances and display their hopes.

By March 9th, 1818, almost a year since he had gathered his biggest ever crowd for what had become the Blanketeers' debacle, Bagguley was again attracting sizeable audiences to the same place. He had Drummond and Johnston alongside him. But the older, more experienced and now more cynical reformers were still willing to give their support. John Knight, with both his health and his cotton business broken after spells in the cold damp cells of several prisons, was in attendance. So too was Joseph Mitchell, after having been held for 240 days without trial. The experiences of neither had shaken their resolve to achieve one vote for one man. And in spite of the obvious shortcomings of Bagguley and his violent supporters, it was clear to those older reformers that the young demagogue could attract crowds of workers in a size and in a fashion they themselves had never experienced in their lives.

John Lloyd, in his turn, was unshaken in his determination to police the reformers' activities in his own energetic fashion. On the morning of March 9th he was told that a sizeable crowd had gathered in St Peter's Field. Bagguley, Drummond and Johnston were said to be haranguing workers from the hustings. With no delay, and without any support, he was soon mounted, and heading for the Field. Joseph Mitchell was speaking. Lloyd pushed his horse towards the edge of the attentive throng. Inevitably, he knew any response to his presence would be hostile. There can be no doubt, however, that Lloyd had immense, even foolish, physical courage. He would not otherwise have been where he was, alone and unarmed.

Mitchell, in the middle of an embittered speech, spotted Lloyd and pointed him out. The crowd turned and Lloyd watched a thousand pairs of eyes filled with hatred swivel on him. In studied understatement, he told the Home Office how he felt 'rather conspicuous on horseback'. The crowd now began to yell at him. The cry of, 'Turn him out!' was taken up. In return, 'I laughed,' Lloyd reported. He stayed his ground.[1] No worker moved towards him. He listened unmolested to the rest of the proceedings that day.

But the part of the fearless hero, unmoved by the threats of a potentially vicious mob, was not a role Lloyd could continue to play with such confidence of success. Throughout that spring and summer the frequency and size of workers' meetings in and around Manchester began to grow. So too did the possibilities for violence. Magistrates in Oldham, Middleton, Bolton and Rochdale, besides those in Manchester and Stockport, became increasingly confused as, week by week, policing these gatherings with a few special constables or militiamen became ever more difficult. The young working-class reformers' efforts were again showing results which were already of considerable concern to the middle class.

Now, for the first time in his long career as Home Secretary, the guardian of that middle class was less than enthusiastic – as far as a man of such frigid temperament was capable of enthusiasm – about his task. He was tired and ill and had spent a good portion of that year away from his Office of State. Worse was to come. His Parliamentary Under Secretary, his brother Hiley, too was now permanently absent. There was no question of his failing to do battle with his hypochondria or with his gluttony. He was now unmistakeably, genuinely and grievously sick.

On April 22nd, Hiley left his office after six years' unmatchable service manipulating rich and poor, laymen and clergy, commoners and kings – and anybody else who was malleable – on behalf of his brother. He never returned. He took to his sick-bed at his country home to nurse an inflamed bladder. By June 11th he was dead. His brother arrived next day distraught at having missed Hiley's last hours. Sidmouth wrote to impart, what was for him devastating news, to the Prince Regent. 'I have lost a limb which cannot be replaced,' he mourned.[2]

The official obituary for Hiley was written in terms of which his brother could only approve. It described his 'good sense, knowledge of mankind and suavity of manner'. Ziegler, Sidmouth's modern biographer, has other epithets to describe Hiley's character: self-centred, vain, indolent, malicious. There is no good reason to disagree with this view.[3]

Notwithstanding Hiley's shortcomings, and in spite of his relatively obscure and menial position serving his brother in government, his manipulative techniques left a lasting scar on the way of life of many ordinary men and women during these years of the early nineteenth century. The network of spies which Hiley both operated and paid for, effectively transformed the nature and the atmosphere of the society in his brother's charge. His system was one which controlled the most troublesome part of the nation by rewarding working men who spied on other working men. It oiled falsehood and fuelled distrust. It led more than one foolish worker deceived by it to the gallows, and many more to transportation for the rest of their lives. It contributed in no small measure to the dissatisfaction and unhappiness within an already deeply troubled and inequitable society.

And so, at this critical point in the affairs of the country, the Home Secretary, as well as being ill and tired, was now also deeply affected by the death of the closest member of his family who had been his most assiduous Under Secretary. The result was that the Office responsible for the stability of the nation was effectively left in the hands of a lawyer who had been at his post for only a few months.

The young man, Henry Hobhouse, who had just replaced John Beckett, Lord Sidmouth's Permanent Under Secretary, was by no means unknown to the Home Office. 'This intelligent person', Sidmouth called him.[4] Eager and ambitious, with a large family to support – he had eight children and he was to send all four of his sons to his own school, Eton – Hobhouse's appointment to the post of Treasury Solicitor at the time of the Luddite Revolt five years earlier had come at a most propitious time in his career. A large man, approaching 17 stones, he had gone to the north and thrown himself into the task of subduing the rebellious workers with great energy. His prosecuting skills achieved maximum sentences for the accused Luddites. At some point in the riots he had become too closely involved, had been attacked and injured, and was left with periodic headaches for the rest of his life.[5] The experience did nothing to endear to him the manufacturing workers whose peaceable behaviour was now his direct responsibility at the Home Office.

As it happened, soon after Hobhouse had moved in to his new office, a second highly motivated and ambitious character appeared on the doorstep attempting to further his own career. John Lloyd had travelled to London hoping to see the new Under Secretary and to renew the friendship they had struck up during the Luddite trials. At first sight it would seem that these two young lawyers would have little to bind them together: Hobhouse, the Etonian depending much on family connections for his advancement in government in London, and Lloyd, the orphaned clerk who had clambered with merit and a thick skin to his ill-defined but respected station in society in the north country manufacturing town.

Against the odds this couple, five years earlier, had formed a close personal bond. It had been of considerable importance in applying a controlling force to the backs of the working classes during the Luddite Revolt. It was to be of even more spectacular importance in the period ahead.

Lloyd had appeared at the Home Office soon after Hobhouse's new appointment, in order to ask Lord Sidmouth for the tenured post of Prothonotary of Chester. For Lloyd to have been given the job would have meant a substantial rise in salary as well as social standing. That the holder of the office, a Mr Humphries, was not yet dead but merely seriously ill had not in any way inhibited John Lloyd from making his request.

To his disappointment, his journey to London was wasted. Sidmouth was absent from the Home Office, ill, and Hobhouse was away on business. Nevertheless, Hobhouse wrote him a letter brimming with enthusiasm at the possibility of the renewal of their friendship on a full working basis. He had to tell Lloyd that he knew Sidmouth was already considering some other lawyer for the post of Prothonotary, when it became vacant. Nevertheless, Hobhouse assured him that he would 'be ever ready in my new situation to act towards you upon the good opinion which I formed in my old one of your loyalty and zeal'.[6]

For the next many months, Lloyd and Hobhouse were to be in close regular contact. The degree of intimacy discernible from their letters is in great contrast to the stiff, formal letters of magistrates reporting the country's problems to central government. Lloyd's notes contain none of the trivia and second-hand information of such correspondents as the Reverend Mr Ethelston, Colonel Fletcher or Mr Chippindale. His reports are invariably concise, sharply to the point and based entirely on his own observations. The years that had passed since the exciting period in which he was involved with Luddite violence, with murder and with hangings, had not left him unchanged. In 1812 General Thomas Maitland had despised Lloyd for his brutality – without doubt it went as far as torture – and his single-mindedness in bringing rebellious workers to the gallows. Now, however, Lloyd was noticeably more mature in his views. Still as energetically zealous and fervently patriotic as ever, his refreshed relationship with Hobhouse presented an opportunity to show that he now viewed the condition of the working man with a new understanding based on his experience of life in a working-class manufacturing community.

In February, 1818 he was reporting to Hobhouse, 'it is known that the manufacturers do not pay their work people proper wages according to their present profits.'[7] He gave precise figures which graphically showed the astonishing influence of the technological changes in the cotton industry in the district in which he lived. In 1813, 141,500 bags of raw cotton had been imported 'from New Orleans, Charleston, Savannah, Brazil, Demarara, West Indies, East Indies, etc.'. In 1817 this had risen to 477,160 bags – '£8,000,000 worth of bags converted into £32,000,000 worth of cloth.' Only a small proportion of this added value was finding its way into the pockets of workers. Lloyd went on, 'If the present system is continued much longer the only difference between the work people of the cotton *planters* and the work people of the cotton manufacturers will be in the colour of their skins.'[8]

Nor had Lloyd remained merely a passive observer of the state of the poor. He had organised a meeting to try to ensure that 'manufacturers should pay workers in coin of the realm and not in kind'.[9] Several Stockport manufacturers had been guilty of attempting to pay off their employees with food and clothing. Lloyd also attempted to organise a Savings Bank for workers. To his disgust he could muster no support whatever from the town's Establishment.

Nevertheless, in spite of this nascent social conscience and the realisation that the roots of discontent now spreading beneath the whole of the cotton manufacturing district were deeply embedded in economic causes, Lloyd's commitment was unwaveringly that of a keeper of the law. When, as they did in early 1819, signs of reformist activities again surfaced in East Lancashire, Lloyd was providing full reports for Hobhouse at the Home Office in the expectation of reciprocal support for firm action.

He was not to be disappointed. The determination and zeal of these two young lawyers and the unwavering support they were prepared to give each other in policing the working class, were to become key factors leading to the traumatic events to come.

# 16

## Strike and Action

Since the end of the war, the wages for spun yarn paid to spinners had fallen from 3d. to 2d. a pound. This reduced their income to about 15s. for a six-day working week. If these seemed like extortionate rates, they were luxury in comparison to what a hand weaver could expect. Even the accomplished spy and reactionary, Mr Chippindale was moved to point out to his magistrate, Colonel Fletcher, just how distressing were the conditions of the weavers of Oldham, his home town. In 1803 their pay had been about 15s. a week – the figure the spinners were complaining of. But as 1818 advanced and as the slump in trade following the war's end suddenly became worse, it was now 4s. 6d. to 5s. Manufacturers, Chippindale pointed out in July, were doing nothing to allay the extreme suffering such wages caused. And yet, as he told Fletcher, and to his own evident astonishment, the weavers continued to conduct themselves in an orderly way.[1]

As the summer drew on, so the slump in trade deepened. And as its effects became more severe, even the most partisan among the middle classes could not fail to observe that the condition of the unemployed, and even of the increasing numbers of the low paid, was descending to desperation level.

Manchester and its district, like other places before and since, was experiencing the problems of an uncontrolled technology. The communities of these East Lancashire towns – the nature of the work they depended on, the condition under which their inhabitants lived, and even their very size – were almost wholly the creation of this technology. Once its function was constrained, so manifestly dependent on it was every supporting trade in the district, that large communities were unbalanced at a speed never before experienced.

Reaction from those most severely affected was inevitable. No longer were magistrates concerned only with the surge of potentially violent reform meetings. Action by workers with a more immediate end in view – the raising of their poverty-line wages – suddenly became of considerable concern to the law-keepers. The passive conduct of the poor suddenly seemed less assured.

The building trades were first to go out on strike. They were soon followed by colliers, then by spinners and weavers. By mid-July the spinners' dispute with factory owners had turned to unpleasant violence. Ten thousand poured on to the streets of Manchester, causing havoc. In Stockport too, on several occasions power-loom workers gathered in worryingly large numbers outside factories where a few blackleg workers had kept their machines turning.

Like a red rag to John Lloyd's bull, it was to Stockport that John Bagguley had now shifted his base from Manchester.

He had moved to live with his uncle, a local tailor. There, in an old windmill in Edward Street he had set up both a day and an evening school for working men. He was ideally situated to latch his cause for reform to that of the striking workers in this, the most volatile of the cotton towns.

Lloyd was scandalised. As weeks passed and the lengthening evenings encouraged larger crowds at open air meetings, on several occasions he found himself being jostled by angry workers. He told Hobhouse, 'That infamous Bagguley has given the common people of the town a sort of confidence to abuse and traduce every one in authority or in superiority of situation.'[2]

Matters came to a head on July 17th. That day spinners massed around the factory of Thomas Garside who was continuing to run his machines with low-paid women spinners – so it was said – from nearby towns. Whilst the Stockport magistrates pleaded with the Home Office to send in troops, Lloyd took matters into his own hands. With eight dismounted troopers from Sir John Leicester's Yeomanry, he waded into the crowd surrounding the mill and emerged with 20 manacled prisoners.[3]

It was also during these tumultuous days that, for the first time, a troop of the Manchester Yeomanry Cavalry was seen in action at Stockport. John Bagguley described what happened in a scathing letter to the newly published radical newspaper, the *Manchester Observer*.[4] He left no doubt in any reader's mind, that he had witnessed the behaviour of tyrants on horseback. He claimed that more than one Stockport worker had been ridden down and injured by the amateur cavalrymen. On the same day the window frames of another well-known reformer, Dr Thomas Cheetham, had been shattered by bullets from the pistol of a frightened Cheshire yeoman. If this was the behaviour of yeomanry regiments against unarmed civilians, what, it might be asked, was the response of these untrained soldiers likely to be against cudgel-waving rioters?

Henry Hobhouse's mind needed no more urging to conclude that Bagguley should be locked safely back behind the bars from which he had so recently been released. When the *Manchester Observer* was put in front of him, with Bagguley's description of the yeomanry's behaviour, he scanned it with a lawyer's eye. Bagguley's remarks, he believed, were libellous and proceedings could thus be brought against him. Moreover, he was also sure from reports he had received that a case could be made against Bagguley under the Combinations Act for attempting to unionise workers.[5]

The first group to which Hobhouse turned to initiate action against Bagguley, was that of the Manchester magistrates. But the Reverend Mr Hay had been unwell recently and had been failing to communicate with both Hobhouse and General Byng. To Hobhouse's intense annoyance, Hay took no action whatever against Bagguley. Nor did any of his colleagues. They seemed to Hobhouse, as they did to Byng, to be impotent. It was not the first time that Hobhouse felt Manchester's law-keepers to be inadequate to their task.

He therefore did what he believed he should have done in the first place: he turned to his energetic friend in Stockport.

For Lloyd, the request to deal personally with Bagguley

came as nothing less than a pleasure. He saw the presence of this young demagogue in the town as a personal affront. On August 10th at Sandy Brow, on the edge of Stockport, he had listened to him give a reform speech lasting more than three hours. He loathed the thin and drawn orator's mannerisms – his waving arms, his piercing voice – as much as he did his words. Haranguing the crowd on this occasion Bagguley had not stopped short of personal abuse of the monarchy, of the government in general and of Lord Sidmouth in particular. He spoke of Christ himself as 'the greatest Reformer that ever appeared on the horizon of liberty'.[6]

Undoubtedly it seemed to Lloyd, listening to these words, that Bagguley was doing no less than encourage the huge, suggestible crowd to see in his own person the shape of Christ. God, and the King and all they represented – all that Lloyd held dear – were under attack. The signal had been given to reach to their defence.

John Lloyd and John Bagguley personified the clear division of class in northern England and manifested the extreme attitudes on either side of the divide. The conflict between these attitudes was always likely to be violent. In the days following Bagguley's published letter of hatred against the Manchester Yeomanry, after yet another riot by Stockport spinners, Lloyd spelled out for Hobhouse how he would deal with these workers: 'I could even now gallop them down by cavalry,' he said.[7]

Bagguley was by now arranging as many of his meetings as possible on days when he knew Lloyd to be occupied elsewhere. Two days later, on August 22nd, he stood in front of a crowded meeting waving a pistol and, so it was reported, threatened to shoot Lloyd if he put in an appearance. Lloyd, on hearing this news, rushed to assure the Home Office that 'I should like the opportunity of trying the Braggadacio.'[8]

However, his plans to use the report to silence the reformer once and for all were not so easily fulfilled as he had hoped. The legal application for an indictment for sedition against Bagguley, which he speedily submitted to London as a formality, was curtly refused by Mr Topping, the Solicitor General. Topping believed that, on the evidence available from Lloyd, a prosecution might not stand up in a court of law. Lloyd was furious at this high-level dithering. The best he could do as a result, was to persuade the elderly magistrates of Stockport to allow him to plan to arrest Bagguley on the spot should he personally hear him utter a single seditious word.[9]

In spite of this setback, from the Home Office there was nothing but praise for Lloyd's firm handling of the Stockport workers. The government's view of Manchester's law-keepers, however, was very different. As Hobhouse told Byng, 'There certainly is *something wrong* ... There is a grievous want of spirit at Manchester and its neighbourhood.'[10]

Manchester's magistrates were wringing their hands at each new turn of events. The Reverend Mr Hay had become so troubled and ill that he could not complete his work at the bench and handed over many of his functions, including that of reporting to government, to Mr Norris, the recently appointed Manchester stipendiary magistrate.

A gentlemanly and amicable man, Norris, in spite of Hay's

reassurances to the Home Office, could not have been a worse choice at this particular moment. Timorous and indecisive, his experience of civil disturbance was too limited for him to be able to deal competently with the violence into which he suddenly found himself pushed. To add to his nervousness, his involvement was subject to a new, close scrutiny from the Home Secretary. Lord Sidmouth had returned to his desk to give Hobhouse a brief, well-deserved rest.

Norris was soon involved. On August 28th at Gray's mill in the Ancoats district of Manchester, standing below locked factory gates, he tried ineffectually to read the Riot Act, then dithered before sending in militia and yeomanry to disperse the crowds of strikers. There, women shouting and screaming, put their children to the fore, delaying the approach of the troops so that their menfolk, if they chose, could run off. Norris watched, uncertain how to act when 'the military found it requisite to use the butt end of the freelock' on many members of the crowd.[11]

Meanwhile, during Lloyd's absence at Chester, Bagguley, Drummond and Johnston had gathered another large crowd of reformers at Sandy Brow, preparing them to march on Manchester. One spy reported how Johnston, in a powerful speech, brought this large gathering of workers to silence. Anticipating the presence of the now despised Manchester Yeomanry at their march, he urged the crowd to take courage from their own numbers: 'The Yeomanry Cavalry will cut a very awkward figure when you all come out . . . I will assure you they will run in every direction crying Murder.' The spy, John Livesey, described how Johnston 'screamed out this last word'.[12]

Next day, September 2nd, the three young orators led their supporters down the Manchester road to join thousands of strikers milling in the town's centre. Huge numbers of striking spinners – some said as many as 30,000 – were again seen heading for Benjamin Gray's Ancoats mill. Mr Norris was terrified as much by the reports reaching him as by what he saw. 'I know not where it may end,' he moaned.

In spite of the turmoil, the evening ended peacefully with the crowds easily dispersed before midnight. Unfortunately, while earlier passing one crowd, Norris saw a soldier hit full in the face by a flying brick. Another struck Norris on the knee. He was frightened literally sick by the incidents. The tale he reported to Lord Sidmouth did not seek to hide the panic he felt. It was, he said, a momentous crisis exacerbated by the presence of young Bagguley and Drummond, who were now getting the Manchester strikers to yell for 'Death or Liberty'. He recommended the government should immediately send artillery to the town. He said,

> If the thing continue a day longer it will be necessary to put every mill on its defence and many lives will be lost. In short I do look to some bloodshed in this affair and perhaps it may be for the best.[13]

These were historically noteworthy, if ill-chosen words. And the historically equally important reply was no comfort for this nervous, inexperienced magistrate. The new Parliamentary Under Secretary at the Home Office, Henry Clive, in his letter to Norris, made his employer's views of the abilities of the Manchester magistrates in general, and of the recipient in particular, unequivocally clear. Lord Sidmouth had directed him to point out, Clive wrote icily, that in Norris's report of the attack on Gray's factory, no reason had been given,

> For not having resorted to speedy and effectual measures for dispersing the mob after the Riot Act had been read and the subsequent hour had elapsed, and the military had been called in. The slow and imperfect manner in which they separated showed that the proper impression had not been made and it is therefore not be wondered at that in the course of the day, and in the evening the rioting was renewed.[14]

Next day, by contrast, Clive was sending off Lord Sidmouth's congratulations to John Lloyd on the 'promptitude and vigour' with which he had acted and which was so 'well suited to the present crisis'.[15]

Lloyd had in fact just returned from a flying visit to consult General Byng in Chester. He galloped back to Stockport, arriving in the early evening of Sunday, September 3rd.

There he found the streets of his home town once again bulging with workers. A parade of weavers was in progress. Lloyd stood his horse quietly and, in his precise fashion, began to count: 1,222 men and 355 women passed him. They were marching in an orderly way.

The only ominous air to the proceedings was that given by the presence of two pipers playing fifes. Lloyd noticed the interesting psychological effect of the music. It transformed an otherwise peaceful occasion into one with a decidedly worrying militaristic purpose.

But this was not the only assembly Lloyd found in Stockport that day. Bagguley was back and had attracted yet another large crowd. Three thousand reformers were gathered round him in the town's centre on this fine early autumn evening. Lloyd noticed that there were many striking spinners in the crowd, but was able to report with some satisfaction that the weavers kept their distance and did not mingle. Bagguley had yet to unite the cause of most of the striking workers to that of reform.

More important still for Lloyd's immediate purposes, he could clearly hear what was being yelled from the hustings. Bagguley was not only speaking, he was using the same words and phrases of sedition and violence that had been reported for many days past now. Soon Johnston and Drummond too were on their feet calling for spilt blood as the only solution to Britain's problems. Several spinners also found their way to the platform to draw attention to their plight.

It was enough for Lloyd. He personally made notes of all the speeches. Then, having recruited a number of what he called 'honest witnesses' to verify what he had recorded, he was once more astride his horse and riding back to Chester. There he had the local magistrates issue Bench Warrants against Bagguley, Drummond and Johnston for sedition. Another was against five spinners for a conspiracy to raise wages.

It was not long before the first of the spinners was locked away in Chester Castle gaol. Lloyd meanwhile, for the third night in succession without sleep, was riding into the darkness on the trail of Bagguley and his henchmen.[16]

The news that Lloyd was fast moving towards them with arrest warrants reached the three young orators ahead of him. They were soon making for the port of Liverpool, thence, they hoped, to what Lloyd sarcastically called 'the true land of liberty – America!'[17]

They were never to see it. By next day Lloyd's constables had arrested Johnston. Bagguley and Drummond having ridden round the countryside trying to raise money for their passage, survived two days longer. At the dockside, half an hour before a boat was due to sail, they were grabbed by that least sensitive of men, Joseph Nadin. He had been enrolled by Lloyd to ensure Bagguley did not slip away to join Cobbett across the Atlantic Ocean.

Bagguley, with his customary fluency, describes the process of being manacled by the Deputy Constable of Manchester:

He is a villan – while he was ironing me he seemed to enjoy the labour as a treat. His eyeballs rolled in his Bullhead and with all the feelings of another Shyloc – Oh for a second Shakespear to draw in nature this uncommon savage 'Oran Outang.'[18]

Within hours all three were in a chaise en route to Chester Castle where Lloyd, with great satisfaction, personally locked them away. To reassure himself at least that there would be no escape, neither for the trio, nor for the arrested spinners, he took up residence alongside them in person in a cell of the gaol itself.

The effect of this high profile and vigorous activity by Lloyd and his constables, was salutary. By September 7th factories had reopened. A day later colliers were all back at their pits and spinners were making their way to the mills. Moreover, as far as Stockport went, the subsiding troubles were the result of 'neither concessions nor compromises on the part of the Masters'.[19] Lloyd was able to reassure the Home Secretary on this important point. Vigour and firmness had triumphed in the maintenance of the status quo. Lord Sidmouth's admiration for Lloyd's work knew no bounds. The Home Secretary instructed that a message be passed to the Stockport clerk that he wished 'such conduct in the course of loyalty and due subordination were initiated in other parts of the kingdom'.[20]

# 17

# The Populist

The popular press of 1819 was not markedly different in its style and range of political reportage from that of today. In its serious attention to one subject area, however, there is a most notable contrast. On a day at the height of the recent troubles, for example, Cowdroy's *Manchester Gazette* devoted as much space to *Science & c.* – and by that it meant technology – as it did to the spinners' and weavers' riots in the town. In detail, the paper described the patent applied for by a Mr Hill of Glamorgan for improving iron smelting by using a mixture of limestone and mine rubbish to produce a free flux of the metal. It also gave a description of a gun, newly invented by Captain Wheeler of New York – in effect, a repeating rifle.[1]

Cowdroy, like so many others in the town in which he lived, was fully aware of what it was that created the wealth of nations. But not every man agreed as to how the wealth of the north country, and hence of England, could be sustained. Sir Robert Peel, whose family fortunes had been built on cotton, was at that time trying to bring in his bill regulating the

employment of children in the newly mechanised cotton factories. The bill attempted to limit the time worked by children
under 16 to 12½ hours a day – including one hour for dinner,
and a half hour for breakfast.

Benjamin Gray, the factory owner who had faced a hail of
strikers' bricks during the recent attacks, had no hesitation in
making known to the Home Secretary his opinion of the
views of those he sarcastically called 'visionary enthusiasts'.
The economic argument, to him, was simple:

> The obvious effect of shortening the hours of labour must be
> to enhance the price or cost of our manufactures and conse-
> quently to injure us in our competition with other countries.

He argued that the result of interfering with current working practices would be to lessen wages and harm, rather than
help, the workers.[2]

Gray was a member of the Committee of Cotton Spinners
set up to prove 'that the allegation charging the occupiers of
cotton spinning mills with exciting a degree of labor from
children, exceeding that of all other trades, is not founded in
fact.' In support of their claim, the committee sent to Lord
Sidmouth a collection of statistics analysing the hours worked
in 287 cotton factories. Five of these showed in a week an
average of 66 hours worked by each worker, 130 factories
showed 72 hours, while 8 factories in Wigan had an *average* of
82.93 hours.[3]

If these figures are correct, and the likelihood is that they
were not overstated, they mean that in these 8 Wigan mills,

half the workforce, which included children of from 9–16 years, worked in excess of 14 hours each day. The cotton masters' case rested on figures showing that children in Yorkshire worsted mills were working for longer hours than these.

But as Peel's bill made its slow way through Parliament at the beginning of 1819, even the radical *Manchester Observer* was more concerned not with the excess of hours worked, but the absence of work: 'when all used to be bustle and activity – when our tradesmen had scarcely time to bid you good morning – we are now a mass of worse than still life – all now is doubt and despondency.'[4]

It was during this period of yet another swing in the cycle of trade and in the resulting severe trade depression that the popular press discovered a new hero – or villain. To whichever category they allocated him, depending on the paper's political stance, he was tailor-made to fill many column inches for many months to come. Whether he deserved either the fame or the opprobrium is open to much debate.

Henry Hunt, quite by chance, was to walk into the gaping political vacuum left when John Lloyd locked away John Bagguley in Chester Castle. Hunt recognised both the vacuum and his luck with the ease of a born opportunist.

A great deal can be said of Hunt. Some of it he said himself in his unreliable memoirs. He was, by others' as well as his own accounts, a physically striking man who used his voice and his body well when addressing a crowd.

Physical attributes were most important to him and a great deal of his autobiography is given over to descriptions, many unbelievable, of his superiority as a fighter, or a swimmer or even as a worker in his own fields. On his own admission, one of his most powerful early memories was his love of the adulation of the crowd. As a boy he had sneaked aboard the gun-ship *The Prince of Wales*, at Portsmouth, just before her launch in the presence of the King and Queen. In front of many thousands of people, an attempt was made roughly to handle him ashore, until an old admiral intervened and gave him permission to stay. The crowd, for some reason inspired by the incident, gave Hunt three cheers. It thrilled him as nothing had ever done. Much of the rest of his life was spent in trying to recapture that sensation of being centre stage, and of exciting the attention and adulation of the throng. It was the same sensation that John Bagguley had felt. That much, at least, the two had in common.

Hunt was from a prosperous farming family of the south-west. Until 1819, he had never visited the north, and knew nothing of the industrial working class which was such a key element in Britain's economy. As early as 1812 he had fought the Bristol election as a radical, but it was not until 1817 and the part he played as orator to the crowds of Spa Fields that the government had payed particular and anxious attention to this florid and excitable man.

Hunt, with his powerful voice and overpowering manner, had the characteristics of a modern entertainer: he was a personality. He would have been capable of commanding a mass following whatever the cause. That which he had chosen – and it was sincerely as well as passionately held – was parliamentary reform. The old Major Cartwright was deeply suspicious of his techniques, just as Hunt despised Cartwright's as outdated. Many in the middle class shared Cartwright's opinion. At the Westminster election of 1818, in which Sir Francis Burdett was elected in a poll of more than 15,000, Hunt gathered only 84 votes.

Reports of Hunt's popular fame, however, had long ago reached Manchester's radical reformers. One of these, Joseph Johnson, a brushmaker who lived in Stockport, now that the local orators were confined to gaol, had written to Hunt to invite him to the next meeting on St Peter's Field on January 18th. Its purpose would be to petition for parliamentary reform and for repeal of the Corn Laws.

Hunt had no hesitation in accepting the flattering letter from the obsequious, lower-middle-class brushmaker who, when the time came, he would also unhesitatingly choose to despise. He was quickly on the road to the north.

John Lloyd was well prepared for him. Hobhouse, regularly informed by His Majesty's postmasters of the contents of Hunt's letters, was able to provide details so that Lloyd was on hand to watch the orator's arrival in his town. Lloyd was surprised by the cheap showmanship he saw on display. When Hunt got down from the Birmingham–Manchester mail coach, he immediately hired an open barouche. Lloyd watched him as he drove about the streets of Stockport where, with much arm and hat waving, he 'gave audience to all the ragamuffins in town'.[5]

Next day Hunt set off in the same barouche for Manchester. The crowds, now well used to the ritual street marches to St Peter's Field, as a result of Bagguley's efforts, were already in the streets ready to greet him. But Hunt had fresh pieces of showmanship with which to stir their feelings. At the town's outskirts he ordered the carriage-horses to be uncoupled and soon had the shafts being pulled by the hands of more than willing townsfolk to give style to his public entry.

As the carriage passed the Exchange building a group of cotton manufacturers had gathered in the news room. From its bow window they hissed Hunt, the flamboyant figure, sporting his trade mark – a large white hat. Hunt was delighted by the barracking and used it well. To cheers, he stopped the coach, doffed his hat and bowed contemptuously. Before the parade, which had grown to a great throng, reached the meeting ground, the barouche passed John Knight, waiting at a street corner. The crowd recognised him and a yell of 'Let the old veteran get in', went up. Again, Hunt manipulated the situation brilliantly. Stopping the coach, he called for Knight to be lifted up alongside him, and called too for a glass of water to be brought. He then raised it high in a dramatic toast to Knight – or to himself – shouting, 'Liberty or Death!' The crowd was delighted.

As the barouche reached St Peter's Field, the mob, as it had learnt to do over many months, responded outrageously. Hunt, the flashy gentleman-farmer, stood on the hustings where Bagguley had stood and reaped from 10,000 workers the harvest sown by the working-class hero.

At one point there was near farce. The cart being used as the hustings collapsed, with Hunt on it. It deterred him not in the least. He was soon reminding the crowd of the manner in which the authorities had treated the Blanketeers: 'They introduced the soldiers to insult, assault and shoot, an injured and peaceable people,' he shouted. 'They dare this day attempt the same measure with us!'[6] And for good measure, he voiced the opinion that the recent convictions of Brandreth and other Derbyshire workers were the results of managed trials: spies' work. The hangings, he yelled, were nothing better than bloody and unfeeling murders.

The jubilant crowd which followed him out of St Peter's Field filled the streets for half a mile on its route to the Spread Eagle Hotel. It was led by Hunt and banner waving workers. Among the banners, magistrates noted, was a 'Cap of Liberty'. This symbol – a tall pole with its ancient cap – was a device descended from Roman times, when slaves had been given their freedom. It had been used effectively on many bloody occasions in the French Revolution. It had now appeared, and had acquired a worrying, threatening significance, in England. It was waved provocatively by a young man as the crowd passed the Manchester Exchange.

Once at the Spread Eagle, as the *Manchester Chronicle* pointedly observed, the crowd divided and 'the high associations of liberty and equality were separated for the night.' For those rich enough to file into the Hotel, there was an expensive subscription dinner at which Hunt described his political career at length. For the rest – and there were many – there was the shuffle back through the cold January night to their homes in the warren-like backstreets of Manchester.

For Hunt, it had been a triumphant first day in the industrial heart of the north.[7]

# 18

## Grand Theatre

That week 'the magnet of attraction' – as the *Manchester Exchange Herald* described her – at Manchester's Theatre Royal was Miss S. Booth playing seven of her favourite characters, including the Hoyden in Sheridan's *The Trip to Scarbro'*. On the Friday, January 22nd, 1819, she took the lead in *The Honey Moon* and, according to the newspaper, 'never was a performance better received.'[1]

The play's reception, however, had little to do with Miss Booth's performance. Henry Hunt, encouraged by his own first success in the heartland of the north had decided to extend his stay and capitalise on the theatre audience gathered by the celebrated actress. Accordingly, in order to advertise further his presence in Manchester, he had taken a box at the theatre for himself, Joseph Johnson, the brushmaker, and two other tradesmen, Nicholas Whitworth, the secretary of the Manchester Reform Society and Thomas Chapman, a fruiterer.

James Norris, the magistrate, when he heard of Hunt's

plan, immediately rushed into a flurry of protective measures. The result was that there was that night at least as distinguished a cast among the audience as among the players. Seated in scarlet dress uniforms in a box almost immediately opposite that awaiting Hunt's arrival, were five officers of the 7th Hussars, one of whom was Lord Uxbridge, and an infantry officer of the 80th Regiment, while in the pit was the town's boroughreeve, Edward Clayton accompanied by his deputy constable, Joseph Nadin, a magistrate, Mr Sylvester and several constables.

As Hunt and his party entered their box, the cry of 'Hunt and Liberty!' went up from the gallery. In loud reply a shout of 'God Save the King!' was taken up from below. Soon the National Anthem was being sung both from the stage and the auditorium accompanied by a cacophony from the gallery and other parts of the house.

There are a number of versions of what happened next during the ensuing rowdy and unrehearsed piece of theatre. Some said that Hunt's party hissed the National Anthem. This seems unlikely; Hunt, if nothing else, was fervently patriotic. Some said that Hunt's hat was knocked off his head and that Chapman, the fruiterer, kept his firmly on. The Colonel of the 7th Hussars, in his report, insisted that all Hunt's party remained seated during the Anthem with heads covered.

Whatever the provocation, the six red-coated officers rapidly left their box, flung open that of Hunt, took him by the collar, and man-handled him and his three companions out of the theatre. Hunt, in his autobiography, concedes this incident as the only physical encounter of his life in which he was bested. The uncharacteristic admission is explicable in the light of the fact that his humiliation was witnessed by many hundreds of spectators.

Hunt nevertheless was resilient. Within a few minutes he was back in his box standing hatless to the strains of more verses of 'God Save the King' with, according to the *Manchester Exchange Herald*, 'a sardonic smile' on his face.

The evening ended with cheers for the military and, from other parts of the house, equally enthusiastic applause for Hunt.

But Hunt was not finished with the theatre. Encouraged by the ease with which he had stolen the limelight in front of a ready-made audience, he announced his intention of holding a repeat performance with an appearance by him there on the following Monday, this time with a bodyguard of 18 supporters. The management, fearing matters might, on this second occasion, get out of hand, closed the theatre. A crowd of 1,500 appeared that night outside the building simply on the off-chance of clapping eyes on this man with the rapidly growing reputation of glamorous crowd-stirrer.[2]

And so within the space of a few days, Hunt had established himself in the political void left by John Bagguley. The absence of Bagguley, moreover, was unlikely to be a temporary affair. John Lloyd had succeeded in setting bail for him and his two companions at the unheard of level of £2,000 each. It was a figure far out of the reach of working men. When Sir Charles Wolseley, the Birmingham reformer, and Sir Francis Burdett offered to raise this amount, Lloyd was able to refuse it on the grounds that the baronets were not residents of the county in which it was set. The trial of the three young orators was unlikely to be held for many weeks, and the chances appeared good that Bagguley at least would be found guilty and imprisoned for a lengthy term.

It had taken Bagguley two years to establish himself as the workers' acknowledged leader for reform. The longer-established front runners such as John Knight and James Mitchell had months before fallen into his shadow. It was Bagguley's maturing methods, his organisation, his persistence and his unusual qualities of leadership which had resulted in the establishment of St Peter's Field as the focal point for the working class of Manchester and its district. Hunt had no similar qualities of leadership to offer the working man, nor was his prime concern the lot of the poor factory workers of the north of England. What he had to hand was a compelling theatrical presence and the cause of reform which coincided with that of Bagguley. Beyond that there was nothing to link him to a people aching to be led. He was an opportunist whose first love was that of being the focus for the eyes of an audience. What he could do for that audience once he had won their attention was a secondary consideration.

Chance and theatrical flair had combined in these few days to turn Henry Hunt, a southern farmer on his first visit to the north, into a figure which the greatest concentration of factory workers in the world would momentarily perceive as their leader.

The local leadership vacuum at potentially the most active of the townships surrounding Manchester – Stockport – was quickly filled. At the Windmill Rooms, Bagguley had formed a friendship with another energetic teacher and preacher: a young man who styled himself the Reverend Joseph Harrison.

John Lloyd had been quick to investigate this radical parson when he appeared in Stockport during previous years. As was his consistent habit, Lloyd discovered at least one fact missed by others. Not only was Harrison, like Bagguley, a passionate and dynamic reformer, Lloyd was able to reveal triumphantly that he had been forced to leave his previous employment in Derbyshire 'for improper liberties taken with young female scholars'.[3]

If the parson's sexual proclivities concerned Lloyd, they were no deterrent to the workers of Stockport. The attendance at Harrison's Windmill Rooms' classes frequently reached several hundred and there he formed the new flourishing Stockport Union. In the days now approaching the trial of Bagguley, Drummond and Johnston, he provided friendship and raised money for their comfort.

Harrison was also at the forefront of attempts to preserve the dynamism Bagguley had given to the working-class reform movement in Stockport, copying the way in which he had organised meetings. On February 15th Harrison took the platform of a rowdy gathering of several thousand held at Sandy Brow. Lloyd was quickly on the scene accompanied by his teenaged younger son, a detachment of the 80th Regiment, a troop of the Cheshire Yeomanry and his magistrate, the elderly Reverend Mr Prescot. The presence of this 75-year-old was necessary since Lloyd required him to read the Riot Act.

The crowd's response to this legal proceeding was simply to break up and reassemble in just as rowdy a fashion at the Windmill Rooms. Again Lloyd repeated the same procedure of having the Riot Act read, and again the crowd dispersed. But this time, as soon as the soldiers had marched off, a section of the crowd grabbed the young Lloyd, roughed him up, threw him to the ground and repeatedly kicked him.

The effect on Lloyd, seeing this brutal treatment of the son on whom he doted, was powerful. It can be measured in his report of the incident to the Home Office, which, for the first time in the several years of such correspondence with his superiors, is emotional and irrational.[4]

Lloyd was not the only one present to have been provoked. One of Byng's officers, Captain Maclean of the 80th Regiment, who was present during the worst of the rioting, told his General next day,

> I trust Sir, you will approve of my forbearance on this occasion, as I could have dispersed the mob by means of the bayonet and butt end of the musket, had not Mr. Prescott expressed a wish to avoid coercive measures – I must say, it has never been my fate, at any period of my life, to come in contact with such a miscreant and cowardly race of reptiles.

Maclean also reported that there were good hopes that Lloyd would be able to send Harrison 'to join his friends, Bagguley and Johnston at Chester'.[5]

Lloyd would not easily forget the insult to a member of his

family. A strong believer in punishment of the guilty, he also had a markedly vengeful streak in his character. It manifested itself not only by his immediate imprisonment in Chester Castle of one of his son's suspected attackers, but also in the trial of John Bagguley.

On April 15th, Bagguley, Drummond and Johnston at last appeared at Chester Spring Assizes indicted with conspiracy and unlawful assembly. Bagguley, as he told Harrison, had little reason to be optimistic about the outcome, especially, as he observed, since the jury consisted of 'nothing but baronets and esquires'.[6] Lloyd, who had stated his intention of supplying 'honest witnesses', on this occasion fell short of the spirit of his promise. One was John Livesey, the Reverend Ethelston's spy, whom Lloyd himself observed was 'a prattling fool' and frequently drunk. Another was William Boulter, the owner of a local billiard room who also played in pantomime. But his star witness was his elder son, John Horatio Lloyd, named after his father and Lord Nelson.

John Horatio had shown exceptional scholastic promise at the local grammar school and Lloyd had succeeded in drawing his son's achievements to the attention of Henry Hobhouse. With the Home Secretary's approval, Hobhouse directed a Treasury loan towards Lloyd – who had little income from his self-appointed task of law-keeper of Stockport and Manchester – so that he could afford to send his son to Oxford. John Horatio was currently an undergraduate of Queen's College.

During Bagguley's reform meeting that previous September the son had stood alongside his father and made detailed notes of speeches from the hustings. It was the son's evidence which did for Bagguley.

Bagguley, Drummond and Johnston were found guilty. Before sentence was passed, Bagguley was allowed to speak. He pointed out to Chief Justice Copley that he had already been imprisoned for seven months on excessive bail set by John Lloyd. He asked for no mercy – only justice. He was sentenced, as were his two friends, to two years in gaol with sureties of £500 each for a further two years.[7]

# 19

## Sharpening Swords

It was clear even before the middle months of 1819 arrived that for its third successive summer, with or without Bagguley's presence, industrial Manchester was sitting uncertainly on the edge of violence. In the absence of the sick Reverend Mr Hay, James Norris was the magistrate on whom most of the burden of law keeping now fell. In spite of the successful curb placed on the working-class leadership by Lloyd, the length and hysterical pitch of Norris's communications to those from whom he sought support were rising as each day brought a rumour of yet another gathering of workers.

A meeting of cotton weavers, he discovered, was planned in Manchester on Midsummer's Day and yet another of reformers a week later. Norris had heard that the 'Cap of Liberty' was to be carried by the reformers. He was thoroughly scared of the likely consequences, having by now been assured of its bloody effects when it had been borne as a symbol in revolutionary France. He was so worried about its appearance in Manchester that he hurried to Stockport to ask

John Lloyd's advice about what to do should the threat to parade it be carried out.[1]

He was even more panicked to hear the rumour that Henry Hunt was again planning to visit the north. Here, as in all things, he feared the worst. He assured the Home Office, 'I have little doubt it will be the signal for *general* measures amongst the disaffected and commotion will ensue.'[2] But with Lord Sidmouth still unwell and once more absent, Hobhouse had again taken firm control of Home Office policy. In unequivocal terms Hobhouse spelled out the course Norris should follow should he be drawn into action. He wrote:

> Yourself and your brother magistrates may depend on being supported by his Majesty's Government in an act of vigour, temperately considered, and firmly executed.[3]

The conditions under which the industrial cotton workers were now having to live were all too visible and few realists could believe that when they gathered *en masse*, they would remain so unnervingly passive as on previous occasions. Worst affected were the weavers. John Lloyd, clear about the iron-fisted policy he believed should be used on rioters, was equally plain about the desperate state to which workers had sunk by mid-1819. He suggested that the government should send some form of relief: 'It is quite impossible that weavers can live upon their earnings,' he insisted.[4]

His magistrate, the old Reverend Mr Prescot, had been deeply moved by the poverty stricken delegates of 4,000 weavers who had visited him. They proposed to attend in force a reform meeting planned for Sandy Brow on June 28th. It was to be addressed by the 'Reverend' Joseph Harrison and by the aristocratic landowner Sir Charles Wolseley, both of whom had a growing reputation for crowd-stirring. Prescot, like Norris, feared the worst as a result of it. 'The state of this district is now truly alarming,' he confided to a neighbour.[5]

Upwards of 20,000 workers attended that meeting. Even more – some reports said as many as 40,000 – turned out at Blackburn a week later. At neither did serious violent incidents erupt. However, across the north country the scale and the frequency of similar meetings were reaching alarming proportions.

Again James Norris asked for advice should the 'Cap of Liberty' be raised on its pole and carried at the Stockport meeting. Hobhouse's reply was as firm as Norris's question was dithering:

> This symbol gives a character to the meeting which cannot be mistaken . . . If it shall be displayed again with impunity, it will be a subject of regret – And if the Magistrates shall see an opportunity of acting with vigour they will recollect that there is no situation in which their energy can be so easily backed by military as at Manchester, where the troops are at hand, and may be kept on the alert, if the Civil Power should appear likely to stand in need of their assistance.[6]

Twice, therefore, in the space of less than a week, Hobhouse had spelled out how Manchester magistrates should react when provoked – even if only symbolically – by civilian crowds.

Many outside this northern melting pot of the underprivileged, the unrepresented, the poor and the desperate, were now suddenly beginning to see in its bubbling interior the source of great political powers. Irrespective of the fact that they were only vaguely aware of the critical technology responsible for generating the heat of change, several men in both the south and the north were simultaneously looking to harness this force. Major Cartwright, Sir Charles Wolseley, the 'Reverend' Joseph Harrison were a few. Karl Marx and Friedrich Engels, a few years later, with more understanding of the technological imperatives, would be others. In 1819 another was the individual with probably least knowledge of, or least care for the source of the north of England's turbulence. Nevertheless, Henry Hunt, who as a result of his already more than adequately demonstrated success at the epicentre, Manchester, combined with the luck of the natural showman, was leading the pack in gaining the following of the masses.

Hunt had taken the initiative by writing a flattering letter to Joseph Johnson, the obsequious brushmaker. Johnson, who by now had become part-owner of the *Manchester Observer* and secretary to a newly formed reform society, the Manchester Patriotic Union, was unnaturally inflated with pride that Hunt had remembered him from his January visit. In an ingratiating reply, he compared Hunt's chairmanship on that occasion to the inferior performance given by Sir Charles Wolseley at the recent Stockport meeting. He used the occasion to invite Hunt, on behalf of the Manchester Patriotic Union, to chair a large meeting planned for Manchester on August 2nd.

In addition to its sycophancy, Johnson's letter, like those of many observers, could not avoid mentioning the conditions met with by anyone walking the depressing streets of Manchester and its surrounding towns during these summer months of 1819:

Nothing but ruin and starvation stare one in the face, the state of this district is truly dreadful, and I believe nothing but the greatest exertions can prevent an insurrection. Oh, that you in London were prepared for it.[7]

If, when he read these ambiguous sentences, Hunt was unsure whether they were an invitation to lead or to suppress an insurrection, others had no such doubts. Johnson's letter had already been intercepted on government orders and copied. Its contents were read by a greatly concerned Henry Hobhouse at the Home Office before it even reached its intended destination. His reaction to what 'the effect of a Man of Rank at the head of the Mob Orators' was likely to produce, was swift. He immediately made sure that General Byng had the 15th Hussars on the march in the direction of Manchester, at the earliest opportunity.[8]

Hunt, however, was quite unaware, even if he had known the contents had been read, that Johnson's letter could have been interpreted to mean that he was planning insurrection. Since he recognised a rival in Sir Charles Wolseley, he was delighted by the flattering words he saw there. Quickly, he drafted an enthusiastic reply, accepting the offer of the chairmanship of the meeting – provided, as he put it, 'the *largest assemblage* may be procured that ever was seen in this country.'

Johnson was willing to try to fulfil the condition literally. He already had in his mind a basic plan to involve the established reformers, such as John Knight and James Wroe, the new editor of the *Manchester Observer*, but also the working-class agitators such as Samuel Bamford, the weaver, and his friend, 'Doctor' Healey. Such men as these could be recruited to organise mass groups of workers in surrounding towns – Middleton, Saddleworth, Lees, Oldham, Stockport and the rest – and have them march on Manchester simultaneously on August 2nd. They could be preceded by bands and banners and each contingent could carry a 'Cap of Liberty'. Hunt, Johnson believed, should prepare and deliver a 'Declaration of Rights' at what could be, with proper organisation, the most important and impressive meeting the country had ever seen.[9]

The government had other cities than Manchester to fret over. At a great radical meeting of 60,000 in Birmingham that week, Sir Charles Wolseley – who was not present – had been elected 'legislatorial attorney' for the city. The radical plan, of which this was a part, was that the unrepresented peoples of all parts of England, irrespective of the existing system, would send their own elected representatives to the House of Commons. The idea behind this was that, since the existing Parliament had not been chosen by the largest proportion of members of the State, the laws it enacted and the taxes it imposed should not apply to those excluded from the franchise. The dramatic, if naive proposal, therefore, was to swamp an unwilling Parliament with new, unauthorised members who would be more truly representative of the people. Long before any such proposal could be put into practice, however, warrants for the arrest of Sir Charles Wolseley and the 'Reverend' Joseph Harrison were issued.

On July 21st yet another vast meeting was held at Smithfield Market in London. Estimates of crowd numbers, as on all such occasions, varied with the political leaning of the observer. Hunt, who was the principal speaker, estimated there were 70,000–80,000 present. Joseph Harrison, who had travelled from Stockport to be present, told John Bagguley there were 150,000, while Henry Hobhouse had been assured there were only 10,000.[10]

One of several resolutions produced by Henry Hunt at that meeting and adopted there, was worded,

That from and after the 1st day of January 1820, we cannot conscientiously consider ourselves as bound in equity by any future enactments which may be made by persons styling themselves our representatives, other than those who shall be fully, freely and fairly chosen by the voices or votes of the largest proportion of the members of the State.[11]

It was an unambiguous challenge to government which the government could not ignore. But this was not the only dramatic content to the Smithfield Market gathering. John Lloyd had by now gained the Home Office's agreement to arrest Joseph Harrison for his part in the last Stockport meeting. He had therefore sent two of his special constables, including his favourite, William Birch, to report to the Lord Mayor of London, John Atkins, and ask for assistance in making the arrest.

For some reason Atkins chose to send his city marshals, accompanied by soldiers, into the great Smithfield crowd at the precise time that it was at its most dense and potentially at its most explosive. The arrest of Harrison on the hustings could have been the prelude to a major riot had it not been for Hunt, who used his considerable powers of crowd control, calling for restraint to prevent what could easily have become an ugly scene.[12]

Without further incident, the handcuffed Harrison was taken through the crowd to the office of the Lord Mayor and handed over to William Birch who was to be responsible for his safe custody on the road back to Stockport.

Henry Hunt, meanwhile, had been given a letter from the brushmaker of Manchester, Joseph Johnson, suggesting that Hunt should become 'legislatorial attorney' for London. Hunt suspected that Johnson himself had his eye on becoming 'legislatorial attorney' for Manchester. The whole idea of electing mock Members of Parliament, Hunt believed – at least the hindsight of his memoirs tells us – was folly.[13]

Hunt was not alone in viewing this plan as foolhardy. Henry Hobhouse had not only already taken legal advice on the subject, he had also instructed the Manchester magistrates how to deal with such pretensions to an election. He told Mr Norris, who was now desperately worried about the consequences of a Manchester assembly at which Henry Hunt would be present,

> On the subject of the expected meeting at Manchester on Monday, I have now to acquaint you that the Attorney and Solicitor General have given their opinion that the election of a Member of Parliament without the King's Writ, is a high misdemeanour and that the parties engaged and acting therein, may be prosecuted for a Conspiracy.

A meeting held for such purpose, Hobhouse went on, would be an unlawful assembly and it would be a matter of prudence and expediency for the magistrates to decide 'on the spot' whether or not to disperse it.[14]

Again Norris's instructions from Hobhouse could not have been clearer. But before he was forced to act on their initiative, an incident occurred which had a profound effect on Norris in particular, and on the middle classes of Manchester and its surrounding districts in general. It again involved John Lloyd but, more cruelly, his constable, William Birch.

At about eight o'clock on the evening of July 24th, 1819, Birch arrived safely back in Stockport with Joseph Harrison. After the prisoner had been questioned by Lloyd, Birch led him through the streets of Stockport to Birch's own house, where Harrison was to be lodged. Following behind was a substantial crowd of hostile workers.

Shortly after ten o'clock that night Birch left his home to walk the short distance to the house of the magistrate, Mr Prescot, which stood next to that of John Lloyd. In the dining-room of Lloyd's house, eating supper, were his two sisters, his two sons and a local surgeon.

As Birch approached Prescot's house, he was quickly surrounded by several men from the crowd, one of whom, John Bruce, the secretary of the Stockport Reform Society, lived with Harrison. Suddenly, from behind Bruce, a second man produced a pistol and, from a point close to Bruce's left cheek, aimed point blank at Birch, and fired.

With blood pouring from his chest, Birch jumped the fence into John Lloyd's garden. Passing the window where the family and its friend were dining, Birch was soon in safe arms, and being examined by the surgeon.[15]

John Lloyd was quickly on the scene. As was his habit throughout life, he was again close to awful violence. By the time he had ministered to Birch the assailants had escaped. He had the Reverend Prescot immediately give orders for a troop of the 15th Hussars to be called. He also arranged for the surgeon of the regiment – an officer well acquainted with bullet wounds – to attend. An exploratory operation on Birch was begun by the two doctors. In spite of inflicting what can only have been hideous pain on their patient, they could find no bullet.[16] Such was the nature of the wound that Birch was not expected to live many hours. He languished in a hopeless state, Lloyd reported to Hobhouse.[17]

As also was his customary response to violence, Lloyd spent the next days in prolonged hyperactivity, neither sleeping nor resting, until he had found suspects. During the first night he arrested two young men, one of whom was Bruce. His left cheek was visibly singed by gunpowder. At six o'clock in the morning Lloyd recruited three magistrates to take over the interrogation of these and other witnesses so that he could rush after other likely assailants. None of those in custody, however, appeared to be the real villains.[18]

The alarmist reaction to the news of the attempted murder was not restricted to Manchester. Lord Sidmouth feared it was a signal for far worse physical violence in the north country. He immediately recommended to the Prince Regent that a reward of £200 should be offered to any man discovering who shot Birch. A pardon would be given to any accomplice supplying evidence. It was this temptation which had brought down Luddite murderers a few years earlier. There was every chance that the same venal motives could again be triggered.[19]

The effect of this incident on the nation as a whole, as it had been on the Prince Regent and his government, was salutary. Within hours, a rumour had spread that Lord Fitzwilliam, the Lord Lieutenant of the West Riding of Yorkshire, had been killed in Leeds when rioters gathered round him and presented papers for his signature. He was supposed to have refused to sign, then been shot.[20]

The rumour was unfounded. It was true, however, that Fitzwilliam had suddenly returned to the north, as had the Lords Lieutenant of Lancashire, Cheshire and Warwickshire. Earlier that month, fearing that civil violence was about to erupt, Lord Sidmouth had ordered each of them to put their yeomanry cavalry regiments on stand-by.[21] The recent brutality appeared to confirm the wisdom of this precautionary measure.

As a result of the Home Secretary's instruction, the Earl of Derby, the Lord Lieutenant of Lancashire, briefed Thomas Trafford, the eager commanding officer of the new Manchester Yeomanry Cavalry. Trafford's active response was to order that his regiment's swords be prepared for action. In the week preceding the shooting of Birch, Daniel Kennedy, a journeyman cutler, received 63 of the Yeomanry's sabres. He had been asked to clean swords in the past. But never had he been instructed, as on this occasion, that they should 'be made very sharp'.[22]

# 20

## An Uncertain Meeting

Throughout that hot summer of 1819, with Lord Sidmouth still sickly and depressed, vital decisions relating to the internal security of an insecure nation continued to be taken by the astute young lawyer, Henry Hobhouse. From the Home Office he issued the instructions which would now affect the nation's future. However, on documents which were really of his own invention, he less and less frequently kept up the charade that they emanated from his chief, Lord Sidmouth.

Hobhouse was as fully aware as need be that the custodianship of the short fuse leading to any explosion in Manchester lay with the magistrates. James Norris's nervousness and inexperience, therefore, worried him greatly. Hobhouse did not shrink from making his own feelings plain. On July 28th, the Reverend William Hay broke the news that he was unwell, suffering in the exceptional heat. He needed a rest from his courtroom work, preferably away from Manchester.[1] Hobhouse's concern was instantaneous. The idea of the control of this place and the huge meeting it was soon to experience, being in the hands of Norris, and of the likes of the Reverend Mr Ethelston, alarmed him greatly. He quickly wrote off to Hay to try to persuade him to stay on in the town. He added: 'Without flattery we find when you are there a something which makes matters proceed better than in your absence.'[2] But it was too late. Hay had already left for Yorkshire. In any case, Hobhouse was by now beginning to suspect that time had taken its toll on this once uncompromising clergyman. He was no longer the same ruthless character Hobhouse had discovered when first they met in 1812 during the Luddite Revolt.

Fortunately, Hobhouse suddenly found himself presented with an unexpected opportunity to take stock. The Manchester reformers had delayed the anticipated date of the meeting which Henry Hunt was to attend. On July 31st, the *Manchester Observer* announced it would take place on August 9th. Moreover, the notice was a clear public statement of the meeting's purpose. This was, the advertisement said, 'to take into consideration the most speedy and effectual mode of obtaining Radical Reform in the Common House of Parliament' and 'to consider the propriety of the "Unrepresented Inhabitants of Manchester" electing a person to represent them in Parliament.'

On that same Saturday as the *Manchester Observer* appeared, the newly convened Select Committee of Magistrates anxiously scanned its contents. Its members had quickly gathered in the Police Office to consider how to act in the face of what now seemed to them to constitute a direct threat. The threat, however, had been overestimated.

The chairman of this group, elected in the Reverend Hay's absence, was the young, handsome, rich and – some said – effeminate William Hulton. Whatever his qualities, they were unequal to coordinating the thoughts of the seven worried men who met with him and James Norris that day. In the first place, Norris had already had firm instructions from Hobhouse regarding what should be done if the expected meeting gathered to elect a Member of Parliament without the King's writ. As Hobhouse had said two weeks earlier, 'if the meeting is not convened for the unlawful purpose, the illegality will not commence until the purpose is developed.'[3] And had these magistrates taken the care to read carefully the announcement in the *Manchester Observer*, they would have seen that the meeting's purpose was most clearly defined as being merely *'to consider* the propriety of . . . electing a person to represent them in Parliament.'

Rushing in to print where only angels should have been allowed to make their delicate mark, William Hulton that day authorised the appearance of huge posters headed with the words ILLEGAL MEETING in banner type. Worse, the notice contained a grammatical error which gave it the opposite sense from that intended. It read,

Whereas it appears by an Advertisement in the *Manchester Observer* Paper of this day, that a PUBLIC and ILLEGAL MEETING is convened for *Monday the 9th day of August next*, to be held on the AREA, NEAR ST. PETER'S CHURCH, in Manchester; We, the Undersigned Magistrates, acting for the Counties Palatine of Lancaster and Chester, *do hereby*

*Caution all Persons to abstain* AT THEIR PERIL from attending such ILLEGAL MEETING.[4]

Not that grammar mattered to many who read it when it was posted in the streets of Manchester on August 3rd. Several beadles who nailed up the sheet were stoned and beaten about the head by crowds of workers who resented what they believed to be its message.

Henry Hobhouse's precise mind, when he saw his copy of the poster which urged citizens 'to abstain at their peril' from attending the meeting, could now only expect the worst of Manchester's magistrates should they be called upon to make key decisions at a potentially explosive meeting.

The magistrates' behaviour, nevertheless, must be seen in the context of what was happening in the towns and particularly in the countryside surrounding Manchester during these few days. In response to Henry Hunt's call for the proper organisation to create the most impressive meeting the country had ever seen, Joseph Johnson had had surprising results. Key working-class reformers, many of them already prominent in the Hampden Clubs, had taken on the leadership of groups of large numbers of workers in order to prepare them for the forthcoming event. They had met with enormous success.

Samuel Bamford was one of these organisers. He had been delegated the task of preparing thousands of Middleton workers for the meeting which, he had been told, 'should exhibit a spectacle such as had never before been witnessed in England'.

As he later pointed out, in the past the press had had no problem in making mocking copy out of gatherings of working men. Customarily, those present were often ragged and dirty and their behaviour confused and disorganised. The Blanketeers' was only the most notorious of those meetings that had ended in chaos. For this new St Peter's Field meeting, a well-coordinated attempt was to be made to ensure that all delegates were neatly turned out, and that they marched in good order. The order was to be realised by rehearsing each contingent in drill.

Men like Bamford, therefore, recruited retired infantry soldiers and local militiamen to put spinners, weavers, bricklayers, colliers and many other tradesmen through their paces. Nightly the contingents gathered in the fields of Middleton, on the moors of Saddleworth and in and around every other town surrounding Manchester and began marching, halting, facing-about and countermarching to shouted commands. There were bugles and drums to keep the recruits in time. In the days leading up to the meeting a passable sense of order began to appear in the workers' squads. The experience was for many a novelty and for others it brought a sense of enjoyment in its contrast with a 12-hour day spent in a spinning mill.[5]

There is no reason whatever to doubt Henry Hunt's word that he intended both the delegations and the meeting itself on St Peter's Field to be entirely peaceful. Equally, most of those preparing to be at the ground on the great day intended it to be one of ordered behaviour – or even more lightheartedly, an enjoyable Monday off work in the middle of a hot summer.

But it requires great naivety to believe that all of those who were drilling in those days before the meeting had nothing other than peaceable thoughts in mind. Before their arrest, the orators led by Bagguley had consistently drummed up an enthusiastic response when calling for violence as a means to end the country's inequities. Many of those marching in the fields and on the wasteland of the Lancashire countryside carried thick sticks or cudgels. That they had been told they were never to use them is probably true. But equally probable is that among the tens of thousands preparing for August 9th, there was a substantial group of thugs who, given the chance, would be more than pleased to turn it into an opportunity to take revenge on special constables, militia, yeomanry and any other supporters of the Establishment. Even Samuel Bamford in his autobiography admits to planning to take 'a score or two of cudgels' – for self-defence.

Nor is there any doubt that numbers of workers had access to arms. Local merchants and manufacturers still had not forgotten the violent shootings of the Luddite period. Closer in time, Jeremiah Brandreth had killed with a pistol. Even closer, William Birch's would-be assassin had also used one. Birch was believed to be still only just clinging to life.

Now, with only days to go before the St Peter's Field meeting, in dozens of places, workers could be seen assembling to a trumpet call, drilling with precision in the evening sun, responding to commands echoing across lonely valleys and sloping arms before marching off into the mists of nightfall. For many miles around, the middle class of the north watched, deeply worried. Every magistrate, Mr Norris and the Reverend Mr Ethelston among them, received reports, many exaggerated through fear, of the nightly drillings.

Colonel Fletcher, the Bolton magistrate, had no doubts about either the reality or the threat. One evening he set off with a company of foot soldiers along the road to Bury and surprised 500 drilling workers. He took ten prisoners for good measure.[6]

For many, these assemblies could have only one purpose. Hobhouse described exactly how the northern middle class interpreted the events in their midst; they were, he said, 'meetings held for the professed purpose of Reform, but really with a view to revolution.'[7]

By August 3rd a royal proclamation had been posted in Manchester forbidding the practice of drilling.

On the same day the full implication of the magistrates' decision to ban the August 9th meeting had struck the Home Secretary, now returned to his office, as soon as Hobhouse revealed it to him. The very notion that magistrates themselves should not have acted within the strict letter of the law was anathema to Lord Sidmouth's well-ordered mind. Indeed, he immediately consulted the Attorney General to confirm his understanding of the legality of the meeting, and had Hobhouse write to Norris to get the magistrates to agree to reconsider their decision.[8]

Next day, he had Hobhouse write yet again to remind Norris how unfortunate it would be if, at the meeting, the magistrates ordered violence to be used. Twice in the same letter Hobhouse emphasised this point. He added, 'it will be the wisest course to abstain from any endeavour to disperse the mob, unless they should proceed to acts of felony or riot.'[9]

There can be no doubt that, coldly and calculatedly as Lord Sidmouth viewed the mob behaviour of the working classes, his unambiguous opinion was that violence should be used on a crowd only as a last resort. This was the message he had Henry Hobhouse transmit firmly during the days in which, as the letters dispatched from the Home Office show, he was clearly back at its head and personally leading its policy.

But equally there can be no doubt, that although Hobhouse faithfully passed on his master's views to the magistrates beneath him, he held back from sharing all Lord Sidmouth's scruples. For weeks past, in Sidmouth's absence, spurred by John Lloyd's descriptions of the success of his iron-fisted activities in Stockport, Hobhouse had been telling Manchester's feeble magistrates to act with more determination and, if necessary, with force. Only a few hours earlier, he had written to General Byng – whom he addressed in the same relaxed and intimate fashion as he did John Lloyd – to say just how weak that spirit was. He also added that he had been ordered to dissuade the magistrates from treating the meeting as illegal. Nevertheless, Hobhouse went on, 'If a riot ensues, that riot must be put down at all hazard'.[10] This was the undiluted view of Henry Hobhouse. Moreover, there was every reason for him to know he could further it in the short term rather than in the long. Lord Sidmouth was again unwell and, even at the hour of crisis, was considering leaving the Home Office in Hobhouse's hands whilst he took a short recuperative holiday.

Even before Lord Sidmouth's bags were packed, Hobhouse wrote to James Norris asking for immediate news about how decisions on the St Peter's Field meeting were progressing. Hobhouse instructed him to send letters to his home address in Grosvenor Place, marked 'Confidential and Immediate', and not to Lord Sidmouth himself, 'as Lord Sidmouth', he told Norris, 'sleeps out of town'.[11]

## 21

## Decisions of Propriety

On August 7th, 1819 the *Manchester Observer* carried its second announcement of the meeting intended for St Peter's Field. This time the date was fixed for Monday, August 16th. To remain even more firmly within the law, however, its aim was now defined differently from that of the first meeting. No mention was made of the election of a Member of Parliament. Its purpose was

> To consider the propriety of adopting the most LEGAL and EFFECTUAL means of obtaining a REFORM in the Commons House of Parliament.

The meeting was to be held at twelve o'clock, and it would be chaired by Henry Hunt. Major Cartwright was one of several well-known reformers named as having been invited to attend.

The announcement, as had its predecessor, listed as its signatories more than 700 householders, most of them handloom weavers.[1]

The consequence of the magistrates' hesitancy was that Manchester's reformers had gratefully capitalised on the cancellation of their first meeting. The result of a banning order, a week's delay, and now a second round of advertising was that there could be no one in the neighbourhood of Manchester who did not know of the great event to be held on the 16th.

No one, that is, except the glamorous central figure. Henry Hunt had not been told.

On the day of the announcement he had set off in his own gig from the south. Next evening, August 8th, he arrived within 3 miles of Stockport. There the news was broken to him that the meeting planned for the next day had been cancelled. In spite of a large and excitable crowd waiting to greet him in Stockport itself, Hunt at first refused to complete his journey.

He was furious. Never an admirer of Johnson, he was now confirmed in his low opinion of the brushmaker. He was convinced that he had been made a fool of deliberately, and decided to return to Hampshire immediately. However, the news of an idolatrous crowd of Stockport workers, combined with a little persuasion, restored his lost dignity. He concluded that the least he could consider would be to stay the night in the welcoming town. Before his gig had completed its short journey, however, it was met on the road by Joseph Johnson and John Thacker Saxton, the managing editor of the *Manchester Observer*. In spite of what Hunt would have posterity believe was his great disinclination, he overcame with ease any reluctance engendered by Johnson's obsequiousness.[2]

Next day, closely watched by John Lloyd and government

spies, Johnson and Saxton led Hunt in triumph into Manchester. Thousands turned out along the Stockport–Manchester road to cheer his open carriage and to acknowledge its chief occupant as their leader. Hunt was not alone. The patrician and much respected reformer Sir Charles Wolseley had turned out to accompany him. Wolseley, however, took both a metaphorical and a literal back seat in the proceedings as his gig trailed behind that of Hunt. The overwhelming reception given to Hunt unquestionably relegated the baronet to second rank.

The spy who watched the procession into Manchester noted Hunt's movements as best he could. The crowds round Hunt's carriage were so thick that the government agent could not get within 100 yards of it. The only reassuring report he could make was that, as Hunt passed by the Manchester Exchange waving his white hat, some hissing was heard.[3]

James Norris had been thrown into immediate panic as soon as he heard of the arrival of Hunt in the north. A messenger had galloped from Stockport with the news, at one o'clock in the morning of the previous day. With Hunt in the vicinity, Manchester, as Norris's eyes saw it, was in a state of 'enormous confusion'.[4] By now, however, he had a supportive influence alongside him. Mr Hay, hearing from his home of the St Peter's Field meeting, in spite of his exhaustion, had immediately set off on the long journey across the Pennines back to Manchester.

As he and Norris watched Hunt's flashy but triumphal progress through their town, they conferred anxiously to see whether they could make a case for arresting Hunt for a breach of the peace. They considered that they could. But the once unbending authority of the Reverend Mr Hay was manifestly no longer what it had been. Once it could never have allowed Norris's uncertainty to rub on to him as it now did. They reflected on the matter yet again and this time came to the conclusion that it would be 'inexpedient' to issue a warrant for Hunt's detention.[5]

With only four days to go before the meeting, fear of its consequences was endemic. Norris now had his brother magistrates agree that the time had come to call out both the Cheshire and the Manchester Yeomanry. In words, he painted the scene of the day in question in the only way his much stretched imagination could visualise:

What the result will be God only knows. The day can scarcely be expected under such circumstances to pass in peace – although the revolutionaries will affect to wish it. The order of the day with them will be peace but many of them I have little doubt will come secretly armed.[6]

Henry Hunt, on the other hand, with other matters in mind, had been alerted to the magistrates' fear of violence. But he was far from being concerned that crowds of the size expected for St Peter's Field could become death traps for great numbers of their members. He was at that moment sitting motionless in Joseph Johnson's cottage at Smedley. His portrait was being touched up by the painter, Tuke. As he sat with poised profile, he listened to the weaver Samuel Bamford suggest to him that his Middleton contingent, once it had peacefully assembled near St Peter's Field, would have no protection from Nadin's armed constables. Cudgels, Bamford insisted, were needed for self-defence. But Hunt would not hear of it.[7] In the hope that no other of Bamford's colleagues would likewise be tempted to break the law and give the authorities, as he said, 'every opportunity . . . to excite a riot that they may have a pretence for spilling our blood', Hunt had a large poster printed and published from Smedley Cottage. It beseeched the people of Manchester to come to next Monday's meeting, 'armed with *no other* weapon but that of a self-approving conscience; determined not to suffer yourselves to be irritated or excited by any means whatever, to commit any breach of the public peace.'[8]

Hunt, as proud of his ability with his tongue, as he was vain of the agility of his body, believed he alone could control and subdue the anticipated great crowd. He made his view clear to Joseph Johnson who, after a week spent in his cottage, Hunt could by now barely bear the sight of. In any case, Hunt argued, if the crowd got out of hand the magistrates could easily disperse it by reading the Riot Act.

In the days he spent at Johnson's home, Hunt had ample time to indulge in one of his favourite diversions: writing to the press. The letter of August 12th which he composed to *The Times* could not have been better calculated to antagonise the magistrates, merchants and manufacturers he was now among. In it he repeated and embellished the rumour that, not only had William Birch not been shot in the chest – indeed, Hunt claimed, he was up and about practising sword exercises with a stick – but that his would-be assassin was none other than John Lloyd's son, John Horatio Lloyd.[9]

It says a great deal of Hunt and of his lack of mature judgement that he would repeat such a silly rumour in a national newspaper without making the slightest attempt to check its factual accuracy. It was true that Birch was now making a recovery. Hunt, had he chosen, could have checked with Birch himself that, far from being the gunman, John Horatio had extended a pair of the arms to which he had fled after being shot.

Factual accuracy was not then, and never would be, Hunt's strong point. Rumours stirred him to exaggerated action more readily than most men were swayed by facts. A second rumour to which he paid attention during the few days he spent in Manchester was that the magistrates planned to arrest him. To prevent any such arrest from interfering with his plans, 48 hours before the St Peter's Field meeting was due to be held, therefore, Hunt decided to offer himself up to the magistrates and then seek bail. With this in mind, he drove to the New Bailey and dramatically presented himself to the sitting magistrates. Politely, they told Hunt they had no charge to prefer against him.[10]

That night, one of these magistrates took up his pen to write to the Home Office. Yet in spite of the fact that Hobhouse had asked for letters to be addressed to him personally, the agitated Norris persisted in the belief that Lord Sidmouth was receiving his increasingly troubled notes. He described the uncertain situation in Manchester, and added,

Your Lordship may easily imagine that under the circumstances the magistrates are placed in the most anxious state with respect to the propriety of their ultimate decision.[11]

But Lord Sidmouth could imagine no such thing. He had left with his family for a short, restful holiday by the seaside. He had chosen Broadstairs.

Hobhouse's letter telling Norris this fact was already well on its way.[12] Hobhouse was again fully in charge and Norris was painfully alert to the Under Secretary's previously unequivocally expressed views on the firmness with which magistrates should act.

# 22

## A Conflict of Interests

History has not been kind to Sir John Byng's famous ancestor and namesake. For his failure to do battle with the French, Admiral John Byng was shot by a firing squad on the quarter-deck of HMS *Monarque* in Portsmouth harbour. Voltaire's prescriptive phrase, *pour encourager les autres*, thus entered the English language.

To Sir John Byng himself, however, historians have been more than kind. They have been especially so in answer to the question, why, in the few nervous days preceding the planned meeting of August 16th, 1819, was the supreme commander of Britain's Northern Forces not in Manchester at the head of his troops as he had been at the Blanketeers' gathering two years earlier? This event, which was likely to be more demanding than any other of the key military post he had held for more than two years, should surely have required his closest on-the-spot attention. Byng's explanation that his absence was simply and only due to the fact that Manchester's magistrates had informed him that his presence would not be necessary that day, has been universally accepted. But an examination of the details of the plainly recorded facts suggests the matter cannot be explained so simply.

It is certain that, besides being precise and efficient, Byng was a kind and liberal man. Unlike his predecessor, Lieutenant General Thomas Maitland, he did not cultivate a mental and physical ruthlessness towards the working class he had come to police. Byng frequently expressed his sympathy with the manufacturing poor of northern England and for the appalling conditions under which they lived and worked – conditions which he was observing for the first time: 'The peaceable demeanour of so many thousand unemployed men is not natural,' he once remarked with astonishment as he watched their cowed and resigned behaviour.[1]

On another occasion during the weavers' strike of 1818, rather than send his cavalry into a large and threatening crowd of workers, he stood in front of them in his civilian dress – 'my coloured cloaths', as he called his outfit – and told them that he 'commanded the troops, but preferred an attempt to convince them by words than to frighten them by force'. To his delight, he talked them into dispersing and considering going back to work. There, he promised, the Masters would be persuaded to give whatever pay rises they could afford. He proudly told the Home Secretary of his success as a public orator.[2]

He also held advanced views about how the workers' complaints should be dealt with. Even as late as the first few days of August, 1819, he was advocating that meetings should be set up, with 'Gentry, Clergy and Master manufacturers' appearing on the same platform, and that these gatherings should be run as debates where the working man's voice should be heard and attended to. He was, he said, in favour of 'communicating with these men' and of the use of 'conciliating language'. These were attitudes not to be incorporated into industrial relations until well past the beginning of the twentieth century.

But on other matters Byng's behaviour is less admirable. His concern for his personal wellbeing, his retrospective views of his own behaviour, and in particular, when need be, his economy with the truth, are cases in point.

During the Oliver scandal, Byng had categorically denied that he ever employed spies. But even allowing that Byng might not have been fully aware of Oliver's real role when, at Wakefield, in 1817, he offered him the hospitality of his carriage, there is nevertheless ample correspondence to show that he benefited from the secret information of others such as 'XY' and the several agents used by the inventive Mr Chippindale.[3]

It is also notable that whenever Byng involved himself in any controversial incident – or more to the point, when he failed to involve himself in a controversial incident, as he was shortly to do – he would make sure to leave an account in his careful hand which, equally carefully, exonerated him from blame.

His absorption by, and his protection of his self-interest are on occasion startling. His Waterloo wounds could be called into play whenever he needed to argue a case in his own interest.

And his self-interest during this important military command was only thinly veiled. On his travels through the northern district during the past few weeks he had seen how the hot summer was going to bring the best grain crop for years. He himself was farming a substantial acreage of wheat. But, like all farmers, he preferred pessimism. He told Hobhouse the price of corn was falling: therefore, so would his profits.[4]

Harvest was approaching and, if at all possible, he intended to be close by his crops where the Master's eye could be used to best effect. Indeed, he was to complain to Hobhouse of the Manchester magistrates' annoying habit of distracting him from his business affairs.

However, the other of his interests which, as with so many Englishmen, irrespective of class, was all-consuming, was his love of the turf. From his Campsmount base, Byng was now deeply involved as a race-horse owner, and was becoming ever more obsessed with his possessions and their performance.

That summer there was, as usual, a clutch of race meetings, all within easy reach of Sir John Byng's headquarters. First, in mid-August, came the fashionable York meeting. In early September, in Byng's neighbouring town, the Pontefract meeting was to take place. Then lastly, in late September were to be held the Doncaster races. And it was in Doncaster, on September 20th, that the great English classic, established 43 years earlier by Lieutenant Colonel Anthony St Leger, was to be run.

The St Leger, a sweepstake for 3-year-olds run over a

2-mile course, had set the pattern of the classic race through-out the world. It broke the mould of every other important race in that it was run off in one heat, rather than in several heats run over much longer distances. Since it was held suffi-ciently late in the season for 3-year-olds to mature, it had registered itself as the ultimate measure of stamina for the young horse. The saying was to develop, 'The fittest horse wins the Two Thousand Guineas, the luckiest horse wins the Derby, but the best horse wins the St Leger.'

For weeks before the event books would be open. As early as 1806 over a million guineas were reported to have been laid in bets on this one race before the end of July.[5]

Throughout the whole of the summer of 1819 local newspapers reported not only on entries for the race but gave the fluctuations of the odds being called in different towns. John Byng was caught up in this extended fever. For many weeks now he had had in training from his string, his favourite – his 3-year-old brown colt, Sir Arthur – preparing for the great event. During the Spring Meeting at York in May, Sir Arthur had performed twice and shown great promise.

The August York meeting was most suitably placed in the calendar for Byng to use for Sir Arthur to show his paces before the St Leger. But there were other not insubstantial temptations surrounding this August meeting. Traditionally, a most fashionable event, the race of 1819 held even more glamorous promise than that of any previous year.

The tone was set by Lord Fitzwilliam, the Lord Lieutenant of the West Riding. Already, on his arrival on July 28th, the

Minster and parish churches throughout York had rung their bells in peals of welcome.[6]

It was now known that Fitzwilliam planned to have royalty in his party. Prince Leopold, the Prince Regent's son-in-law, and his suite were to join the Lord Lieutenant. Also to be present were Lord Grantham, Lord Gavagh, Lord and Lady Muncaster, Lady Downes, Viscount Milton (Fitzwilliam's son), Lord Molyneux, Lady Lowther and Lady Sheffield. When Sir John Byng received a personal request from Fitzwilliam asking him to be a member of the most fashionable group at this gathering of high fashion, he was deeply flattered.[7] Byng was one of the few invited guests who did not rate a peerage.

The racing itself held great promise. In spite of being hard going, the course was reported to be in excellent condition. Lord Fitzwilliam had entries in four races, Sir John Byng in two. The first race, for 4-year-olds, the King's Plate, was for 100 guineas prize money given by the now terminally ill monarch. Run on Monday the 2nd, it would signal the start of six crowded days of racing. Byng's Sir Arthur was entered for the Sweepstake of August 12th.[8]

But the racing that week was merely the hub of a substantial whirl of alternative activities. The Assembly Room Ball, for example, was very fully subscribed, as were other balls, and the theatre too would be crowded. Accommodation in nearby spas – Harrogate and Scarborough in particular – was at a premium.[9] And although the races were due to end on the Saturday, celebrations were to continue until the following

Wednesday, August 18th, reaching a finale with the post-race ball that evening.

When, in the middle of July, it seemed that the reformers' great meeting on St Peter's Field was fixed for August 2nd there was, therefore, no question of a clash of General Byng's duty with his most passionate interest. On July 16th, with considerable enthusiasm, he told the Home Office that he hoped Manchester's magistrates would show firmness on the day in question, clamp down on seditious speeches and deal ruthlessly with any marchers who dared to hoist 'the insignia of treason', the 'Cap of Liberty'. If the magistrates behaved with this degree of firmness then, Byng said,

> I will be prepared to go there, and will have in that neigh-bourhood, that is within an easy day's march, 8 squadron of cavalry, 18 companies of infantry and the guns. I am sure I can add to the Yeomanry if requisite. I hope therefore the civil authorities will not be deterred from doing their duty.[10]

*His* duty, he is unambiguously saying here, he will be ready to perform in Manchester, in person.

Byng had already contacted the rich and hospitable Sir John Leicester and asked him to prepare to stand-to his Cheshire Yeomanry regiment. But Byng, who knew that Lady Leicester was just about to set off for the seaside with her near 60-year-old husband, added that, since he did 'not anticipate any commotion' in Manchester, and since the regiment had such an excellent lieutenant colonel, it was quite unnecessary for Leicester himself to be debarred 'from accompanying his lady'.[11]

But the fiery patron of the arts had no intention whatsoever of being separated from his expensively and brilliantly uniformed body of men on what others promised would be a day of considerable excitement. He responded to Byng with enormous enthusiasm, leaving no doubt that his entire regiment would be present, with Leicester himself at its head, astride his charger.[12]

Hearing this news from Byng, Lord Sidmouth could not restrain himself from personally offering his congratulations to the Prince Regent's aristocratic bosom companion. Attentively, he assured Leicester,

> I am satisfied that the appearance of so fine a Body of Cavalry, can not fail to give confidence to the well disposed at the same time that it will strike terror in the minds of the disaffected.[13]

As for Byng's personal attendance in Manchester, Lord Sidmouth had made clear from the start of Byng's command, that Byng had the autonomy to choose for himself. On July 23rd, 1819, Hobhouse told Byng,

> With respect to your going to Manchester on or before the 2nd of August, Lord Sidmouth does not at all wish that you should do so, unless you see it expedient yourself, or should receive a pressing invitation from the magistrates of Manchester.[14]

But Byng still had no hesitation in going to Manchester at that time. He was furious at having had so little information from Norris about the state of unrest in the town.[15] When the Home Secretary suggested on July 30th that Byng should visit Manchester personally, it was an unnecessary request. Byng was already on his way. Next evening he sat down in the Manchester Police Office to discuss the tense situation with all the magistrates at their Select Committee meeting under the chairmanship of young Mr Hulton.

At this gathering Byng discovered that the St Peter's Field reform meeting intended for August 2nd had been delayed until the 9th. Moreover, the Select Committee also confirmed that it would like to have the General in attendance there.

It was at this juncture, therefore, that the conflict between Byng's interest and his duty surfaced. If he was expected in Manchester on Monday the 9th, he would be forced to forgo the personal invitation of Lord Fitzwilliam to join the royal party at York Races. Even assuming that no problems presented themselves at the St Peter's Field meeting itself, it would be necessary to police the town and the thousands who would congregate there for one or two days after the event until the potentially violent crowds had fully dispersed. This responsibility, if fully undertaken by Byng, would make it impossible for him to return to York in time even to see Sir Arthur run in his key race on Thursday.

Though he occasionally manifested the characteristics of a snob, there is no evidence that Byng was a sybarite, nor that he found the social attractions of York an overwhelming reason for his presence in the city. Nevertheless, he undoubtedly suffered the compulsions of all race-goers and particularly all horse owners. His letter of decision to Hobhouse required careful composition.

He told the Under Secretary that, naturally, if it was really necessary he would be in command on St Peter's Field. But he also made clear that he could easily be in touch from nearby York, where he had a regiment of cavalry in reserve. Moreover, not only had Lord Grantham, his fellow guest at the races, told him that he would be glad to assemble his regiment at the first sign of trouble in Lancashire,[16] but Lord Fitzwilliam too had several yeomanry regiments at his disposal in the West Riding. Byng's revised intention was now to leave Manchester in the charge of Lieutenant Colonel L'Estrange in whom, so Byng claimed, he wished to demonstrate his absolute confidence. L'Estrange had been with his regiment in Byng's brigade in the Peninsula: 'We therefore understand each other,' Byng reassured Hobhouse, should the Under Secretary have had any hidden doubts about the plan.[17]

With this exceptionally warm summer still at its height, Byng hurried back to York. He was in Lord Fitzwilliam's party on Monday, the 9th, to see the first race, the King's Plate, won by Ranter. His Lordship had some success in the second race when his black colt Belianis came third.

But enjoyable as the day was, Byng was given only a few hours' respite from the mounting unrest in Manchester. On the evening after the first day's races, Byng retired to bed early with what he called a 'nervous headache', only to be woken from his sleep at half past eleven by a post messenger. What he read in the Reverend Mr Hay's letter put him in a furious temper. It told him that Hay, Norris and Ethelston had just heard the news that Henry Hunt had arrived in Stockport. At a panicky meeting the trio had decided to request Byng's presence in Manchester immediately.[18]

Sweating, in what he described as intolerably hot weather, Byng deliberately delayed his reply to Hay until the following morning since, he claimed, his headache was so bad he could not write. Then in a manner which anticipated no contradiction, he told Hay he was fully confident that L'Estrange could handle the situation in Manchester. He went on,

> And if no serious disturbance occurs, I am not aware of any particular service my presence can render.

But in order that neither Hay nor any other magistrate should jump to any unwarranted conclusions as to a more pressing personal reason for his protracted stay in York, Byng added,

> I must request you to believe that I stay not here from the unworthy motive of seeing the Races, from which circumstances have occurred to prevent my receiving any interest or pleasure.

This letter, which already smacks of special pleading, ends with a postscript:

> I will trouble you to give me as full information as you can, that I may better be able to decide on the necessary

arrangements and my attention is at this moment being called *to two other Quarters*.[19]

What these two other quarters were, that were so important that they could divert his attention from the St Peter's Field gathering, Byng did not specify here. However, next day, he again confided in Henry Hobhouse, giving what he plainly considered were two very good reasons for his absence from Manchester. He told Hobhouse he was more than a little vexed at the magistrates unnecessarily distracting him, 'considering the extensive commerce I have and business to attend to'.[20]

Mr Hay's response to Byng's firmly expressed position was, in the circumstances, predictable. The additional heat generated by Hunt's arrival in the north had subsided somewhat. Much chastened by being accused of panic, Hay now wrote in an apologetic fashion to Byng on Tuesday, August 10th, sending the letter by ordinary post, rather than by express, telling him of the new aspect in Manchester, and adding,

I am happy to say that that aspect has been materially altered from the reports which we have since rec'd & in such a degree as to do away with the propriety of applying to you in any further instance with the same view as in the first instance we felt it our duty to do.[21]

Byng had been formally let off the hook. The document telling him that his presence in Manchester was not necessary, was there for posterity to see, should the evidence be needed. He could now rest in the heat and enjoy what was left of the races with a clear conscience. On the day before the St Peter's Field meeting, he told Henry Hobhouse, 'I am not going to Manchester tomorrow as I have not been applied to.'[22]

As for the remainder of the military presence in Manchester Byng had made proper and ample preparations. There was more than a sufficiency of troops. Both local yeomanry regiments were on the alert. Thomas Trafford, the commanding officer of the Manchester Yeomanry, had his force prepared; the 63 sabres had been returned from their recent sharpening and had been distributed.

The Cheshire Yeomanry too had been made ready. When the cancellation of the August 2nd meeting had been notified, Sir John Leicester had been most bitterly disappointed that his regiment would not be used. There was even worse news. The following week arsonists, undoubtedly local manufacturing workers, set fire to his Tabley House mansion in which he kept part of his art collection, including works by Turner and Lawrence. Only the exertions of devoted servants prevented it from being gutted.[23]

By the time the 16th was fixed upon for the St Peter's Field gathering, Sir John, like Lord Sidmouth, had set off for the seaside with his wife, reluctantly leaving his regiment in the hands of its commanding officer, Lieutenant Colonel Townshend.

In addition to the yeomanry, all Byng's requested regular

reinforcement troops had arrived in the Manchester area, including two more squadrons of cavalry and a regiment of foot which had sailed from Ireland and then marched from Liverpool. As a dramatic further gesture, Byng had requested and received from the Duke of Wellington two horse-drawn six-pounder guns. Byng had made sure that they arrived in Manchester, and were pulled through the town, on market day. No Mancunian could then doubt that they would be present near St Peter's Field ready to be used should the occasion demand it.

Byng listed the full complement of troops under his command in Manchester and its district:[24]

| | | |
|---|---|---|
| Manchester | 6 troops of cavalry: | 15th Hussars |
| | 7 companies of infantry: | 31st & 88th Regt. |
| Bolton | 2 troops of cavalry: | 6th Dragoon Guards |
| Oldham | 2 troops of cavalry: | 6th Dragoon Guards |
| Ashton | 2 troops of cavalry: | 7th Dragoon Guards |
| Rochdale | 2 companies of infantry: | 88th Regt. |
| Stockport | 1 troop of yeomanry cavalry: | (*Cheshire Yeomanry*) |
| | 4 companies of infantry: | 31st & 88th Regt. |
| Macclesfield | 1 squadron of | |
| | yeomanry cavalry: | (*Cheshire Yeomanry*) |
| | 3 companies of infantry: | 31st Regt. |
| Altrincham | | |
| and Knutsford | 5 troops of yeomanry cavalry: | (*Cheshire Yeomanry*) |
| Warrington | 3 companies of infantry: | 31st Regt. |
| Preston | 1 troop of cavalry: | 15th Hussars |
| Blackburn | 1 troop of cavalry: | 15th Hussars |

There is one notable omission in Byng's list. He makes no mention whatever of the one other military group at his disposal – the Manchester Yeomanry Cavalry. The reason for this is plain: on the day of the meeting the troop of the Manchester Yeomanry was to be under the immediate command of the magistrates, should they need its assistance, rather than under that of the military commander.

The contrast between Byng's relaxed approach to the size and deployment of troops under his control and the rigid attitude of his predecessor, 'King' Thomas Maitland, is here starkly revealed. Immediately after Maitland had arrived in the northern counties to suppress the Luddite Revolt, he had firmly taken all yeomanry regiments out of the hands of the Lords Lieutenant of the counties and put them under his personal command. Byng had now left himself – or rather his deputy – in the potentially embarrassing, if not hazardous position of having a small private regiment operating independently alongside his own in Manchester on August 16th.

Discounting this local mounted force, therefore, the number of cavalry troops which Guy L'Estrange had in readiness in Manchester itself, was six. Several others such as that at Stockport were less than an hour's ride away. He had 7 companies of infantry in the town and 12 nearby. In sum, with or without the Manchester Yeomanry, L'Estrange had a most substantial military force at his disposal.

The force was impressive. But what of this deputy commander himself? Much was being asked of him. Guy L'Estrange, as a young officer in the Peninsula War, had risen with lightning swiftness through the ranks. He had been given command of a foot regiment in 1811 while still in his early thirties. But now, the war over and an end having come to rapid preferment, he was still, 8 years later, Lieutenant Colonel. The 31st Foot was now the third infantry regiment he had commanded at that rank. Moreover, on August 16th, the situation was such that the mobile troops most likely to be put to use in the first instance would be those of cavalry regiments, of which he had no direct experience of command.

There can be no doubt that Byng's gesture of showing absolute confidence in L'Estrange was flattering. Whether it was wise was another matter.

# 23

# White Moss

Sunday, the day before the meeting, as so many days before had been, was fine and hot. A tense atmosphere was reported about the town. But there was, as yet, nothing to cause the magistrates, again gathered at the New Bailey, to do other than silently worry.

In the districts surrounding Manchester, however, all was movement. The reformers' contingents from Stockport, Middleton, Oldham, Bury, Bolton, Saddleworth, Rochdale and elsewhere were making final preparations before marching on Manchester, several planning to leave long before daybreak in order to be on the Field in time to take up prominent positions near the hustings.

The news from Middleton, when it arrived, pierced whatever sanguinity the magistrates still possessed. Just before daybreak at White Moss, a piece of ground near the town, a reported 600–800 men had begun drilling in squads, each with a drill sergeant at its head. Though they had no guns, they were responding to commands such as, 'Make ready! Fire!' by clapping their hands to simulate gunshots. Unknown to the marchers, they were being watched by James Murray, a confectioner and special constable in plain clothes, and John Chadwick, a shoemaker and police informer. Suddenly, from within the ranks, the cry of 'Spy!' had gone up. Someone had recognised Murray, the Manchester gingerbread maker. Murray had begun to run. He was quickly chased and overpowered by several dozen men and badly beaten up. He was made to beg forgiveness on his knees before being allowed to crawl away bleeding.[1]

The report of this affair, as was inevitable under these circumstances, convinced the Manchester magistrates that violent behaviour on St Peter's Field next day was virtually certain. They immediately issued a notice forbidding women and children to attend the meeting.

But, panicked as they were, they were not the only inhabitants of Manchester and its district to believe that the following 24 hours would be not only violent, but a watershed in the country's history. John Lloyd, a keen observer of the economic barometer which was such an accurate indicator of the times, noted that, 'The tenants of a gentleman near this town refuse to pay their rent – till they know the result of Monday's meeting': they had sniffed the heady whiff of revolution in the air.[2]

As the hot and uncomfortable day drew to its close, James Norris, the most gentle and the most unsure of the magistrates still present in the Police Office, began his final report of the day. At eleven o'clock, 13 hours before the meeting was due to start, he scribbled a letter to the Home Office, still persisting in addressing it to the absent Lord Sidmouth: 'We are,' he said with understatement, 'in a state of painful uncertainty.'[3]

# 24

## The Road to Manchester

The first man to walk with defined purpose on to St Peter's Field on the morning of August 16th, 1819, was Thomas Worrell. He was Assistant Surveyor of Paving for the town of Manchester. His presence there had been ordered by Edward Clayton, the town's new boroughreeve. Clayton was determined that anything that could tempt by offering itself as a weapon should be removed from the Field. He had ordered Worrell to make an early inspection in person. At seven o'clock, therefore, the Assistant Surveyor walked the ground, saw 'about a quarter of a load' of stones,[1] and had them carted away.

The Field was an irregular quadrilateral. Its broadest dimension was about 170 yards in one direction and 150 yards in the other. Down its eastern edge ran Mount Street. It was from the house of a tradesman living in this street, a Mr Buxton, that the magistrates planned to watch the day's proceedings, just as they had watched from Mr Brown's cottage on the day of the Blanketeers' meeting. Mr Buxton's rear second-floor window gave a good panoramic view over the ground and of the position of the hustings from which Henry Hunt was to speak.

Windmill Street ran the length of the south-western edge of the Field. Houses along it faced directly on to the area where the meeting was to be held, and it was planned that the hustings would be built immediately in front of them. The street's buildings were on slightly raised terrain. From their windows, activity in the roads outside the Field could easily be seen, as it could from the small mound alongside the houses in the south-eastern corner of the ground.

Most of its northern edge was bordered by the 10 feet 3 inches high wall of the Quakers' burial yard, in the middle of which stood their Meeting House. The compounded earth inside the yard was so high that the wall inside measured only 3 feet 7 inches. Spectators could therefore stand protected by the wall and look down on the heads of those standing in St Peter's Field.

St Peter's Church itself lay outside the Field, its classical front approached by Peter Street. Even in 1819, it was clear that one day a paved continuation of the broad street would be built right across the middle of the Field, which was a site, to use the terminology of the next century, ripe for development. Logs suitable for building material already lay untidily in the area near the Quakers' yard. The drainage channels from Windmill Street had been dug across half the Field's width. Any horseman crossing its length, therefore, needed to take care that his mount did not stumble either in these channels, or over the scattered logs. Some horsemen at least were well aware of the existence of these obstacles. A troop of the Cheshire Yeomanry, having paraded in the streets of Manchester on the evening of the 15th, had spent the night close by them. They had slept comfortably enough through the warm dark hours, lying at their tethered horses' heads at the edge of the Field.[2] Early in the morning they had left to join the main body of the regiment.

These obstructions apart, as Thomas Worrell scanned it that day, St Peter's Field was an almost flat, deserted plain. It was not in itself an unusual feature of any English town or village. Many of Manchester's townsfolk still called it the 'green', as was the common name in smaller places. But there was little grass to be seen there after so many weeks of cloudless sky and parching sun. A worn brown surface was all that remained by this mid-August morning. The traditional meeting place for workers for many miles around, its only exceptional characteristic was its size. No other completely enclosed area in the north of England could match it. A simple calculation based on its known area shows that 150,000 people could gather there, without discomfort, effectively sealed in by the irregular walls of the surrounding houses. When densely packed, 200,000 people could have stood on its surface. When Thomas Worrell left shortly after seven o'clock that morning, it was deserted.

It was already by this time, however, at the focus of many minds, particularly of those outside Manchester's 26 old parish townships. Many of the workers intending to march on St Peter's Field from outlying districts such as those at Bury, Royton and Saddleworth had been gathering since before dawn. Even the Oldham contingent had begun to assemble on its green before six o'clock.[3] The numbers there were to grow to as many as 8,000.

At Middleton, important because the leader of its delegation was the well-known activist, Samuel Bamford, almost the whole town had been successfully worked upon to take part in the march on Manchester, or to contribute to it. By eight o'clock, on the Barrowfields ground, Bamford was organising 3,000 men, their wives, children, banners and bands.[4]

He arranged twelve of his best dressed and best looking men in two rows of six, gave them each a branch of laurel to represent peace and friendship, and regimented the growing numbers behind them into ranks of five as they arrived at the assembly point. He allotted a leader to every 100 men. Most had been persuaded to wear their best white shirt, stock and hat, so that the gathering that bright morning in the centre of Middleton could only have been impressive – even an arresting sight – to the government agents monitoring its growth.

To head the march, Bamford had arranged for a turn out of members of the local church band, dressed like the rest. They were carrying their woodwind and brass instruments – including bassoons and 'clarionets', according to James Dyson, one of the weavers present[5] – plus a large drum with which to beat the time of the march and a bugle to add an air of military excitement.

Accompanying every group were the banners specially sewn and painted for the occasion. The brightly coloured wording on each were more expressions of hope than passionate demands: 'Unity and Strength', 'Liberty and Fraternity', 'Parliaments Annual', and 'Suffrage Universal'.

Bamford, the organiser with probably the best grasp of logistics of those who controlled the various towns' assemblies that day, insisted that his still growing gathering should form a hollow square around him before it set off, so that he could address all those intending to complete the 6-mile march into Manchester. Standing on a chair placed in the middle of the square of now keenly attentive workers, Bamford, shouting to be heard above the noisy throng, reminded them of the singular purpose of their march that day: to achieve a reform of Parliament. There is also no doubt that he reminded them not to cause any disturbance, nor to insult anybody they should meet on the road.[6] He had accepted Henry Hunt's recommendation that they come 'armed with no other weapon but that of a self-approving conscience'. But there is also little doubt that, in his own retrospective account of the assembly, written many years later, he considerably exaggerated the number and the force of his exhortations to the workers to make certain that the outcome of that day in Manchester should be peaceable. If Bamford told those preparing for the trek of at least two hours to take with them no weapons or cudgels, some at least clung on to staves and sticks. Most, no doubt, intended to use them only as walking sticks. Others, however, saw other uses for them and other possible conclusions to this day of mass gathering. A few miles distant, John Ashworth had already watched the division of 3,000–5,000 Saddleworth marchers stride down the Manchester road twelve abreast, led by Bamford's little friend, 'Doctor' Healey. As early as eight o'clock that morning, Ashworth had heard one man mutter that that day 'they would make a Moscow of Manchester'. As if to remind those taking part of this possibility, a black flag bearing the white lettering 'Equal Representation or Death', was being held aloft directly behind Healey as he walked along, singing.

As Bamford stepped down from his chair on Barrowfields and a great cheer rose from the men ranged round him, the music of another band was suddenly and dramatically heard in the distance. By the time the Middleton contingent had spread itself into a long column it had been joined by the even greater army of steadily marching workers from Rochdale. Together, the two groups made up more than 10,000.

There were also large groups of workers, not all from the textile industries, moving just as great and sometimes greater distances towards Manchester. At Macclesfield, the colliery owner, Professor Smyth, discovered that his pits had emptied. All his miners had set off with the rest.

Women too were already on the road in considerable numbers. A not insubstantial by-product of the technological changes now sweeping Britain was that a woman, working at a power-driven machine, could equal the output of a man in precisely the same period of time on a handloom; the power of the male muscle was a diminishing asset. In a revolutionary fashion the status of the working woman, thus pushed by technological change, was changing. The beginnings of productive equality, notably in the cotton spinning industry, marked the beginnings of political equality.

The contribution of women to the Luddite Revolt seven

years earlier had been inconsequential. The manifestation of women in the crowds converging on Manchester on August 16th, 1819 was unmistakeable, as was to be its consequences.

From his prison cell, John Bagguley, had astutely realised the potential contribution of women both to his cause of reform and their own ends, and had sent a powerful letter of encouragement to the Stockport Female Union. It launched an all-women delegation of marchers towards St Peter's Field that day. So too did the Oldham and the Royton Unions. The Royton women carried a flag – it was of striking appearance – which can only have been the forerunner of female emancipatory slogans of a century later. It read, 'Let us die like men, and not be sold like slaves.'

Nancy Prestwick, aged 65 and the mother of a wool worker, led her own delegation of up to 300 women.[7] She was not the first, nor the last, to have verbal abuse thrown at her by the women who lined the streets and watched. They shouted to the marching women to go home to their families.

Meanwhile, Samuel Bamford, leading now substantially more than 10,000 people towards the town, had convinced himself that the intimidatory effect of such a large organised body of workers would be such that the civil and military authorities would already have blocked the road at the Collyhurst–Newton toll-gate, and would be preparing to read the Riot Act. He was astonished to find that apart from 'a horseman or two prancing before us' the roads to Manchester were unimpeded.

Striding out with renewed confidence, therefore, he headed his army towards Collyhurst, which would bring it to within

2 miles of Manchester's centre. Not far down this road, however, he was stopped by a messenger from Henry Hunt. The orator had a request to make of the weaver. It was that Bamford should about-face his great column, return it to the toll-gate and bring it forward by the New Town road. From there it could lead Hunt's own procession in to Manchester.

The duenna-like characteristics of both men here stood on display. Bamford, at first, refused to pander to the request of the middle-class southerner and took no heed whatever of the message. But the arrival of a second messenger soon changed the mood of the crowd following the weaver. Eventually Bamford was forced into the complex manoeuvre of redirecting his whole column in accordance with Hunt's wishes. As Bamford sarcastically put it, he had 'administered to the vanity of our "great leader" '.[8]

# 25

## Strangers on the Streets

During the next two hours, first from the hills to the west and the north, then from the flatter country nearer the town itself, but subsequently down every road which led to the place, broad columns of workers descended simultaneously on Manchester. The atmosphere of menace created by this highly successful synchronisation was not inconsiderable. Nor was it slow to percolate the consciousness of the government officials and informers watching the scene.

Joseph Travis, a grocer and special constable employed by the Oldham magistrates specifically to observe the marchers, watched the crowds pass through his town at nine o'clock. He then hastily rode on to join Mr Chippindale closer to Manchester. As Travis counted worker after worker, Chippindale wrote down the numbers and the names of the divisions – identifiable by the banners each waved – which had by now begun to unite on the roads from the north-west: Royton, Crompton, Chatterton, Saddleworth, Oldham. Travis saw that in addition to the ordered ranks of workers, there were many hundreds of stragglers also intent on reaching the Field.[1]

The Oldham and Saddleworth divisions converged at the New Cross district of Manchester and there some were persuaded by their leaders to throw away the sticks they carried. But not all were discarded. It was at about eleven o'clock that the manufacturer Francis Phillips rode out to the south-east down the Stockport road along with Joseph Birley, also a manufacturer. Birley's brother, Hugh, was at that moment assembling his troop of yeomanry cavalry in Manchester. Phillips and Joseph Birley had not ridden far before they were confronted by the Stockport contingent of workers marching towards them 'with all the regularity of a regiment'. Phillips guessed there were from 1,400–1,500 people facing them, though other estimates put the Stockport attendance as high as 5,000. He noted most particularly that, although they were not armed, 'a number of them had sticks. They carried them in a different manner, as they liked, not in order. One had a stick like a club, which he shook at me in a threatening manner.'[2] Phillips turned his horse's head and hurried back in the direction of Manchester.

He was merely one of the first of Manchester's middle class to be alarmed by the ordered mass he could see descending on the town. Roger Entwhistle, the clerk of Manchester race course, stood outside the Albion Hotel where the Stockport road passed the railings of Manchester's infirmary. His alarm mounted in proportion to the increasing density of the columns. As he strode past, one ragged worker put the fear of God into this member of the property-owning class by shouting at him, as Entwhistle recalled, 'that before night he would have as good a coat on his back as I had'.[3]

Thomas Sharp, an ironmonger and special constable, watched the marchers as they swept towards where he stood on the steps of the portico of the Mosley Street newsroom. Many of the youths he saw were carrying thick sticks. One of them, in Sharp's earshot, shouted to his companions that he would dearly like to go into the newsroom. The others shouted back that 'with patience he might do so before night – and many another building or many another house'.[4]

But as in all potentially perilous human activity, none is so sensitive to smouldering danger as the one charged with the responsibility for snuffing it. Of all members of the middle class, the magistrates were most fearful of the likely consequences from the masses now pouring into the town. At nine o'clock they had met – the Reverend Mr Hay, the Reverend Mr Ethelston, Mr Norris, Mr Evans and several others – at the Star Inn to breakfast and review the situation. It cannot have helped that the chairman of this group, the Select Committee, was William Hulton. This fair-haired young man in his coloured clothes not only had effeminate mannerisms, he readily admitted his over-sensitivity to the possibility of even having to witness any acts of violence, let alone participate in them.

By half past ten that morning the assembled magistrates had still reached no unanimous conclusion as to what actions they should take either before or after Henry Hunt's arrival at the meeting. Apprehensive and uncertain, at sometime during the next half hour, they left the Inn and began to make their way through the converging crowds to Mr Buxton's house on the edge of St Peter's Field.

It was during this journey that Mr Hay made the estimate, which he later confirmed to Lord Sidmouth, that there were already at least 20,000 strangers alone on the streets of Manchester.[5] Roger Entwhistle guessed the total number of townsfolk and visitors on the move at 100,000. So powerful was its emotional effect on those who experienced it, that the day was to be characterised by wildly differing estimates of the numbers involved.

The individual to whom a knowledge of crowd numbers was essential, but who received no reliable estimates, was the military commander, Lieutenant Colonel Guy L'Estrange. Left with nothing better than the knowledge that his notably absent superior officer, Sir John Byng, had expressed confidence in his abilities, and having been requested the previous evening by Mr Hay to put his troops on the alert, L'Estrange had been able to make few detailed plans for this unpredictable occasion. He ensured that his detachments of troops in surrounding towns were well-placed, but lacking instructions as to strategy from either Byng or the magistrates, he had to guess as to what would be the best tactical positions for his force within Manchester and in particular in the streets surrounding St Peter's Field. A considerable proportion of L'Estrange's own regiment, 250 men of the 31st Foot, was at his disposal. Also available were several companies of the 88th Regiment. However, since he considered it most likely that initial activity would be demanded of the more mobile cavalry, he had elected to place himself in Byrom Street, a quarter of a mile to the west of the Field, along with two squadrons of the 15th Hussars, one squadron of Cheshire Yeomanry and one troop of Manchester Yeomanry.[6]

He moved his position early in the day, well before the greatest mass of workers had begun to descend on the Field. He had alongside him two other officers of his own rank.

The first was an exceptional character with every bit of L'Estrange's experience in the field of battle. He was Lieutenant Colonel Leighton Dalrymple, the officer commanding the 15th Hussars. The most extraordinary feature of Dalrymple's leadership of a regiment of horse – and he was himself astride that day – was that he had only one leg, the other had been shot off at Waterloo. The circumstances under which his limb was severed give an idea of the drama and the violence already experienced by many of the regular soldiers present in Manchester.

Four years earlier, as Dalrymple had sat in his saddle on a Waterloo hill-top, a cannon ball had struck him on the leg, felling both him and his mount. The ball then continued on to where Sir Colquhoun Grant, the brigade commander, was talking to a group of cavalry officers. It bounced from the top of the hill and passed through the body of Grant's horse; the animal was one of five horses to be shot from under Grant that day.

These stories were already legend and admired as examples of military heroism and glamour not only by the regular cavalrymen, but by the amateurs of the Cheshire and Manchester Yeomanry Cavalry who had so willingly volunteered their services in the hopes, perhaps, of one day sharing in such unpredictable deeds on the battlefield.

They were also well-known to William Jolliffe, the 18-year-old cornet serving in the 15th Hussars under Dalrymple.[7] But rather than anticipating action leading to glory, Jolliffe found himself looking for the first time at crowds of workers of a drab manufacturing community, quite different in bearing, dress and manners from the population of the southern villages near the vicarage in which he had grown up.

He had paraded with his troop in field service order on this warm morning, at about half past eight, and then ridden into town, reaching Byrom Street at about ten o'clock. Within an hour, he and his fellow Hussars were joined by troopers of the Cheshire Yeomanry, riding in from Sale Moor. This regiment too was commanded by an officer of field rank, Lieutenant Colonel Townshend. Remarkably, Townshend had succeeded in mustering 420 men. Of the 20 who had reported sick, one was the regimental colonel: dispirited by the repeated postponements of the meeting, at which he had proposed to head his beautifully turned-out force, Sir John Leicester had now reached the seaside.

One other, however, had succeeded in attaching himself to the roll of Leicester's regiment. John Lloyd described the circumstances to Henry Hobhouse of how, 'Altho' a Capt. of Infantry for many years I thought it an honour to enlist into the Stockport troop of Cheshire Yeomanry – and to volunteer my services.'[8] And no mean horseman – so he had. Lloyd's knack of putting himself in situations which were to overflow into extraordinary violence was uncanny.

The Manchester Yeomanry Cavalry troop alongside the Cheshires was led by a well-known local manufacturer,

Captain Richard Withington. The remainder of the Manchester Yeomanry, however, was more than half a mile away, standing equidistant from St Peter's Field, but almost diametrically opposite Withington's troop in Portland Street, to the east of the ground.

There at the head of two troops was Major Thomas Trafford, the commanding officer. Alongside him was his second-in-command, a manufacturer like himself, Hugh Hornby Birley. They brought the total numbers of Manchester Yeomanry parading that day up to 101. It seems that it had already been agreed, that if their assistance was called for, Trafford would liaise with the magistrates while Birley would stay at the head of the two troops.

It might well have been expected that, since the mill owners of the town had much property to protect, there would have been more manufacturers represented among the volunteer horsemen than any other occupation. But this was not the case. Among the 101 were only 7 cotton manufacturers and 4 merchants. In addition there were 13 publicans, 8 others who, to a greater or lesser extent, were connected with the horse trade and therefore likely to be competent horsemen – 2 saddlers, a horse breaker, a farrier and so on – plus, among others, a cheese monger, a quack doctor, 2 tobacconists, 2 watchmakers, an insurance agent – and a dancing master.[9]

In other words, there was little to bind this group together by way of common craft, skill or knowledge. There was, however, the customary freemasonry which exists among those who own and enjoy horses and indeed, a prerequisite of attendance that day was that each man should be able to mount himself on his own mare or gelding.

There was one other attraction which forged yet another link between those who joined territorial regiments: as was the case with Lord Sidmouth himself, it was the love of dressing up in uniform.

The finery with which the Manchester Yeomanry had to compete that morning was not insubstantial. Most conspicuous was the flattering dark blue field dress with its scarlet facings, fur Busby hat and scarlet plume, worn by the 15th Hussars. But even this did not overshadow the men of the Cheshire Yeomanry, so brilliantly and expensively clad by the absent Sir John Leicester.

In one sense the Manchester Yeomanry had risen to the challenge. The uniform which had been designed for them was nothing if not distinctive. A sky-blue jacket with white facings, topped by a black shako hat with its truncated cone, made its troopers instantly recognisable. On the other hand, the combination also gave them a toy-soldier appearance which bordered on the comic. The early nineteenth century was still the time, however, when the soldier was meant to be distinguishable by, rather than camouflaged by his dress. In this respect the Manchester Yeomanry had succeeded.

Whereas the new regiment had recently adequately uniformed itself, its experience as a potential fighting unit left much to be desired. It had been in existence for only a few months. Most officers and troopers would have experienced some sword drill but, as with polo, unless indulged in regularly and seriously, the art of handling the sabre with confidence and accuracy is difficult to acquire. As an aid to the use of the broadsword, one enterprising Manchester cotton manufacturer had earlier produced a large machine-printed coloured handkerchief describing and illustrating the drill motions of the sword both on foot and mounted. It emphasised that, 'The recruit should be taught all the cuts quick and as one movement.' It gave such arcane instructions as, 'To the Rear Cut in Two Motions . . . carry the edge round till it arrives in a right line with the arm which will be at its full extent, turn the back of the hand down . . .'[10]

It is just possible that these exhortations were significant to the professional cavalrymen; it is more certain that they meant little to, and even confused the amateur. In truth, there was no abridged course which the freshly mounted yeoman could take to acquire the main skill of his part-time occupation.

There was among the Manchester Yeomanry, however, enthusiasm in abundance. It is not unlikely that as they waited in the yard of Pickford's, the hauliers, in Portland Street the two troops, dismounted, and with the girths of their horses slackened, exchanged flasks. Still today, this is not an uncommon habit among horsemen. That day as they began to sweat, in their thick uniforms, heated by the rising August sun, it is probable that such refreshment was freely offered and accepted. It was later suggested that many of the men of these troops took so much liquor during this period that they were drunk by the time the order came to remount. But there exists no worthwhile evidence to sustain this accusation.

These two groups of cavalry, one to the west which he

himself commanded, and one to the east commanded by Traf-ford, were the military units L'Estrange had deployed in order that they might be rapidly on the scene should civil distur-bance demand their presence at either of the main entrances to St Peter's Field. But he had also positioned his infantry so that they too could strike quickly. He had placed his own regiment, the 31st Foot, in Brazennose Street, 200 yards to the north of the ground, and had stationed a detachment of the 88th Foot under Lieutenant Colonel McGregor in Dickinson Street, less than 100 yards from the Quaker Meeting House. Near the south-east exit stood the two six-pound guns of the Royal Artillery under Major Dyneley. They had been placed in Lower Mosley Street, just out of sight of any spectators standing on the Field itself.

There was one further group that had begun to gather on which L'Estrange knew he could call for help if need be, but which, like the Manchester Yeomanry, was under the immediate command of the magistrates. This was the band of special constables. At about ten o'clock they had begun to col-lect in St James's Square, a short walk from the Field, under the eye of Manchester's Deputy Constable, Joseph Nadin. Like their leader, many of these recruits were burly indi-viduals, chosen not for their intelligence, but for their ability to resist physical violence, or to initiate it as the case demanded. Like him most were distinctively dressed and were recognis-able by the large metal badges of office they wore, and the thick staves they carried.

Nadin had already been instructed by the boroughreeve, Edward Clayton, that they were to be the first of the

Establishment's forces on the Field that day. Moreover, Nadin had ensured that there would be as large a number as any he had ever had reason to call upon on any single occasion in the past.

In total Lieutenant Colonel L'Estrange's support stood at more than 1,000 troops[11] and between 400–500 constables.[12]

# 26

## To the Hustings

Each notable building which the columns of workers encountered as they reached central Manchester, provoked a cheer or a jeer depending on the structure's symbolic stature. The Manchester Exchange building, its newsroom's tall windows sheltering many visibly worried merchants, inevitably attracted boos, hisses and the shaking of clenched fists. So too did the small house of James Murray, the special constable beaten up at White Moss 24 hours earlier, now lying in his bedroom in an unhappy state. Many hundreds made detours from their St Peter's Field road simply to shout their scorn through the windows of the deeply unpopular gingerbread maker.

By half past eleven Bamford's Middleton and Rochdale contingents had reached Smedley where Hunt was waiting at Johnson's cottage. His open carriage, to be pulled by two horses, was full. It included his sponsor, Joseph Johnson, James Moorhouse, the Stockport reformer, John Thacker Saxton, managing editor of the *Manchester Observer*, Richard

Carlile, the pamphleteer, John Knight, the old campaigner without whom no Manchester reform meeting could be complete and, sitting on the driver's box, Mrs Mary Fildes, President of the Manchester Female Reform Union. Standing in the road behind her, ready to walk in line, was her committee of women, each member dressed in white.

Bamford's long contingent passed by. It took – such was its length, some said – more than half an hour to do so. Hunt's barouche, his bands and flags, and the Smedley crowds fell in behind.

Bamford headed for Piccadilly in order to march down Mosley Street thence to St Peter's Church. Long before he reached this point, however, the weaver learned that he had lost Hunt's party in the backstreets of Manchester.

Whether this divergence of the main contingent of the day from the main attraction of the day was accidental or a deliberate manoeuvre by Bamford, is difficult to know. He nevertheless was unequivocal about the result, which gave him considerable satisfaction. 'I must own,' he wrote, 'I was not displeased at this separation. I was of opinion that we had tendered homage quite sufficient to the mere vanity of self-exhibition, too much of which I now thought was apparent.'[1]

But few of the workers lining the streets of Manchester cared about the petty relations between Bamford and Hunt. They yelled their approval of the white-hatted orator in his barouche, now taking the longer route of entry down Shudehill and Hanging Ditch, through the Market Place and along Deansgate. Hunt made a point of halting at Murray's house so that the crowd could scream still more disapproval of the spy.

Similarly, he engineered stops at the Exchange, at the Star Inn in Deansgate where the magistrates had met, and also outside the Police Office where there was a concerted clamour of hisses and groans[2] in the expectation that the din would be heard by Joseph Nadin.

By the time Bamford's great column had swept left-handed round St Peter's Church and into the Peter Street approach to the Field, tens of thousands were already gathered there. Bamford described it as walking into a 'chasm of human beings'. An enormous cheer greeted the contingent's arrival as banners and 'Caps of Liberty', now arranged along the full length of the square, were waved in welcome.

There was not a soldier to be seen from any point on the Field. With the sun at its highest and hottest, to many, the brightly lit scene had the appearance of gaiety and celebration. John Benjamin Smith, a young man who had been taken by his aunt to see the event from a house near to that of Mr Buxton in Mount Street, where the magistrates were at that moment gathering, wrote,

> It seemed to be a gala day with the country people who were mostly dressed in their best and brought with them their wives and when I saw boys and girls taking their father's hand in the procession, I observed to my Aunt: 'These are the guarantees of their peaceable intentions – we need have no fears.'[3]

Smith was by no means the only member of the middle class to notice how so many of those in the crowds had come with the intention of turning the occasion into an excuse for a summer holiday. The reporter of the London newspaper the *Courier*, at half past eleven, saw the entry of one of the delegations into St Peter's Field. Led by flags, and with bands playing, he noticed that all the marchers in the columns were covered in dust, so far had they travelled. He wrote,

> A number of women, boys, and even children, were in the procession, which had from this circumstance, more the appearance of a large village party going to a merry making than that of a body of people advancing to the overthrow of the government of their country.[4]

Outside the ground, the substantial military force, no matter how unobtrusive, was alert to both the mood and the progress of the marchers. William Jolliffe, the young cornet of the 15th Hussars, waiting with his troop, had by this time been dismounted in Byrom Street for nearly two hours. For almost the whole of this period, as the horses fidgeted, he had watched a solid mass of people moving past the end of Quay Street 100 yards away. In order to pass the time, he mounted his horse and followed those of Lieutenant Colonel L'Estrange and Townshend to the street's end to observe the columns and listen to the bands as they passed down Deansgate.[5]

Hunt's barouche, when it too appeared, caused a stir. Decked out with blue and white bunting, accompanied by white-shirted young men, with Mrs Fildes gaily dressed and with Hunt raising a fresh response from the crowd with each wave of his white hat, it was a memorable sight for the impressionable young Jolliffe. As the passing crowd caught sight of the senior officers, quietly sitting their horses, a great jeer went up. Fists were shaken – so too, the magistrates later said, were cudgels,[6] and Hunt once more thrust up his hat in a gesture of defiance.

Shortly before reaching this point Hunt had seen a figure whose clothes marked him as a gentleman, determinedly pushing his way through the crowds to get close to the slowly moving carriage. It was that of John Tyas, the reporter sent to cover the meeting for *The Times*. News of his assignment had been welcomed by Tyas since his uncle lived in Manchester. That day Tyas was feeling most unwell. Nevertheless, a conscientious professional, he had every intention of reporting Hunt's speech from close quarters in spite of his illness. As Hunt's barouche approached, he shouted up to the orator, asking him for permission to join him on the hustings.

Nothing could have pleased Hunt better than to have a reporter from a leading London paper to note his speeches. But there was no room for Tyas in Hunt's crowded barouche, built to hold only four passengers. He therefore shouted down to the newspaperman to stick close by the carriage until it reached the Field and the hustings, where he would be made welcome. It was to come close to being the last request Tyas would make in his life. He took hold of the handle of the barouche's door and clung to it for the rest of the journey.[7]

The hustings was made up of two waggons lashed together. They had been placed near the Windmill, a public house in the street of the same name. At about mid-day, Manchester's boroughreeve, Edward Clayton, appeared from the direction of Mount Street. He was followed by several hundred special constables. They quickly pushed through the crowds and formed themselves into two lines, a few yards apart, leading from Mr Buxton's house, across the Field, directly to the hustings.

In time those nearer the hustings realised that the pathway the constables had thus created was a channel of communication which would join any speakers on the platform to the magistrates in Buxton's house. It was the easy passage, many also realised, by which the magistrates could send their representatives to arrest Hunt, or any other reformer, should they so choose.

To spoil this manoeuvre, therefore, several reformers near the waggons gathered and pushed them several yards further away from the constables' two lines and deeper into the Field. The crowd immediately alongside now quickly pressed round the hustings to form a circle. Some said they linked arms as a human barrier. The result, however they arranged themselves, was never in dispute. The passage created by the constables was effectively broken at the last few yards which led to the hustings.

The reporter from the *Courier* watched Edward Clayton as he organised the constables' lines. He decided to stick close by the boroughreeve, and stay within his earshot, as Clayton made his way through the crowd back to the magistrates in Mount Street. The reporter took particular note that, at no time as he walked did Clayton make any remonstrance to the workers as he pushed past them. Not once did he suggest that the meeting was illegal.[8]

There was still nothing in the crowd's behaviour, however, to provoke such a reaction. Joseph Nadin's unpopular and distinctively cloaked figure proved the point when, unmistakeably, it appeared from the edge of the Field and began to walk up and down the aisle formed by the two rows. The worst abuse Nadin succeeded in attracting was a good-natured yell of 'That is Joseph', followed by a coarse remark on the size of his stomach. 'He has more meat in his belly than we have,' another worker shouted.[9]

When at last, shortly after St John's Church clock had struck one, the crowd saw Hunt's carriage at the edge of the Field, a tremendous cheer exploded from all over the ground. It had taken almost one and a half hours for the vehicle to reach that point. John Tyas was still clinging to the carriage door handle. He later wrote of that moment, that the enthusiasm excited among the crowd at the sight of Hunt 'was certainly beyond anything which we ever before witnessed'.[10] He was not alone in his astonishment at the intense volume of this reception. 'I never heard so loud a shout,' said the Reverend Edward Stanley, watching from the magistrates' house.[11] And certainly the triumphant entry of Hunt on to St Peter's Field imprinted itself on the memory of many of those who later recalled it.

The total numbers present had by now reached what some observers estimated to be more than 150,000. To continuous cheering and singing, Hunt made his way to the hustings. As he did so the massed bands joined together to play 'See the Conquering Hero Comes' and, so that the loyalist fervour of the meeting could not be mistaken, followed it with 'God Save the King'.

The magistrates, watching from Mount Street, counted 18 flags and five 'Caps of Liberty' being waved in a line from St Peter's Street to the ground to the hustings, guiding the orator along his route. The Royton women's red flags – 'Annual Parliaments and Universal Suffrage' now alongside 'Let us die like men and not be sold like slaves' – and the Saddleworth delegation's black banner – inscribed on one side 'Taxation without representation is tyrannical; equal representation or death', and on the other 'Union is strength – Unite and be free' – were most prominent. They were to Hunt plain words of encouragement. To the magistrates, however, these phrases along with, what to them, were the sinister 'Caps of Liberty', could only be interpreted as threats of violence to come. As Hunt reached his destination and began to mount the waggons, another great cheer rose up.

It had been the first of these shouts, both easily audible in Byrom Street, that had alerted Guy L'Estrange. Using it as a signal, he gave the order to the cavalry commanders to stand by. Each troop, including that of the Manchester Yeomanry, now mounted. A half mile away, at the other side of the ground in Portland Street, the remaining two troops of Manchester Yeomanry Cavalry were already astride. A short time earlier, William Buckley, a tradesman from Derby, had stood nearby at the entrance to Pickford's yard, and watched the troopers there dress by the right and left, and load their pistols.[12]

Buckley then made his way to the edge of the Field. Some from the crowd, so dense had it now become, and so sickening was the heat, were trying to leave. Samuel Bamford's wife, neatly dressed in her second best, standing in a good position near the hustings, had seen her husband jump on to one of the carts, then leap off again. Worried at being separated from him, surrounded by strangers and almost suffocating, she began to feel so sick that she was forced to beg the men around her to clear a path so that she could reach help at one of the house doors in Windmill Street. Bamford himself, though he claimed he marvelled at the size of the task Hunt faced with this crowd – now beyond anything in size he had seen before – also decided to leave. Since Hunt's speeches would contain nothing new for him, so he wrote later, he pushed his way off the Field to find some 'refreshment'.[13]

When Hunt arrived, a 17-year-old boy – no doubt attempting to emulate the spectacular success of the absent John Bagguley – was trying out his oratory on the crowd. So far, he had succeeded only in boring his audience and had had to stand down. But now that Hunt was in place, the atmosphere had become electric.

Alongside him on the hustings were several figures well-known to the crowd: John Knight, Joseph Johnson and John Thacker Saxton were local men and had frequently been seen on hustings on this and other grounds. Not so well-known were Richard Carlile, the publisher of Thomas Paine's works, and George Swift, a reformer and shoemaker, who had seated himself next to the young newspaper reporter, Edward Baines Jr. Baines's father, the editor of the *Leeds Mercury*, would have been present in person, had it not been for the fact that he had accepted a prior invitation from Robert Owen. Baines had set off for Scotland to inspect Owen's experiments in proto-socialism at his model factory at New Lanark.

The 19-year-old Baines was not nearly so radical as his distinguished father. Indeed, he was deeply disapproving of both Henry Hunt and his opinions.[14] But the same might have been said of several other reporters who had also crowded on to the hustings. John Tyas, now safely aboard, would be described by *The Times* in its issue of the very next day as being 'about as much a Jacobin, or friend of Jacobins, as is Lord Liverpool himself'.[15] In other words, irrespective of Hunt's kindness, Tyas did not approve of his politics. Nor is there any reason to suppose did John Smith of the *Liverpool Mercury*, who was also on the hustings.

Two notable figures from the middle class were absent. Major Cartwright after giving Union Societies advice to elect 'legislatorial attorneys', had been indicted in Birmingham, placed on bail, and had been forced to return to London. Sir Charles Wolseley, who had also promised to attend, had fared worse. He had been arrested days earlier and was now in gaol.

All those appearing on the hustings – even Johnson, the brushmaker, Swift, the shoemaker, and all the newspaper reporters – were of the middle or lower middle class. So successful had been John Lloyd's policy of arrest, that not a single working-class leader of standing had been left free to take his place on the platform which now faced the greatest gathering of industrial workers ever seen.

# 27

## Magisterial Decision

Hunt's first action on climbing aboard the waggons was to complain to those near him about this stage. First, it faced the prevailing hot breeze, so that his words, difficult enough to project to such a crowd, would be blown back into his face. Second, the deal planks joining the vehicles together seemed insecure. He had reason to be critical. On the only other occasion he had spoken from this spot, the hustings had collapsed beneath him.

After reassurances had been given, Joseph Johnson stepped forward to address the noisy crowd. He had only one purpose: to propose Hunt chairman of the meeting.

Johnson, in this brief foray as orator, phrased himself badly. There was a momentary silence as the great audience waited for some voice to shout a word as seconder of what seemed to be a proposed motion. It never came. Johnson, awkwardly, had now to declare Hunt chairman, unseconded. But after hip, hip, hip – hoorahs were raised for the glamorous figure at the focus of all eyes, the atmosphere of exuberance and the deafening noise returned to fill the ground.

It was a testimony to Hunt's skill that he was quickly able to bring the hubbub of the whole of that vast crowd to a halt. His first word, according to John Tyas, was, 'Gentlemen!' Hunt no doubt immediately recognised the inadequacy of that address. Around him were many hundreds of women – white frocked, their hair decked with laurel, and waving banners. There were even some, including Mrs Fildes, alongside him on the hustings.

Hunt therefore had quickly to find a more all-embracing epithet. It would not have satisfied later feminists but it served Hunt's purpose: 'Fellow countrymen,' was his amendment – and he now launched himself into the seamless oratory for which he had become famous.

His first purpose was to emphasise the need for at least partial quiet for himself and peaceful behaviour from those around. There is no doubt that to achieve this last end was his sincere wish. John Tyas recorded how Hunt declaimed that he hoped those in front of him that day, would 'now exercise the all-powerful right of the people; and if any person would not be quiet that they would put him down and keep him quiet.'[1]

Subsequently, others present put a more threatening interpretation on Hunt's expression, which could have meant that those not in favour of the meeting's purpose should be put down. But neither at this, nor at any other stage, would it have been to Hunt's advantage to have violence erupt against any law-keeper present that day.

In the first-floor room of the house of Mr Buxton, 100 yards away, the magistrates were straining their ears at the open windows to hear Hunt's words. There is no chance that they could have distinguished any of them. The Reverend Stanley in the room above could hear snatches of the well-modulated voice, but caught none of its meaning. For all his oratorical experience, Hunt's speech was heard clearly and recorded only by those on the hustings and by those few thousand in the area directly beneath where he stood. It was left to the magistrates to divine the sentiments being expressed from an interpretation of the sounds projected by the people in the boisterous crowd, and of the movements of their arms and banners.

William Hulton was watching them anxiously through a pair of opera glasses borrowed from one of his colleagues. Though he and his fellow magistrates had not thought to prearrange any concerted plan of action with the military, they at least agreed on one situation to which, should it arise, they would make a response. That was, if violence erupted, and Nadin and his special constables could no longer keep the peace, then they would call for military aid.

Throughout the previous hour, as the crowd had thickened and become more excitable, upwards of 60 manufacturers and merchants had climbed the stairs to the magistrates' room to demand that Hulton take some action – any action – to forestall an eruption.[2] The pressures on this young and inse-cure man to exercise his prepared option were thus immense even before Henry Hunt's cavalcade reached central Man-chester. It was the sheer force of the explosive cheer greeting the arrival of the carriage at the ground that precipitated his decision. By the time the distant figure of Hunt had begun to gesticulate above the heads of the masses, Hulton had already taken the steps necessary to initiate the arrest of the orator and several of his supporters.

The first man to whom he turned to request action was Jonathan Andrews, one of the two Chief Constables. Hulton handed to him an already prepared arrest warrant. On it, in addition to that of Hunt, were the names of three others whom Joseph Nadin had every reason to wish to see behind bars: Johnson, Knight and Moorhouse. Andrews replied, however, that without military assistance, he would be unable to execute the warrant. He later testified that it would have been madness to attempt it and that it would have put Nadin and his special constables' lives at risk had they attempted to break through the wall of bodies now ringing the hustings.[3]

It is possible that Hulton knew full well what answer Andrews would give before he asked his question. Whether or not this was so, he now sat, took a pen and scribbled two notes. The one, addressed to the commanding officer of the Manchester Yeomanry Cavalry, read,

> Sir, as chairman of the select committee of magistrates, I request you to proceed immediately to no.6, Mount Street, where the magistrates are assembled. They consider the Civil Power wholly inadequate to preserve the peace. I have the honour, & c. Wm. Hulton.[4]

It was undated and did not give the time it was written. Hulton then proceeded to write a similar note to Lieutenant Colonel L'Estrange.

With the benefit of hindsight, Hulton later explained why he took this course of action. He said,

> When I wrote these two letters, I considered at that moment that the lives and properties of all the persons in Manchester were in the greatest possible danger. I took this into consideration, that the meeting was part of a great scheme, carrying on throughout the country. We had undoubted information upon that point; of the existence of such a scheme, we had received undoubted information.[5]

That Hulton believed that there existed a conspiracy to throw the country into a state of revolution, is possible. But considering the agitated state in which he and those around him now found themselves, it is inconceivable that he gave proper thought as to whether this was the precise moment in which to act to save the nation from the consequence of that conspiracy. Flustered and under pressure, his purpose was to try to deal with a crowd which he had been convinced was about to turn to violence.

He now handed both notes to Jonathan Andrews. That Andrews was already prepared for some instruction of this kind is plain. Ready in waiting were two horsemen eager to act as messengers to each of the two units of cavalry. One of these was Joseph Birley, who that morning had ridden the Stockport road and had looked with awe at the approaching contingent of workers. The other was Thomas Withington who, like Birley, had a relative serving that day with the Manchester Yeomanry.

Immediately the pair galloped off, Withington to the west and to Colonel L'Estrange, Birley to the east and to Major Trafford. The situation was, therefore, that Hulton had dispatched the identical instruction to two independently commanded military groups. And the location of these groups was such that there was no way in which the action precipitated by this request could be performed other than independently.

Joseph Birley had the shorter distance to travel. It can have taken him only a few minutes to reach Portland Street from Mount Street. There, he handed over his message, not to the officer commanding, but to the second-in-command – his brother. Dutifully, Captain Hugh Birley handed the sheet of paper to Major Trafford and read what was written there over his CO's shoulder.[6]

Immediately Trafford had read the three sentences on the sheet of paper, the order was given to draw swords. Then, in the words of one observer, the two troops of Manchester Yeomanry Cavalry immediately 'galloped furiously'[7] towards St Peter's Field. Their progress down two straight streets – Nicholas Street, then left into Cooper Street – was as direct as any other they could have chosen. It was not without incident. A young woman, by chance like Hunt's companion also named Mrs Fildes, carrying her 2-year-old son William, stepped into the road as, so she thought, the last horse passed. She was struck hard by a galloping trooper, rapidly bringing up the rear. Her child was killed instantly. It was the first fatality of Peterloo.[8]

In as short a time as it had taken Birley to deliver his message, the amateur soldiers of the Manchester Yeomanry

Cavalry retraced his route, sweeping past Cooper's cottage and into the east Peter Street entrance to St Peter's Field, reining to a halt in considerable disorder near the magistrates' house. Here they now tried to reorganise themselves into better military fashion.

Joseph Nadin meanwhile made his way to the distant end of the two lines of constables, telling them to be prepared, when the time came, to pull back to let the Yeomanry through. As he did so, others of the magistrates alongside Hulton also moved into action. They had decided that the time had come to invoke the Riot Act. It was natural, considering the immense hubbub outside Buxton's house, that the man with the loudest voice should read it – or shout it to the crowd. The choice fell on the Reverend Mr Ethelston, the preacher known to be proud of his voice.

Ethelston quickly descended from the first floor of the house to look for his servant whom he had left at the door holding his horse's head. It was his intention to read the Act sitting in his saddle. Nowhere, however, could be seen either horse or servant. He later claimed to have tried several times to get the attention of the crowd from where he stood on his feet. Having failed in this, he now climbed back to the first floor, leaned far out of the lower half of the sash window and began to bellow to the crowd below.

Behind Ethelston stood Mr Hay who also later described how,

He leant so far out, that I stood behind him, ready to catch his skirts for fear he might fall over. Mr. Ethelston is a gentleman who I have occasionally heard sing, and he has a remarkably powerful voice. When he drew back his head into the room, after having read the proclamation, I observed to him, 'Mr. Ethelston, I never heard your voice so powerful.'[9]

Thus did the senior magistrate present that day reassure posterity that the proclamation of the Riot Act *had* been carried out before violent military action was indulged in. If the proclamation was not in doubt, however, its audibility most certainly was. The Reverend Edward Stanley, standing as a visitor at the second-floor window above that at which Ethelston performed, heard not a syllable of the baritone voice.

Nadin had by now made his way back to the magistrates' house where the boroughreeve, Clayton, along with his two constables, Andrews and Moore, were waiting. It was Andrews who approached Captain Hugh Birley, now to the fore of the Manchester Yeomanry troops, telling him that the constables had in their possession an arrest warrant and needed his assistance. 'I desired him to surround the hustings in order that we might take the orators off the stage,' Andrews later said.[10]

Clayton mounted his horse and rode alongside the Cavalry, halting on their left. Moore, however, fearing that he would not be able to keep up with the horses, shouted to Clayton to dismount in order to avoid their becoming separated. The boroughreeve did as he was asked. Andrews, meanwhile, seeing that Birley was ready to give the signal for his troops to advance, prepared to set off on foot ahead of them into the crowd.

Henry Hunt, by this time, was in the full flood of his speech. But, yet again he had been subjected to another annoyance to his vanity. John Knight suddenly rose and whispered something in his ear. Furious, Hunt turned on him and said, 'Sir, I will not be interrupted: when you speak yourself, you will not like to experience such interruption.'[11]

But he had not spoken more than two or three further sentences before he saw over the heads of the crowd the disorganised arrival of the Manchester Yeomanry in front of Mount Street.

At this moment Hugh Birley was giving his order to his force. His troopers responded by raising their swords. There was immediate panic among the crowd nearest the troops' horses. People began to scatter.

Uncertain as to what was happening in the distance, but seeing the blue and white uniforms of the Yeomanry, Hunt felt it necessary to make some response. With the help of Johnson he quickly called for, and got, a great cheer from the crowd. Whether or not the Yeomanry interpreted this as a gesture of defiance, they themselves, sabres in the air, raised a shout in return and put their spurs to their horses. The time was about twenty minutes before two o'clock.

# 28

## The Charge of the Yeomanry

Thomas Withington, leaving the magistrates' house and cantering fast with William Hulton's message to Lieutenant Colonel L'Estrange at the identical moment that Joseph Birley left carrying the same note to Major Trafford, cannot have taken less than double Birley's journey time. In the first place the distance round the streets south of St Peter's Field to Byrom Street was at least double that travelled by Birley, and second, he needed to avoid several streets which were blocked by crowds of workers.

As he placed his message in Guy L'Estrange's hand, he was able to tell the military commander which streets were impassable, and which provided a clear passage back to Mount Street. L'Estrange quickly ordered Lieutenant Colonel Dalrymple and the 15th Hussars to form immediately behind him with the Manchester and the Cheshire Yeomanry – John Lloyd among them – to bring up the rear. Then, telling Withington to lead the way, he set off at a canter. The route Withington chose first took the squadrons towards, and then down Deansgate in a direction away from the west entrance to St Peter's Field before wheeling back along Fleet Street, then Lower Mosley Street and finally towards the east Peter Street entrance to the ground.

But, during this lengthy but ordered progress of the professional cavalry through the back streets, as can only have been obvious from the shouts and screams from within the Field itself, violent military activity had already begun. And L'Estrange was not yet halfway to the scene of the action which he had expected to command.

Inside the ground, much had happened. The Manchester Yeomanry Cavalry's horses, little enough accustomed to military manoeuvres, and wholly unfamiliar with crowd control, had moved forward at their riders' urging. They at first managed to form rough lines facing down lines of constables into the Field. To their front was Hugh Birley and alongside him, two trumpeters on piebald horses.

Edward Clayton and Jonathan Andrews, intent on leading the combined civil and military party which was to arrest Hunt, strode ahead of the three in the direction of the constables. But they quickly found themselves overtaken by the horses. John Moore also tried to keep up the pace, but he quickly found himself stumbling, and finally falling under the pressure from what was clearly increasingly disorganised progress by the Yeomanry behind him.

Joseph Nadin, in whose hands was the arrest warrant, was taken by surprise by the sudden departure of the horses. The result was that he found he had lost sight of his employers, the boroughreeve and his two Chief Constables. He therefore followed in the wake of the Yeomen, now thrusting forward.

From his bird's eye view, the Reverend Stanley saw the mounted soldiers, still led by Hugh Birley and the trumpeters, trying at first to keep some semblance of order, five or six abreast. But, as they moved down to the lines of constables into the thicker part of the crowd, their speed began to increase. Within a few paces it had progressed to the canter which precedes a charge. Stanley noticed how all semblance of order in the ranks quickly disappeared. Then, looking down at the ground over which the prancing horses had passed, he saw the body of a woman. It was the second casualty of the day; but as was obvious from the panic now beginning to manifest itself, it would not be the last. The impact of half-held, half-ton animals on human bodies had begun.

The screams of those hit mingled with the taunts hurled by those at a safer distance: 'Feather bed soldiers!' and 'Church and guts men!'[1] And rather than checking, the pace was seen to increase as, maddened by the insults and frightened at their own inability to control their mounts, the sky-blue uniformed men plunged further into the crowd.

The dust from the threshing hooves had quickly risen several feet into the air. Above it Mr Stanley could see the sabres glistening as the horses plunged towards the hustings.

As the first horsemen reached the wall of workers massed round the platform, some of Nadin's force of special constables raised their truncheons to identify themselves to the fast approaching military. Whether or not the Yeomen mistook the truncheons for workers' cudgels, or whether they were too blinded by dust and fear to differentiate friend from foe, the constables suffered grievously for their gesture. Several were struck down, both by horses and by the flats of swords, as were the men and women reformers alongside them.

The aim of the Yeomen – the arrest of the reformers' leaders on the hustings – was still far from being achieved. Their first rush into the thickest part of the crowd had taken them within 30 yards of the carts. Like the rest of those standing alongside him, Hunt was uncertain how to respond. Edward Baines, the young journalist, saw the orator stretch out an arm and cry, 'Be firm!'[2] But the shout could not possibly have influenced the rows of swaying bodies in front of him.

The uncertainty on the platform quickly turned to fear. Baines did not wait to see the effect of Hunt's shouts. He turned and jumped from the back of the carts. By the time he had pushed his way a few yards into the crowd, he could see one of the Yeomanry trumpeters wheeling his piebald horse up against the platform where, a few seconds earlier, Baines himself had been standing. Again there was panic. In one movement the crowd surged away, carrying Baines with it for 30 yards – and to safety.

The hustings was completely surrounded. Hunt, most of his committee of reformers, the women and some of the newspaper reporters remained standing in their exposed positions. Hugh Birley, waving his sword, pushed his horse up to the carts.

'Sir,' he shouted to the orator, 'I have a warrant against you, and arrest you as my prisoner.'

Hunt at first tried to use this opportunity to quieten the

shouts and screams of the crowd. But, although there was a visible lull in activity on this island at its centre, the crowd was beyond control. Hunt now turned to Birley and said, 'I willingly surrender myself to any civil officer who will show me his warrant.'[3]

That civil officer, against the odds, was on hand to do his duty. The hated Joseph Nadin behaved with the same courage as he had shown on the day of the Blanketeers' March. He pushed his way, behind the cavalry, through the thickest part of the hostile crowd, with his piece of paper. Not all the four named on it were to be seen. James Moorhouse had not reached the hustings that day and John Knight, seeing the approach of the cavalry, had quickly made his escape.

But the remaining pair was within reach. Hunt and Johnson jumped to the ground and into the arms of the constables and their deputy. Nadin grabbed at Johnson's legs. As he did so, a well-aimed brick struck his arm.

This was the moment, according to John Tyas of *The Times* – still standing on the platform – when mayhem broke out around the hustings. As Hunt left the cart, Tyas heard from the Yeomanry, 'Have at their flags!' And with swords above them flashing, the Cavalry horses plunged towards the banners on the hustings itself and towards those in the thick of the crowd.

George Swift, the shoemaker, standing in the exposed position Hunt had just left, watched with alarm, as the Yeomanry began chopping with their swords in his direction. He was forced to jump back to avoid serious injury. Leaping to the ground in an attempt to escape he found there an almost unconscious bleeding young woman. He took hold of her and dragged her through the mêlée towards Windmill Street.

The lunging of the Yeomanry had set people not only running in every direction, it had provoked a great shower of bricks and stones. The result was, Tyas observed, that 'the Manchester Yeomanry Cavalry lost all command of temper.' Alongside him was the well-known reformer John Thacker Saxton of the *Manchester Observer*. Seeing him, two troopers of the Manchester Yeomanry rode up alongside the hustings. According to Tyas, one shouted to the other,

'There is that villain, Saxton; do you run him through the body.' 'No,' replied the other 'I had rather not – I leave it to you.' The man immediately made a lunge at Saxton, and it was only by slipping aside that the blow missed his life. As it was, it cut his coat and waistcoat, but fortunately did him no other injury. A man within five yards of us in another direction had his nose completely taken off by a blow of a sabre; whilst another was laid prostrate, but whether he was dead or had merely thrown himself down to obtain protection we cannot say.[4]

From the magistrates' position the details of the disastrous encounter were indistinguishable through the fog of dust. The blue uniforms had all but disappeared into a sea of outraged bodies. The only events of which the magistrates could be certain were, that sticks were being raised, bricks were being thrown, horses had stumbled and troopers had fallen.

Such was the fracas on the ground as Thomas Withington,

leading Guy L'Estrange and his force, wheeled into Windmill Street and on to the south-east corner of St Peter's Field.

Immediately, L'Estrange, seeing the confusion in front of him, but with no understanding whatever of the reason for it, spurred his horse towards the houses in Mount Street and collected it again beneath the window of the magistrates' room at which Mr Hulton stood. From his saddle, shouting up to the young man, he asked what it was the magistrates wanted him to do.

'Good God, Sir!' Hulton shouted back. 'Do not you see how they are attacking the yeomanry? Disperse the crowd!'[5]

It is most doubtful whether, at that instant, L'Estrange had any idea what function the Manchester Yeomanry was attempting to perform in the middle of the panicking and screaming crowd. But the instruction to disperse the mob was clear. His former commander-in-chief had once encapsulated the problem here facing L'Estrange. Wellington had observed that anyone could get 10,000 men into a space, but it needed a real general to get them out again.[6]

But even now St Peter's Field was being invested with newcomers. Dalrymple's four troops of 15th Hussars, moving in threes, had come on to the ground at a canter and passed in front of the magistrates' house. Within seconds he had received their orders from L'Estrange.

There was scarcely a pause in the movement of the Hussars before the commands 'Front!' and 'Forward!' were shouted. In response, the trumpeter sounded the charge. The threes wheeled into a line which now stretched across the whole eastern side of the ground. It was at this point that young

Cornet Jolliffe, raising his sword and putting his spurs to his horse like the rest of his troop, realised that the great area in front of him 'in all parts was so filled with people that their hats seemed to touch'.[7]

Simultaneously, the Cheshire Yeomanry who, unlike their Manchester counterparts, had arrived on the ground in good order, moved rapidly along its southern edge parallel to Windmill Street so that they were positioned behind the hustings. Then, without pausing, they too wheeled in the direction of the carts.

Thus, within the space of five minutes, three substantial bodies of cavalry had charged into the crowd from different directions. William Jolliffe, at the forefront of this rapid advance by the Hussars was, like the rest of his troop, driving back the crowd with the flat of his sword. But he was already well aware that blood was being spilt even if unintentionally, by the cutting edge of these same weapons. In later years, unlike others, he never tried to shift any share of the blame from the shoulders of his own regiment. He wrote,

> believing though I do that nine out of ten of the sabre-wounds were caused by the Hussars, I must still consider that it redounds to the human forebearance of the men of the 15th that more wounds were not received, when the vast numbers are taken into consideration with whom they were brought into hostile collision.[8]

If the Manchester Yeomanry were sufficiently skilful horsemen to be able to use the flats of their swords, there are few testimonies, other than their own, that they did so. Of all the soldiers on the Field, they were the most easily identifiable by their exotic uniforms. Equally, many of their faces were well-known to those they were now attacking. One worker, John Leigh, trying to escape in the direction of Windmill Street, was slashed at and wounded by a horseman he recognised: it was the Yeomanry commander, Hugh Birley. Three more Yeomen struck at him before he threw himself down in an attempt to escape their blades.[9]

Panicking, and perhaps fearful for their own safety, several members of the Yeomanry – the trumpeter, Meagher in particular – appear to have gone berserk. William Buckley, the Manchester tradesman, watched them as they wielded their weapons. Describing the scene from which he now began to flee, he said, 'the carnage seemed to be indiscriminate.'[10]

Several people – both men and women – were sabred in the first few minutes of sword waving. Meagher's weapon, its owner so easily identified both by his trumpet and his piebald horse, appears to have been responsible for some of the worst injuries inflicted. William Cheetham, a weaver from Bolton, was one of those whose body was badly cut by him. So was a 71-year-old woman, Alice Kearsley, who was struck at twice. With one of the blows Meagher succeeded in almost severing her ear.

Henry Hunt too in that first phase of violence was struck on the head by the flat of a sword.

But the cause of serious injuries was not restricted to the sabre. The collision of horses and humans was by now taking a dreadful toll. Joseph Wrigley and John Lees, who had arrived from Oldham, found themselves swept away from their position close to the hustings by the pressure of the crowd. Wrigley was trapped behind Lees, an ex-soldier who had survived Waterloo. Helpless, he watched as a cavalryman pushed his horse forward and aimed a blow at Lees's head. Lees raised his walking stick in his right hand – whether as protection or to strike the trooper. As soon as he did so, a second soldier struck out, cutting into his right elbow.

Lees collapsed backwards on to Wrigley, pulling them both down under the animal's feet. A shoe was torn from Lees's foot by a horse's hoof.

Wrigley, still trying to rise from under the bodies struggling on the ground, was conscious of swords being slashed above him. He then heard the voice of an officer of the 15th Hussars shouting, 'For shame, won't you give the people time to get away. Don't you see them down?'[11] This gentlemanly cry had been enough to allow Wrigley to get back on his feet. But the sword waving of the soldiers and the truncheon wielding of the special constables had not stopped. He could see more horsemen making cuts at the cart where Mary Fildes and other women still stood. Wrigley turned to run, but not before a Yeoman thrust his sword at him. The blade pierced his hat. Battered by human and animal bodies, he was still able to run. He made a dash for safety behind the horse of the officer of the 15th, and never looked back until he was off the Field.

# 29

## This is Waterloo for You

The 15th Hussars had charged diagonally across St Peter's Field. Several cavalrymen failed to complete the journey. So thick was the crowd through which they rode that the logs of wood left scattered on the ground were completely hidden. At least one officer and several troopers were dislodged and injured at these obstructions. The commanding officer, Guy L'Estrange, survived by good horsemanship, and by luck. An accurately aimed brick struck his cap hard, sending it flying to the ground. He himself managed to stay in the saddle and had led his squadrons half-way across the ground before he tried to check their charge.

John Hulme of the Manchester Yeomanry was less fortunate. He pursued and twice sabred one fleeing worker, William Butterworth. The brick, flung by a woman, that then hit Hulme knocked him to the ground where he was trampled by a horse. So terrible was the injury inflicted that he was subsequently only recognisable by the name in his glove.

Lethal weapons other than bricks were in use. One trooper

of the 15th, William Rooke, suddenly heard a warning shout from one of the Yeomanry alongside him telling him he was just about to lose his horse's entrails. Rooke looked down and saw a reformer swinging a two-handed sickle in his direction. He pulled at his mare in order to avoid the worst of the blow. Nevertheless, the metal slashed the animal from saddle flap to flank.

Lieutenant Charles O'Donnell's horse took him beyond the Quakers' yard to the western edge of Peter Street. There he saw a worker brandishing an iron railing in his direction. He successfully warded off the sharp point until his assailant let the spear fall before running off into the crowd.

Another subaltern of the 15th, Frederic Buckley, whose horse had been brought down, succeeded in remounting. He now found himself being lunged at with a bent iron rail. It was, he later said, a formidable weapon. The attacker in this case was less successful in making an escape. According to Buckley, 'He raised this, as I thought to attack me. I think I made a cut at him, but he happening to fall on a raised ground, my sword only struck him slightly. He fell so quick, I barely did strike him.'[1] Buckley, when later he recalled the incident, never contemplated the possibility that he had just killed a man.

By then, both he and O'Donnell could hear shots being fired in their direction. The farrier of the Manchester Yeomanry was the first to see the gun. Pointing to the roof of an unfinished house, he shouted to his troop commander, Captain Smyth, 'That fellow is boking his gun at either you or me. I have seen him fire at us more than once.'[2]

The infantiers of the 88th Regiment, who had assembled in Dickinson Street, were able to deal quickly with the danger. They needed to move only 100 yards in order to position themselves on the other side of the Quakers' yard. Once there, they quickly cleared the marksman from where he was hiding behind the chimney. The brief episode undoubtedly accounted for the many reports of shots having been fired that day.

In the charge, Cornet William Jolliffe had completely overshot the Quakers' yard. Reaching the end of the Field, he saw to his astonishment that the workers fleeing before the first wave of cavalry were lying 'literally piled up to a considerable elevation above the level of the ground'.[3]

He now turned his horse back towards the yard. As he reached it, he saw one of the regimental farriers riding at a small door in the high wall. The farrier's horse struck the door with such force that it flew open, allowing the cavalryman to ride in and chase the stone throwing workers from its shelter. Sabre slashes on the bark of trees growing in the graveyard, and blood on the ground beneath, later testified to the violence of this encounter.

In the centre of the Field, the exercise which had caused the terrible activity all around – the arrest of the chief speakers on the hustings – had been achieved. Joseph Nadin now had hold of Henry Hunt and Jonathan Andrews was dealing with Joseph Johnson. But the route from the carts to the magistrates' house was perilous. The safe passageway which had been formed by the two lines of constables had been completely destroyed by the first wave of Yeomanry. Nadin was forced to lead the way back to Mount Street through struggling bodies and snorting animals.

Two of the Yeomanry, recognising Hunt, aimed blows at him, which he evaded by making sure that Nadin's body was between his and the troopers' horses. Another hazard was the pistol of Richard Withington. The Yeomanry captain kept it cocked and aimed at Hunt as he dogged the pair. Several times Nadin was forced to strike out with his staff to protect the orator from the blows of his own constables. By the time they reached Buxton's house, Hunt had been hit two or three times.

Even here, he was not safe. Standing in front of him was the figure of a well-known Manchester citizen: that of General Clay. This was the officer who, during the Luddite uprisings had dealt brutally with the town's rioters. Now, seven years later, in spite of being retired on half-pay, he intended to treat Hunt in the same manner. The young businessman John Benjamin Smith watched how, when Hunt reached the confined steps to the house, Clay raised a large stick in both hands and brought it down, packing Hunt's hat over his face. According to Hunt, Nadin himself now pushed through to shout 'Shame!' at Clay and prevent more serious bludgeoning of Hunt by the officer. Nadin replaced the white hat on its owner's head. 'By this means,' Hunt said later, 'Nadin saved my life.'[4] Smith also watched how Clay, ashamed of himself, merged quietly back into the crowd.

The arrest of the meeting's chief speakers concluded, the Yeomanry had one other immediate aim in view: the destruction of the remaining symbols of radical reform. The brightly coloured banners, their painted words and embroidered devices which stretched the length of the ground, the coloured flags on the hustings waving above the rising dust, and in particular the 'Caps of Liberty' here became objects of wroth. The hustings' flags and the platform of planks were quickly chopped down by the swinging swords. The emblems and the 'Caps of Liberty', however, were potential trophies to be won and preserved as battle honours. Both the Cheshire Yeomanry and the unmounted special constables joined the Manchester Yeomanry in the chase for these prizes.

The Reverend Stanley watched one mounted man, apparently the servant of one of the officers, break loose from the cavalry and, unarmed, struggle with a group of workers for possession of their banner. But there was still not the first sign that the wanton use of weapons was about to cease. Thomas Redford, as he tried to make off with the Middleton contingent's green banner, was cut at by a sabre. It slashed a six-inch wound between his shoulder blades.

Having missed the first violent attack on the hustings, the Cheshire Yeomanry could join in this latest activity with vigour. One of the red banners John Lloyd's troop succeeded in wresting from its bearers and holding aloft with pride bore the words, 'Let us die like men and not be sold like slaves': it was the standard of the Royton Women's Union.

Several special constables squabbled over potential booty. One of these, Robert Mutrie, managed to tear a red 'Cap of Liberty' from its owner's standard. To his surprise, it was not the soft cloth he had believed it to be, but a sharp tin-lined object which he could not stuff into his pocket.

During these skirmishes the main body of the terrified crowd running from the Field had had some difficulty escaping into the side streets. At first, the main Peter Street escape route to the east was blocked by the 88th Infantry Regiment standing and using their fixed bayonets. That to the west had quickly become choked with cavalry which had travelled from one end of the ground to the other. And for a time, Captain Richard Withington of the Manchester Yeomanry had stood his horse at the Rogers Row exit, pointing his pistol at fleeing workers. He promised to blow out the brains of one man who tried to pass.

Now, however, the passage ways were open, sucking the mass of people away from the centre of violence. At the periphery, owners of houses with doorways opening on to the Field were taking in some of those unwilling or unable to run for the street exits. Ann Jones saw the iron railing in front of her house in Windmill Street pressed to the ground by the crowd retreating in front of the cavalry.

Her husband, John, meantime watched Richard Withington and another member of the Manchester Yeomanry 'cutting at every one they could reach'. They drew back only when an officer of the 15th Hussars – in all probability the same gentlemanly cavalryman who had earlier protected Joseph Wrigley near the hustings – rode up shaking his sword and crying out, 'For shame! For shame! Gentlemen; forbear, forbear! The people cannot get away!'[5]

Ann Jones was now 'fully employed in pulling people into my house, in order to save their lives. I saw a great quantity of blood on the field near where the hustings had stood.' She later claimed that two people were killed at her doorstep. As she helped with the wounded, one of the special constables strode into the house and shouted in triumph, 'This is Waterloo for you – this is Waterloo!'[6]

As her husband John gave a bowl of water to an injured reformer, another constable struck the bowl from his hand as the bleeding man was drinking.

One householder, Mary Dowlan, a charwoman, took fourteen people into her house and began to dress their wounds. 'My house,' she said, 'was liker to a slaughter-house than to a Christian's house, with human blood.'[7]

Samuel Bamford's wife succeeded in finding shelter in one of these houses. She subsequently told her husband how, horrified by some of the scenes she had witnessed on the Field, she crept into a deserted vault. Here, she put her fingers in her ears to stop out the screams of the injured. Sitting, waiting, the tumult suddenly began to die down. Then, the door to her hiding place opened. Through it came a group of men carrying the dead body of a middle-aged woman. Mima Bamford muffled a scream of terror as the men passed, taking the corpse to another room, leaving her to the sudden silence. Eventually, a kindly special constable helped her away to safety.

Across the other side of the ground, Cornet Jolliffe turned his attention away from the Quakers' yard and moved his horse in the direction of the hustings. To his surprise, he discovered that the space had almost emptied. Only a group of special constables and a few scattered Hussars were near the carts. One of the cavalrymen was his commanding officer,

Leighton Dalrymple, who, in spite of the shortcomings of one leg, had remained in his saddle throughout the whole of the turmoil. Dalrymple ordered him to find a trumpeter to sound 'retreat'.

Jolliffe rode off quickly into the side streets. There, it was apparent, the violent action that had occurred on the ground had not abated as the crowds tried to escape. Indeed, in the more confined space of these alleyways, the activity was, in some ways, more terrifying.

Several of those chased by cavalry into these clogged passages were able to identify unambiguously the faces above several of the sky blue and white uniforms. One 60-year-old woman, Margaret Goodwin, trying to make her way from the edges of the mob, recognised a rider furiously spurring his horse towards her. She had known Thomas Shelmerdine since he was a boy. As he reached her, she shouted up to him. 'Tom Shelmerdine, thee will not hurt me, I know.'[8] At which Shelmerdine rode her down. He then swung his sabre, slashing her on the scalp.

Edward Gilmore, a Manchester tradesman, was sitting at dinner when he heard the noise of the crowd. He walked to the end of the street before seeing the confusion of the retreating workers. As the cavalry advanced, he decided to return to the safety of his house. He was 25 yards from his door when his hat was knocked from his head by a sword. His error was to bend to pick up the hat from the flagstones. As he stooped he was struck at again, but now by a cavalryman he knew. This time the sabre gashed his head. He had recognised – and so had Gilmore's son who witnessed the incident – the Manchester Yeomanry cavalryman, Edward Tebbutt. Others that day could show injuries they claimed were inflicted by the same man. One of these, a young woman, was Tebbutt's neighbour.

The reporter of the *Courier*, running towards Deansgate, passed several people lying wounded and bleeding on the ground – one of them a white-capped young girl covered in blood. In his subsequent description of events he never tried to pretend that he had stopped to give succour. Rather, seeing a troop of the 15th Hussars, he ran straight up to them, swept off his hat and, speaking truthfully as a retired, if ungallant, officer called out, 'Save a fellow soldier!' A courteous officer of the 15th told a trooper: 'See this gentleman to a place of safety!'[9]

William Jolliffe had not ridden more than 100 yards into these streets before he found a regimental trumpeter and led him back to his colonel. The Field on to which they galloped, as well as the adjacent streets, now presented, as he described it,

An extraordinary sight: the ground was quite covered with hats, shoes, musical instruments and other things. Here and there lay the unfortunates who were too much injured to move away, and this sight was rendered the more distressing, by observing some women among the sufferers.[10]

Samuel Bamford described the same scene as that which faced the impressionable young cornet. Approximately a quarter of an hour earlier, this had been the meeting place of an orderly crowd:

The yeomanry had dismounted – some were easing their horses' girths, others adjusting their accoutrements, and some were wiping their sabres. Several mounds of human beings still remained where they had fallen, crushed down and smothered. Some of these still groaning, others with staring eyes, were gasping for breath, and others would never breathe more. All was silent save those low sounds, and the occasional snorting and pawing of steeds. Persons might sometimes be noticed peeping from attics and over the tall ridgings of houses, but they quickly withdrew, as if fearful of being observed.[11]

This, like other celebrated passages by Bamford, can only be a second-hand description. He subsequently describes how the first wave of Yeomanry carried him behind the Quakers' Meeting House from where he was able to escape to the streets.

Jolliffe dismounted. A trooper from his regiment whose horse had been brought down by the logs in front of the Quakers' yard, was badly injured and needed attention. As he ministered to the soldier, he noticed the peculiar silence that had overtaken St Peter's Field suddenly broken by the rattle of Major Dyneley's two pieces of artillery as they were dragged across the ground by a troop of Hussars.

# 30

## A Degree of Peace

John Tyas, *The Times* reporter, with an enormous sense of relief, had been arrested when the violence was at its height. In Hunt's wake, he was escorted off the Field by a special constable. As he hurried away, he passed 'a woman on the ground, insensible to all outward appearance, and with two large gouts of blood on her left breast.'[1]

Soon, he found himself in a room in Mr Buxton's house along with Hunt, Johnson, Saxton and several others including another wounded woman, Mrs Elizabeth Gaunt, in a fainting condition. She had been cut and trampled on. A cruelly libellous poem would soon attach itself to her as 'Hunt's concubine':

His mistress sent to the hospital her face to renew
For she got it closely shaven on the plains of Peter-Loo.[2]

After a brief interview with the Reverend Mr Hay, the prisoners were handed over to Lieutenant Colonel L'Estrange who, with a detachment of 15th Hussars, marched them through the Manchester streets to the prison yard of the New Bailey. There, the remaining pair named on the arrest warrant, John Knight and James Moorhouse, joined those in detention.

The military escort had been essential. Without it Hunt would either have been rescued by his supporters or, more surely, attacked by his detractors. The streets through which they had passed were still crowded with fleeing people, some of whom had turned to rioting and it would be many hours before normality returned.

Such was the outrage at the scale of injury inflicted on, for the most part, peaceful citizens, it was inevitable that a violent reaction would occur. There was a short lull in activity during the afternoon during which detachments of cavalry patrolled the streets. Several constables who had suffered on the Field, realising by now that, as pedestrians, they were the most vulnerable of targets, fetched their horses and joined the cavalry. One of these, Robert Mutrie, got into his saddle soon after he escaped from the ground at two o'clock. Riding for most of this time alongside the ever anxious magistrate, Mr Norris, he was not to leave his horse's back, so he claimed, for 13 hours.

It was not long before those eager for revenge became active. At New Cross, one of the toughest sections of the town, an unfounded rumour spread that a grocer, a Mr Tate, had captured one of the women reformers' flags as a souvenir. Crowds gathered and his shopfront was completely destroyed.

Robert Mutrie by this time had begun to help a troop of the 15th Hussars under Captain Booth which was trying to clear the streets. But since the Riot Act had not been read, Booth, with commendable restraint, deployed his troops without the use of either guns or swords. Dozens of times the Hussars charged, each time exposed to bricks, stones and other weapons. And each time, once the horses had passed, the crowd poured back on to the streets.

Eventually Booth lost his temper, confronted the indecisive Mr Norris and swore that unless the magistrate read the Riot Act he would order his men to their quarters. After dithering, Norris did as he was bidden. Booth, an officer with no similar facets of uncertainty in his character, had no intention of waiting for the statutory hour to elapse after the Act had been read, before taking military action. Mutrie described what occurred:

> The moment it was read Capt. B. ordered the infantry officer to form a hollow square in the centre of the Cross, we all took shelter in the square when the word was given to fire in all directions – the square then opened and the horse charged every way upon the crowd – my mare grew quite mad and carried me over the back of many a poor Devil – two were shot in the first charge just opposite my room window. You may be sure I was (as well as my Mare) very thankful to get relieved at 3 o'clock in the morning.[3]

And so the violence continued. At ten o'clock that night, the Reverend Mr Ethelston wrote to Lord Sidmouth reporting the shooting of the two rioters and telling him that 'the town is in great confusion and alarm.'[4]

Unknown to the magistrates, other reports were at that moment being carried to London. Two middle-class radicals, Archibald Prentice and John Edward Taylor (later to become owner of the *Manchester Guardian*), had by now discovered that John Tyas was imprisoned. They had agreed, therefore, to write to different London newspapers giving full accounts of what they had seen. Their copy was to be in print within twenty-four hours.[5]

Not until nine o'clock on the morning of the 17th was a reasonable degree of peace restored, though in some nearby towns, in particular Stockport and Macclesfield, the returning marchers continued to riot for many hours. In Manchester itself the magistrates took the precaution of having huge handbills printed ordering all shops to be closed for the day. Tyas, when he was released at midday, found that troops had been posted at key points throughout the town. But by three o'clock all soldiers had been withdrawn and a sullen calm had descended on the place.

The streets were empty except for those looking for lost relatives. Cornet Jolliffe followed some medical officers through a ward of the Infirmary. The sight was melancholy. In addition to those who had been crushed and trampled there were as many as 20 people lying there with serious sabre wounds. Among these were two women whom Jolliffe guessed would never recover. One man was dying from a gunshot would to his head; another had just had his leg amputated.

Nobody could yet know the true extent of the human damage. Many of the wounded, fearing retribution from

Nadin's men, or for other reasons, had hidden their injuries and made their way to their homes. John Lees, the ex-soldier struck down near the hustings, was one. Although his clothes covered fearful wounds, within hours he appeared at his workplace.

Many of those unhurt were deeply affected. Some elderly people stopping off on their journey home at the same public houses at which they had drunk on their journey into Manchester, had been seen in tears. Samuel Bamford, after his escape from the Field, made his way to Smedley Cottage to learn that Hunt was under arrest. He now set out to find his wife and as many of the Middleton contingent as he could muster. In the end he succeeded in gathering together about 1,000 people who, led by a worker carrying their one remaining banner, silently shuffled back to their home town.

Bamford himself would be arrested in a few days' time. When, in due course, he arrived at the New Bailey, he found not only Henry Hunt imprisoned there, but also nine others, including two women.

No greater contrast with the grief and sense of failure which permeated the working classes in the towns surrounding Manchester could be provided than by the reaction of one notable group of the middle class of Stockport. The troop of Cheshire Yeomanry, on their return to the town, gave an extraordinary display, waving their captured banners and vowing to continue the fight. It was the euphoric reaction frequently reported in soldiers in the hours following successful but bloody battle.

John Lloyd gave a triumphant description of 'the *glorious* day at Manchester' to his friend in the Home Office, Henry Hobhouse. 'We have come back with honour today,' he wrote, 'having with our troop done essential service and obtained praise – on the *field* on picket and in pursuit of the Pikemen yesterday in the neighbourhood of Oldham.'

With enormous enthusiasm, he reported how they had captured two banners and now intended to present them to their Colonel, Sir John Leicester. He might perhaps have shown less pride in the achievement had he realised that one of these had been wrested from the hands of the women of Royton. Lloyd, however, was unswerving in his prescription for dealing with situations such as that which had developed on St Peter's Field: 'We remain on duty,' he said, 'and now is the time to make a good finish.'[6]

Lloyd need have had no doubts that the efforts of those charged with maintaining law and order would not be properly acknowledged. Lord Sidmouth had by now received several dispatches describing how the St Peter's Field mob had been dispersed. In spite of the fact that the magistrates had used the force which he had specifically implored them to avoid, Sidmouth, on August 18th, sat and personally wrote to the Reverend Mr Hay his congratulations on the outcome of the affair. He said, 'I am gratified equally by the deliberated and spirited manner in which the Magistrates discharged their arduous and important duty on that occasion.' He told Hay also that he had already commended the magistrates' conduct to the Prince Regent, as well as 'the merits of the two corps of Yeomanry Cavalry'.[7]

On incomplete information, Sidmouth had approved the actions of a magistracy even now still in turmoil. John Lloyd's hope of further violent activity was as evident as James Norris's fear of it. Norris had reverted to the edge of panic on August 17th when Constable Moore had returned to Manchester with the report that between 30,000 and 50,000 men had assembled in the outskirts and were preparing to descend on the town.

Having failed utterly to learn from his experience of the previous day, shortly before ten o'clock that night, Norris sat down and wrote to Lord Sidmouth: 'Indeed, my Lord, I feel it my duty to state to you that the town (in particular parts) and the adjoining county threatens to be in a *night* or two in a complete insurrectionary state.'[8]

Lord Sidmouth, however, was as disinclined to take any further precipitate action at Norris's urging, as he was to act on Lloyd's suggestions for a definitive final flourish. Newspaper reports of the affair, it was already plain, ensured a substantial national reaction for which the government would need to prepare itself. Sidmouth now needed a considered and calm report of both what had occurred, and of what the consequences had been.

Manchester, far from being on the point of revolutionary riot, as the town's law officers would have Sidmouth believe, was overcome by a sense of grief and subjugation. It was the response that could have been expected from a defeated army after the decisive victory of some superior force. Five days after the event, one of the Home Office's Manchester informers attempted to get near the office of

James Wroe, the editor of the *Manchester Observer*. He failed because the crowd trying to buy that day's edition, with its account of August 16th, was so large.[9] In its pages, the paper had succeeded in coining the word which encapsulated the fatuity of the day: 'Peter-Loo'.

# 31

# Relief

The size and nature of the calamity was still to be assessed. However, it was obvious to the magistrates that their report to government of the events of the 16th had best be made in person by one of the members of their Select Committee. By August 19th, by fast coach, the Reverend Mr Hay had reached London. But already, not only had Archibald Prentice's and J. E. Taylor's account appeared in print in the capital, so too had that of John Tyas in *The Times*. Tyas's version confirmed all the sensational and bloody details given by the earlier reporters, and included a full description of the waywardness of the cavalry.

That day in Whitehall, Hay faced five members of the Cabinet: Lord Sidmouth, Lord Wellington, Lord Castlereagh, Lord Vansittart and Lord Eldon. But there was no possibility that the statistics he gave them could have been other than misleadingly inadequate. Even several weeks after Peterloo, the magistrates persisted in minimising the size of the St Peter's Field crowd. Hay put the estimate of those who 'took part in the meeting' – as opposed to those who were spectators on the edges of the crowd – at 30,000.[1] *The Times*, the day he visited London, had already published the figure of 80,000. Others placed the numbers considerably higher. Hunt guessed 150,000. The *Manchester Observer* of August 21st calculated that 153,000 people had been present by half past one that afternoon, and the *Monthly Magazine* of October 1st estimated 120,000 on the ground plus 40,000 in the surrounding streets.

On August 19th, Hay's knowledge of the casualties can only have been scant. The Manchester Infirmary's Register Book on August 16th showed that 29 persons injured in the area of St Peter's Church had been admitted that day and that two had died; 34 were admitted on the 17th and one had died.[2] It is likely that, when he arrived in Whitehall, he had been told only of the first day's figures, and that these were the statistics he disclosed to the members of the Cabinet he confronted.

By the following week William Hulton was writing to Lord Sidmouth admitting to the presence of 71 patients in the Infirmary. He added that the Committee of Magistrates hoped that the Home Secretary would see this small number 'as a proof of the extreme forbearance of the military in dispersing an assemblage of 30,000 people.'[3]

Others, aware of the magistrates' efforts to obfuscate the scale of damage, took practical steps to reach more realistic figures. In the last days of August, Charles Pearson, a solicitor, attended a surgery as well as the homes of many who, from fear of arrest or for some other reason, had chosen not to present themselves to a medical practitioner. In one village of less than 50 cottages, Pearson found ten wounded people. He was able to compile a list of 200 names of those he had met who had not attended the Infirmary. He put the total number of injured at not less than 500.[4]

It was only when a committee of middle-class manufacturers raised subscriptions for the relief of victims of Peterloo – and paid out compensation – that a believable account of the extent of the human damage could be made. Deaths, attributable to injuries, either on the day of the St Peter's Field meeting, or in the weeks immediately following, were put at 11. Four hundred and twenty wounded were listed at the time of the report on February 14th, 1820. One hundred and forty were still to be assessed for financial assistance – which averaged about £3 per person.[5]

The actual relief this sum brought to some sufferers was no doubt immeasurably small. It is inevitable that a number must subsequently have died from causes related to their experiences on St Peter's Field.

The *Relief List* gives both a stark and a poignant description of the condition of that section of the working class which absorbed the physical impact of Peterloo. It needs only a few quotations from it to assess the trauma inflicted not simply on individuals, but on whole families; equally, it is a sobering commentary on social attitudes of the time.

Alcock, William, 33    Heaton Norris, nr Stockport, Iron Founder. Rt arm much hurt by a blow from a sabre. This was done by one of the 15th Hussars.

Barron, Thomas, 67 — 6 Edge St., Plasterer. Severely beat on the head with truncheons. 3 weeks disabled. Since fallen from a scaffold, supposed in consequence of his head being bad.

Barlow, Ann, (7 children) — Crushed by the crowd, and had her breast broken; bruised by the Constables' staves. Now ill. Was three weeks in the infirmary. A deplorable object.

Dwyer, Edward, 67 — 40 Jersey St., weaver. Sabred on the head, and bruised in the loins by being trampled on. A poor old man in a deplorable state.

Evans, Mary — 8 Style St., Stabbed with a bayonet in the back of the thigh by a soldier of the 88th Regt. Stopped by the 88th Reg. in getting away; her niece had her clothes pierced by a bayonet but another soldier interfered and saved her.

Greaves, Sarah, 38 — Hollingwood. Left collar bone broke by a blow from a Yeoman with the back of his sabre.

Lees, James, 25 — Delph, Weaver, (2 children). A sabre cut on the top of his head, 5″ long and one near the forehead by one of the 15th Hussars. He was taken to the Infirmary and dressed by one of the junior surgeons who put his name over the bed and ordered him to undress. Dr. Ransome asked him, if he had had enough of meetings? On his reply in the negative he was ordered to leave the place immediately.

Leigh, John, 27 — Sabred on the hip when down in the crowd. Says the trumpeter and Capt. Birley passed him when down; that Birley returned and cut him.

Marsh, William, 57 — Chorlton (6 children). Sabre cut on the back of the head, bone in his leg splintered and crushed on the body by being trampled on. He states he had 3 children working in Birley's factory, who, when he learnt of his being hurt at the meeting, discharged them.

The *Relief List* continues with many scores of other similarly described incidents.

The law-keepers too had suffered, though the injuries they sustained could not be compared with those they had inflicted on civilians. One special constable was dead. The 15th

Hussars reported 2 officers and 21 other ranks struck by stones and sticks. The Manchester and Salford Yeomanry Cavalry named 3 officers and 41 other ranks similarly hurt.[6] For the Cheshire Yeomanry, Lloyd reported, 'The casualties are few – 4 men hurt and wounded, one dangerously.'[7]

Throughout the days that followed, graphic descriptions of incidents on the Field, and the bare statistics of death and injury to which they had given rise, continued to reach the magistrates. The possibility that, by their actions they had wrought an enormous act, if not of criminality, then of evil against a gathering of English working people was placed before them within hours of the affair, by local newspapers and pamphlets and, shortly afterwards, by nationally influential publications such as *The Times* and the *Leeds Mercury*. Three days after Peterloo, whilst their colleague, Mr Hay, was in London a letter in Lord Sidmouth's hand arrived in Manchester. Irrespective of the fact that it was addressed to Hay, Mr Norris and Mr Hulton, knowing full well that the contents of the envelope would be a judgement on their behaviour, tore it open. With relief they read Sidmouth's sentences approving their conduct.[8] Next day they also had in their hands a guarded letter from Hobhouse telling them of Hay's appearance before the Cabinet and of his 'verbal account of the transactions of Monday which have made a deep impression on Lord Sidmouth's mind'.[9]

The truth was, however, that this deep impression was far from favourable. Both Sidmouth and Hobhouse had been taken aback by Hay's inadequate performance before the gathering of senior members of government. Hobhouse's private opinion was that 'Hay is not the man he was two years ago.' Hay's account of the debacle had been so incomplete that Hobhouse had been forced to check the facts from other sources.[10]

The situation was deeply worrying for Sidmouth. Not only had he already expressed his written approval of the Manchester magistrates' behaviour, he had persuaded the country's Head of State to do the same. Relaxing on board the *Royal George* yacht off Christchurch, the Prince Regent, not troubling to wait for any considered reports of the outcome of the St Peter's Field meeting, had had his personal secretary, Sir Basil Bloomfield, pen a fulsome letter approving the actions of both the magistrates and the regular and yeomanry cavalry.[11] By August 21st, the day the word Peterloo was added to the English language, Sidmouth had transmitted these royal thanks via the Lords Lieutenant of Lancashire and Cheshire.

Accusations of wanton bungling were now rising up on every side. Against these Sidmouth presented his unchanging front. But a crack had appeared in that hitherto unyielding surface. It showed itself when, two days after he had received the Prince Regent's paean of praise, a letter from young Mr Hulton of Manchester was handed to him.

Now facing deep censure in Manchester for his critical role as Chairman of the Select Committee of Magistrates, Hulton desperately needed support. The higher the quarter from which it came, the better. Hulton therefore looked to Sidmouth to be his saviour. He asked for permission to publish the letter the Home Secretary had written on August 18th, approving the actions of the magistrates on the 16th.

Sidmouth, however, quickly shifted away from the burden of responsibility Hulton was trying to load on his back. He had Hobhouse pen his firm refusal. Hobhouse wrote, 'His Lordship presumes that it can no longer appear to the magistrates to be of any consequence to give publicity to his letter.' Sidmouth's communication to the Lords Lieutenant setting out the Prince Regent's approval of their action, Hobhouse went on, 'must be of greater value . . . His Lordship would accordingly prefer that it shall not be published.'[12]

Hulton's sense that blame would soon be apportioned and that he would be required to bear his share was correct. He and his fellow magistrates had tried to head off public criticism by calling a meeting on Thursday, the 19th, in order that loyal inhabitants of Manchester and Salford could publish resolutions supporting the action on the 16th.

The meeting – supposedly public – held at the Star Inn, was undisguisedly rigged. Its Chairman, the mill-owner and manufacturer Francis Phillips, began by asking 'any persons present who do not approve of the objects of this meeting' to withdraw.[13] With such a predetermined composition, it came as no surprise that Manchester's magistrates received a whole-hearted vote of thanks from their audience.

In response, the reporter of Peterloo, the radical manufacturer Archibald Prentice, set about organising a petition of protest against both the violence on St Peter's Field, and the validity of the magistrates' 'public' meeting. Within two or three days Prentice had 4,800 signatures on his petition, many of which, to his gratification, were, as he put it, those of members of the 'respectable classes'.[14]

## 32

## Sustaining a Reputation

Now it was clear that the working classes of the industrial north were looking on Peterloo, not as a battle which they had knowingly joined, but as a tragedy into which they had been unwittingly dragged. The consequence was equally clear: there was to be no violent revolutionary reaction from among the lower orders of Manchester or any other part of Great Britain. What was sought, however, was that the perpetrators of the atrocity should be brought to justice. And increasingly, as the possibility of large-scale working-class violence receded, the 'respectable classes' were willing to be seen joining this clamour for accountability.

The newspaper carrying a full description of the events of August 16th did not reach Sir Francis Burdett's hunting box at Kirby Park in Leicestershire until five days after Peterloo. Undoubtedly genuinely shocked, but dramatic in thought and deed as ever, Burdett stood at a large stone in the park, and there placed on it a sheet of paper. On this he addressed a letter to the electors of his parliamentary constituency,

Westminster. His intention was – and in this he was successful – that it should be published widely by London and other papers. The letter began,

> Gentlemen – On reading the newspapers this morning, having arrived late yesterday evening, I was filled with shame, grief, and indignation at the account of the blood spilt at Manchester.

Like so many others who read of Peterloo, he was appalled that fellow countrymen had carried out an attack on their own people. Unquenchably xenophobic, he wrote of the perpetrators,

> Would to heaven that they had been Dutchmen or Switzers or Hessians or Hanoverians or anything rather than Englishmen who had done such deeds. What kill men unarmed, unresisting and Gracious God! women too, disfigured, maimed, cut down, and trampled on by dragoons.[1]

By September 2nd, Burdett was back in London where, supported by Major Cartwright and John Cam Hobhouse, he held a meeting in Palace Yard, Westminster. There he was able to give to a crowd of 30,000 a theatrical condemnation of Peterloo.

During the next few weeks large meetings of protest were held in many parts of the country. And with some of these, members of both the upper and the middle classes were involved. Lord Sidmouth, meanwhile, was calculatedly waiting, preparing to use whatever means were necessary to deal with those prominent members of society daring, or foolish enough to put their heads above the parapets. The first to appear outside London was both prominent and surprising. It was that of the Lord Lieutenant of the West Riding, Lord Fitzwilliam.

Sidmouth had no reason to suppose that, when the Establishment was under pressure, Fitzwilliam in his capacity as Lord Lieutenant of his county, would do other than lend his solid support. True, he was a Whig, and a soft-centred one at that, but in the past he had proved a pillar of the Establishment. Moreover, the Yorkshire Racing Calendar was still far from complete, and it was well-known that Fitzwilliam was making serious preparations for its major event. But Sidmouth had misjudged his man.

Shortly after the York race meeting, Sir John Byng had sold Sir Arthur, his colt much favoured for the St Leger, to Lord Fitzwilliam. But it was his own bay, Palmerin, which Fitzwilliam had qualified for the Doncaster classic on September 18th. This race, it so happened, would be the most sensational in the history of the St Leger. It was won that day, not by Palmerin, but by an outsider, Antonio. Immediately, however, an objection was raised. Several horses had failed to start with the rest. A false start was declared and the race re-run – without Fitzwilliam's Palmerin. The atmosphere on course, where such vast sums of money were at stake, was highly charged. In due course, the Stewards of the Jockey Club added to the consternation by over-ruling the second result and adjudging Antonio the winner.

Amid all this diversion and uproar, however, Fitzwilliam was far from allowing matters of conscience to go by default. Just as he had at York Races, he had that week arranged at his house, Wentworth, a large and fashionable party for the Doncaster event. From this party Fitzwilliam gathered round him a group – and Sir John Byng was not one – whose purpose was to organise the Yorkshire meeting of protest calling for a governmental inquiry into Peterloo.

Sidmouth had already written a speech which was to be delivered by the Prince Regent from the throne, condemning a meeting of the Common Council of London which had called for an immediate inquiry and punishment for those guilty of carrying out the St Peter's Field assault. In the case of Fitzwilliam, Sidmouth was able to take action of a more direct kind. On October 19th, he heard that Fitzwilliam's meeting had been held earlier that week in York. It took place in the Castle Yard where the Yorkshire Luddites had been hanged. Sidmouth immediately contacted the Prime Minister. By October 20th, a Cabinet meeting had been held, and the Prince Regent consulted. Next day Sidmouth asked for, and got, Fitzwilliam's resignation as Lord Lieutenant of the West Riding.

Sidmouth had taken firm action of a different kind against Sir Francis Burdett. The result was equally definitive. He had approved of an action for seditious libel against the baronet. On March 23rd, 1820, Burdett was tried at Leicester Assizes. Conducting his own defence, quoting Magna Carta and Shakespeare, evoking the Star Chamber, the despotism of the Roman emperors, the Constitution, Homer, John

Locke and Aesop, he addressed the jury in a speech lasting 70 minutes. Without retiring, the jury found him guilty. In due course Burdett was fined £2,000 and imprisoned for three months.

Sidmouth, still not fully recovered from his illness, stood cold, but unwavering throughout the whole of a sustained period of pressure for governmental action. From here on he never budged in his loyalty to his subordinates in Manchester. As late as May, 1821, Burdett tried to introduce a motion into Parliament demanding an inquiry. It was powerfully supported by John Cam Hobhouse, the cousin of Sidmouth's own Permanent Under Secretary, Henry Hobhouse. All this, like the rest of the forces applied, had no influence with the man who was probably the most unbending of those ever to have held the office of Secretary of State.

Far from being purged of fear for the country's stability by the peaceful and reasoned response of those civic meetings which had so far been held, Sidmouth believed that even stronger measures were necessary to maintain the nation in the tourniquet which he, as Home Secretary, had applied. Sedition, treason, insurrection and rebellion, he believed, could only be avoided by preventive means. He emphasised the seriousness of his beliefs in a deeply emotional letter to his Prime Minister, Lord Liverpool:

> As I have repeatedly spoken, in the fulness of my heart – Health and comfort I have willingly sacrificed to a sense of private honour and public duty; and there is no further sacrifice, be what it might, that I am not ready and determined to

make, if required by such considerations – But I feel, and have felt for some time past, that whilst the country is suffering from the want, as I conceive, of these decisive and efficient measures, which the crisis calls for, my reputation is suffering also.[2]

His reputation, as he saw it, was saved by the wholehearted support of the reactionary Cabinet of which he was a member, and by the four bills which he had laid before Parliament before the end of 1819. One was to prevent drilling and training in the use of firearms by civilian groups, a second gave magistrates the power to search for arms and to arrest those found carrying them, the third made it no longer possible for certain objections to be raised to delay the administration of justice, and the fourth effectively prevented all public meetings of more than 50 people with severe restrictions on even those meetings that were allowed.

Two more bills were subsequently passed. These gave courts powers to seize newspapers and pamphlets after a conviction for publication of a blasphemous and seditious libel, and introduced stamp duties to a wider range of cheaper newspapers.

Together, when they became law, these were known as the Six Acts. The British government had now placed the radical elements of the working class in an iron grip. They could no longer organise, their affairs could be investigated and disrupted with ease, there were fewer constraints on the laws which could be used to detain them, the newspapers which supported their activities could be priced out of the reach of those for whom they were intended and, worse, these newspapers could be gagged when necessary.

Lord Liverpool's government, driven by the Home Office's obsession to control the citizens of the nation, had now completed the institution of the most repressive regime in modern British history.

# 33

## Great Expectations

In the days following Peterloo the working classes of Manchester waited with an expectation they were certain would be fulfilled. Those who had been affected – and the violence had touched many hundreds of families – now needed the reassurance that there would be legal retribution, particularly against those who had been visibly identified with sword in hand, cutting down their fellow townsfolk on or near St Peter's Field.

When two weeks had passed and not only had no such action started, but no statement of intent had been issued from government or any other quarter, some workers looked around to try to find for themselves suitable targets for punishment. Closest to hand, in that not only did he live within the town, but was himself of the working class, was the Manchester Yeomanry Cavalry trumpeter, Edward Meagher.

It had been Meagher who, alongside the factory owner Hugh Birley, had first spurred his horse into the St Peter's Field crowd. A few minutes later, near the hustings and then in the side streets near the ground, he had been seen to go berserk, cutting in an uncontrolled fashion at whatever and whomever came within reach of his sabre. Several survivors, both men and women, would eventually testify that his was the sword that had slashed them.

In the early hours of the morning of Sunday, September 5th, a crowd gathered outside Meagher's lodgings in Queen Street. Inside, it was reported, well fortified by alcohol from a Saturday night's revelry, Meagher held two loaded pistols. Harassed by and afraid of the taunts from below, Meagher loosed off several shots into the crowd. As a result of the incident, two men had to be carried off with gunshot wounds to their legs.

Even after this piece of widely witnessed violence neither Meagher nor any other was brought to account. A month later he was acquitted by Manchester magistrates after a trial in which his action with the pistols was successfully argued to have been justified because of the danger he had faced from the crowd. And still he had not been called to account for his behaviour on August 16th.

Expectations during this period were lifted even higher when, on September 7th, one of those who had managed to walk off St Peter's Field in spite of a severe sabre wound, died in a pitiful condition. Radicals succeeded in mounting an inquest on the death which, if it were properly convened, would have to investigate the Manchester magistrates' actions, and those of the cavalry, and thus apportion blame.

The victim was the Oldham cloth-worker and ex-soldier John Lees, whom Joseph Wrigley had seen struck down on

St Peter's Field. The formalities to the inquest began the day after Lees's death and attracted substantial national interest. The editor of *The Times*, one of his staff and a reporter from the *Morning Chronicle* were among the representatives of several newspapers present when the hearing began.

The proceedings had a cathartic effect upon Manchester's manufacturing population. They provided a new stage and an extended time-frame in which the events of August 16th could be replayed. Witness after witness appeared to tell again frightening and intimate details of experiences on the ground that day. Wrigley, at great length, described how he and Lees had been overwhelmed by the cavalry and how Lees was sabred by a mounted trooper.

Lees's father, Robert, described how his son appeared at his workplace next morning, his shirt covered in blood, unable to move properly.

William Harrison described how he had visited his weak and failing friend shortly before he died. He found that Lees had lost the sight of his left eye and the use of his left side. Some of his last words to Harrison were that, although he had been at the battle of Waterloo, he had never been in such danger as on St Peter's Field. 'At Waterloo,' he said, 'there was man to man but there it was downright murder.'[1]

Each working-class witness successively added to the evidence damning the behaviour of both the civilian and the military law-keeping force of August 16th. Crucially, no evidence of the identity of the cavalryman who sabred Lees was offered. The compilation of dramatic narrative was so powerful and protracted that, on October 13th, the coroner, who scarcely bothered to disguise his partiality towards both magistrates and constables, looked for and found an excuse to adjourn the inquest. His grounds were that the jury was by now so fatigued that the health of several was suffering.

The adjournment proved to be a disaster for the radicals' cause. During this period, it was shown that the jury and the coroner had viewed Lees's body, not at the same time, as the law required, but on different occasions. On this procedural irregularity the inquest was declared void and peremptorily terminated. The vivid, traumatic and moving recall of the events of Peterloo by some of those most deeply involved had been for nought.

Whilst the inquest on John Lees was in progress a second hearing was being instituted which would, in due course, again provide a platform for a reworking of the events of Peterloo. On September 4th, the male prisoners who had been held in Manchester's New Bailey prison were arraigned at Lancaster Assizes. Mrs Grant, after 12 days in solitary confinement with her wounds, had simply been discharged, along with others, for want of evidence. Ten remained. Henry Hunt was described as a yeoman; Joseph Johnson, a brushmaker; James Moorhouse, a coach-maker; and the rest, John Knight, Robert Jones, Joseph Healey, George Swift, John Thacker Saxton, Samuel Bamford and Robert Wilde, as labourers. This last description might have fitted the weavers, Bamford and Jones, the shoemaker, Swift, and even the unemployed Wilde; it covered neither the pretensions of 'Doctor' Healey, nor the achievements of the journalist, Thacker Saxton, nor of the manufacturer-turned-orator, Knight.

All ten were indicted for conspiracy and unlawful assembly and given bail. The true labourers were soon identified when Sir Charles Wolseley and others present in court had to offer the sureties and the £200 bail which the working men could under no circumstances find from their own pockets.

Hunt used the return journey to Manchester as a great parade of reassurance for both the radical cause and for himself. Enormous gatherings waited to cheer him in the small Lancashire towns and villages through which he passed. At Pendleton 80,000 people were said to have waited on his carriage.[2]

He finally reached Manchester in triumph on September 9th. From there he left for London and another rapturous reception which proved to Hunt, if proof were necessary, that the carnage on St Peter's Field, of which he had been the focal point, had now become of monumental national concern. *The Times* reported 300,000 people in the streets of the capital, cheering the orator on.[3]

In the weeks that followed this surge of public attention, many meetings of protest were held in many towns echoing that which Hunt had addressed in London. The protests took other forms: petitions to Parliament, attempts to bring members of the Manchester Yeomanry before the criminal court and even, it was alleged, an assassination attempt on the life of Joseph Nadin. But large as these gatherings of reformers and protestors were, other than from the manifestations of a few isolated acts of violence, if was clear that these would remain essentially controlled and unquestionably peaceable affairs. And as the winter months approached neither the government nor the magistracy, taking their example from

Lord Sidmouth, needed to waver. They needed to show neither their military strength, nor any sign of guilt.

The policy proved most effective in a nation where temperament was such that human behaviour of the kind experienced at Peterloo was a relatively infrequent occurrence. By the end of the year, the activity of radical reform groups had already begun to drop to a remarkably low level.

Henry Hunt used every means at his disposal to bring the magistrates to account. He had no more success than any other leading radical. In one of the speeches he gave in London after Peterloo, he said that he would be 'the most complete idiot that ever existed, if he did not allow that the late events of Manchester had placed him on the pinnacle of popularity'.[4] He cannot have guessed how quickly the slide from that great height would occur as a result of an efficiently operating governmental and legal machine.

His trial, and that of the nine other reformers, was fixed for York Spring Assizes on March 16th, 1820. The distance from Manchester and the distance in time from the day of Peterloo, were both considerable. They successfully removed this fresh public replay of the bloody events from the intimate interest of the workers of the manufacturing heartland of Lancashire. Unlike the Yorkshire Luddite trial, held in the same place, the road to York did not become a pilgrims' way for the working class. The Pennine hills proved a satisfactory barrier to any remaining embers of passion.

Hunt was found guilty of seditious assembly and sentenced to two and a half years in Ilchester gaol. Bamford, Johnson and Healey were found guilty on the same charge and sentenced to a year in Lincoln gaol. John Knight, also found guilty, was given two years' imprisonment on a subsequent charge. The rest were acquitted.

There was to be yet one more attempt to have the events of Peterloo rerun like some constantly repeated horror film. A test case was brought against four members of the Manchester Yeomanry Cavalry: Captain Hugh Hornby Birley, Captain Richard Withington, Trumpeter Edward Meagher, and Private Alexander Oliver. The plaintiff was the Middleton hatter Thomas Redford who, on St Peter's Field on August 16th had carried his town contingent's banner. Significantly exposed that day, he had been cut by sabres several times as he held on to his flag. He had subsequently suffered great pain over many weeks.

The trial began at Lancaster on April 4th, 1822 – nearly three years after the events took place. In court, Redford's counsel's thrust was that the assault of any one of them was the assault of all of them – Oliver had been clearly identified as he struck at least one of the blows.

Many by now familiar witnesses appeared to tell their stories, including several newspaper reporters who had been on St Peter's Field, among them Edward Baines of the *Leeds Mercury*. But, as with a replayed film, the capacity of their stories to shock had become dulled.

The defendants were acquitted. Their action, it was held, was justified in dispersing an illegal gathering. Their costs were met by His Majesty's government. There was resentment at this outcome but, after three years, no outcry. Peterloo was already slipping into history.

# 34

## Responsibility

Who should be held responsible for Peterloo?

The man charged with the task of maintaining the internal stability of the nation at the time of the Massacre, to whom all law officers reported, and who commanded all military forces dealing with civil disorder, was the Home Secretary, Lord Sidmouth. This cold, singular politician, both during his lifetime and after his death faced many confidently pointed fingers accusing him of the responsibility for the fracas, and thus of the deaths and the suffering that followed. Magistrates, soldiers and constables, it was held, had responded to a situation he controlled by virtue of his office, and to decisions he made in Whitehall. His was the ultimate guilt.

But the nature of the events leading to that summer of 1819 is too complicated to allow such a simple interpretation. In the first place, the Home Office – that is to say, Lord Sidmouth and his Permanent Under Secretary, Henry Hobhouse – were dealing at a critical period with an uncommonly weak Manchester magistracy. The figure they assumed on past experience to be one of great strength, that of the Reverend Mr Hay, was, in reality, worn out. In the early days of August, of his own admission, he was suffering from a number of unspecified, but clearly debilitating, 'awkward symptoms'.[1]

The Chairman of the newly appointed Select Committee of Magistrates, William Hulton, was young, effeminate and lacking any experience of the kind he was to face on August 16th. And the Home Officer's main point of contact, James Norris, was the most insecure and nervous of men.

On more than one occasion, Lord Sidmouth had had Henry Hobhouse spell out to Norris his precise views on the subject of the use of violence when dealing with large crowds. On July 26th, he had Hobhouse specifically write that a magistrate must take care not to ascribe to a meeting 'the character which he suspects to belong to it, but that which he can establish by evidence'.[2] Furthermore, Norris was assured, Lord Sidmouth presumed there would be few cases in which force would be necessary. Subsequently – twice in the same letter – Norris was warned of Sidmouth's concern that the meeting should not be used as an excuse for violent repression. In that letter of August 4th, Hobhouse had written, 'Lord Sidmouth is of opinion that it will be the wisest course to abstain from any endeavour to disperse the mob, unless they proceed to acts of felony or riot.'[3] And no such acts had occurred before the Manchester Yeomanry Cavalry was ordered on to St Peter's Field on August 16th.

But equally, responsibility cannot wholly be shifted to the magistrates because of their shortcomings. The Home Office was understaffed and overburdened. Its inadequacies were not negligible. Its cumbersome and strained method of transmitting information to magistrates could, and did, give rise to ambiguities.

There can be no doubt that, in the weeks preceding the meeting, Norris had been receiving two contradictory sets of signals from the Home Office. One set, derived from Hobhouse's master, Lord Sidmouth, recommended firmness: but a firmness tempered with caution and peaceable methods. The second set emanated from what seemed to be the same source, but which in fact was subtly different, and it implied that very different action should be taken.

For many months before the St Peter's Field meeting Hobhouse had received detailed personal reports of the rough and tough methods of J.S. Lloyd in Stockport. Those invariably involved rapid response to the first signs of undesirable activity, they were usually carried out on horseback, and they frequently ended with the deviants being unceremoniously bundled into prison. They had become Lloyd's stock in trade and had earned him Hobhouse's frequently expressed admiration. They had been the techniques Lloyd had so successfully used to ensure that Bagguley, Drummond and Johnston were not on the Field on August 16th.

Time and again Hobhouse complained of the insipidity and ineffectiveness of Manchester's law-keepers compared with those to be found in Stockport. Privately, Hobhouse had confided to Sir John Byng, 'At Manchester a directing spirit is evidently wanted.'[4] And in Stockport that extraordinary, energetic spirit was provided by Lloyd, who had a dominating influence over the elderly magistrates, whose clerk he was. John Lloyd had been given no authority to do what he did on behalf of the Establishment. He simply took it. Mr Norris had been forced to suffer the indignity of being sent to Stockport by Hobhouse in order to study Lloyd's unofficial methods. It was no wonder if Norris felt inadequate.

The relationship of Hobhouse and Lloyd and its pressure on Norris had been critical because it had been applied at its most forceful when Sidmouth, depressed and ill, had been absent from the Home Office and when Hobhouse was in sole command. But even when Sidmouth returned to his post, Norris was made to realise that Hobhouse was monitoring his performance and measuring it against the neighbouring yardstick. Ten days before Peterloo, Hobhouse had told Norris to send letters to his Grosvenor Place house marked 'Confidential and immediate'.[5]

Thus even in the period immediately preceding Peterloo, ambiguous signals from the Home Office were still reaching Manchester.

Under the circumstances it is not surprising that the magistrates elected to take violent action. But if guilt for the direction of that action is to be apportioned, less must fall on the shoulders of the subsequently derided Home Secretary. Sidmouth's wishes to avoid attempting to disperse the crowd, unless acts of rioting occurred, were clear and unequivocal. Rather, a significant share must fall on Henry Hobhouse who wished to be seen to act independently of his Secretary of State, advocating the vigorous physical techniques of his friend, John Lloyd. This energetic and ambitious pair succeeded in insinuating their ideas well beyond those of their employer. Lloyd, irrespective of the calamity that resulted, believed to the end that their actions had been both successful, and morally unchallengeable.

But even further down the hierarchy, substantial responsibility can still be apportioned. After Manchester's inadequate magistrates' decision to call on a substantial military force to attack a civilian crowd, need the consequence of the resulting action have been mayhem, butchery and bloodshed?

Seven years earlier Lieutenant General the Hon. Thomas Maitland, faced with the Luddite Revolt, had also had to control magistrates whom he considered weak and inadequate. He had dealt personally with both the Reverend Mr Hay and J. S. Lloyd, liked neither, and thoroughly mistrusted the ambitions of the latter.

Maitland's leadership and generalship were unquestioned by the civil authorities, as by the army. He had no resistance when he swept every available force, including local yeomanry regiments, under his command. And the strength of that command was such that, when the blood of the workers he had been sent to police was let, it was done in a fashion he rigidly controlled.

The consequence was chilling. The numbers of men who died on gallows he erected at York, were greater than the numbers who perished on the day of Peterloo. But whether or not their hangings were unjust, they were not carried out in panic.

The commander of the Northern Forces at Peterloo, Maitland's successor, Sir John Byng, having been absent at

York on August 16th, when he heard of the Massacre, immediately abandoned the race meeting and its celebratory Grand
Ball, and returned to Manchester. His reasons for being in
York – his headache, his war wounds, his other business, his
intentions to force the civil authorities to deal with civil
unrest, his trust in his inexperienced deputy – were never
questioned. His protestation that it would be unworthy to
suggest his absence from Manchester was due to his passionate wish to be at York Races, was equally readily accepted.

On his return to investigate the debris on St Peter's Field,
he was soon able to reveal to the Home Office that, along
with Mr Norris, he had interviewed Henry Hunt's acolyte,
Joseph Johnson. The brushmaker, now scared and repentant,
had offered his personal correspondence with Hunt in
exchange for lenient treatment for his participation on St
Peter's Field.

Byng, however, in his letters to Hobhouse, in the few
days following August 16th, had as much to say of James
Norris, as he did of Johnson. His remarks were incriminatory
of the magistrate who, as the executor of government policy,
must bear greater responsibility than any other for the decision to charge at Peterloo. Byng painted for Hobhouse the
picture of a weak man, timorous and easily frightened by the
press, which was now clamouring for action against those
responsible.[6]

Hobhouse, in his response, readily latched on to the idea of
making Norris a clearly recognisable scapegoat for the hor-
rors which had occurred. He wrote, 'I should very much
doubt whether in Norris's present temperament he would

continue and Lord S. is therefore (entre nous) casting about for an able successor.'[7]

On the morning following Peterloo, Byng had received Lieutenant Colonel L'Estrange's military report and forwarded it to the Home Secretary. In response, Lord Sidmouth thanked Byng and congratulated the officers and troops on their conduct and their forbearance of 'the insults unwarrantedly directed against them on this trying occasion'.[8] Byng had escaped implication in this great episode of history with his reputation totally unsullied, and so it has remained. But do the facts justify allowing the behaviour of this urbane and likeable man to remain unquestioned?

Two and a half years earlier, Byng had held the identical military rank and position as that he now occupied. On March 10th, 1817 the Blanketeers had taken up their positions on St Peter's Field in much the same way as they had done on August 16th, 1819. The crowd at the earlier meeting was less than at Peterloo and so too had been the nervousness of the magistrates. But in many other respects, the similarities between the two meetings were considerable. A great mob of workers, some of them carrying sticks and cudgels, faced a military force of cavalry and infantry armed with swords, bayonets and guns.

One significant difference was that, in 1817, when the military force had moved on to the Field, in command had been a senior and most experienced officer – Byng himself. Having made careful preparation, and under clear orders, the cavalry executed their 'neat' manoeuvres to arrest the ringleaders and bring the crowd to order. They left the Field with no blood having been shed.

In August, 1819 Byng abnegated his responsibility in favour of York Races. The man he left in command was considerably his junior: a regimental officer whose experience was inadequate to deal with the complex situation he suddenly found he had inherited. On the evening of August 15th, 1819, Lieutenant Colonel L'Estrange had left his discussions with the Manchester magistrates having been told of the threat posed by the anticipated size of the meeting next day, having decided on his troops' positions, and knowing that he would be expected to support, and receive support from the magistrates' constables and the Yeomanry under their command.

However, beyond these simple logistical arrangements, no attempt was made to coordinate the action of the civil and military forces. At the inquest on John Lees, the Deputy Constable, Joseph Nadin, who was present at the key consultations on the 15th, clearly said, 'I knew of no arrangements that day betwixt the civil and military power, for the dispersion of the meeting.'[9]

This error by L'Estrange, when dealing for the first time with civil authorities and potential civil disorder, is perhaps understandable. But what is not comprehensible is that he should accept supreme military command and not ensure that all active military forces were in fact under that command. The ability of the magistrates to call in the Manchester and Salford Yeomanry, independent of L'Estrange's force, proved the calamity of Peterloo. The havoc wreaked by the swords of amateur cavalrymen acting independently and answerable to no experienced superior was unstoppable once begun. When the professional forces followed in their wake, there was nothing L'Estrange could do to retrieve the situation other than inflict more of what he could see already happening.

The military failure at Peterloo was palpable. The true supreme commander, Byng, should have been made to acknowledge it. But there was never any question that this would happen. Lord Sidmouth was publicly as congratulatory and unwaveringly loyal to his Northern Forces' commanding officer as he was to his Manchester magistrates. The government fell into line behind the Home Secretary. There was to be neither an inquiry nor censure of any individual, and this included Lord Sidmouth himself.

Lord Redesdale echoed the enduring view of the Establishment when he wrote to the Home Secretary three days after Peterloo. He congratulated Sidmouth, 'on the bursting of the storm, notwithstanding the dreadful consequences'. He added, 'no doubt some of our friends will whine over the victims of their ambition.'[10]

# 35

## Technological Imperatives

It was evident within hours of Peterloo – such was the manner in which blood had been shed by Englishmen using swords on their own unarmed compatriots – that the episode would permanently figure large and importantly in history. And so it has. Equally, it seemed, its consequences for the rights of the individual could not be other than seminal and enduring. J. E. Taylor, soon to become editor of the new *Manchester Guardian*, was quickly in print with his assessment: 'In one brief hour,' he said, 'it has done more for the sacred cause of liberty, at the field of Peterloo, than the slow but certain progress of opinion could have operated in *half a century*.'[1]

But was this the case? Whereas the answer to the question, who was responsible for Peterloo? is complex, the answer to that other question, what had it achieved for liberty? is simple. It achieved tragically little – particularly for those who suffered most from it, the manufacturing working class.

It was true that, in reaction against Peterloo, much had occurred. The Six Acts reduced civil liberties within the nation to an even more unacceptable level. It is not fanciful to compare the restricted freedoms of the British worker in the post-Peterloo period of the early nineteenth century with those of the black South African in the post-Sharpeville period of the late twentieth century.

In human terms, the machine of the repressive government following the Six Acts continued to show its efficiency. Before the end of 1820, every leading working-class radical reformer of importance was in gaol, several in solitary confinement. So too were several of the middle class. Bagguley, Drummond and Johnston were already incarcerated. To their numbers had been added Henry Hunt, Samuel Bamford and the remainder arrested on St Peter's Field. John Knight was again behind bars with five others indicted with him for conspiracy. Sir Francis Burdett was serving his term for seditious libel. Those who had not been compromised in positions leading to indictment were soon mopped up. John Lloyd took pleasure from this operation, and in particular, in his arrest of the 'Reverend' Joseph Harrison. Lloyd discovered, and he described the fact with relish, that yet again the sexually active minister had been found 'making free with one of his female scholars'.[2]

Lloyd then added Sir Charles Wolseley to his bag. Both Wolseley and Harrison were tried for speaking seditious words in the spring of 1820. Wolseley received 18 months' and Harrison a total of no less than three and a half years' imprisonment. It was a swingeing sentence for the wayward parson whose sermons had wandered too far into politics.

Twice within ten years the British government had shown

how easily a relatively small force of arms could be used to subdue the most dense manufacturing population in the world. This, followed again by the legalised removal of the whole of its working-class leadership, completed the process of emasculation.

Support for radical reform slipped rapidly into decline. Before the end of 1820 the easing of the manufacturing economy in yet another cyclical swing of trade, released any remaining internal political head of steam. Workers willingly walked back to the factories where the machines of spinning and weaving mills were beginning to turn to supply a reviving export trade.

It has been said that the consequence of the drilling and discipline of Peterloo was the translation of workers into a class.[3] But such drilling and discipline had been well demonstrated in earlier episodes, involving large numbers of workers, not least the Luddite Revolt. And all evidence suggests that attitudes and patterns of behaviour had already been moulded by this earlier period. The people of the northern communities already looked upon themselves as being of a distinct class, identifiable by low income derived from labouring in manufacturing industries.

Peterloo, rather than being the device, was merely the banner. The condition of the working class in Manchester and its surrounding districts, like that of much of northern Britain, had been created by technological invention. The technology of Kay's flying shuttle, Arkwright's spinning frame, Cartwright's weaving machine and many other key inventions had assembled a template which shaped people's lives. It put vast numbers of people in social conditions – acceptable or not – which could not have been imagined in a previous century. The effects were eventually to be felt world-wide, but were most strikingly visible in the north of England.

This technology created a culture. It determined the hours people worked, the times they ate their meals, the conditions in the places in which they spent as much as half their lives, the clothes they wore, the type and situation of houses in which they lived, the hours available for leisure, the size of the buildings which dominated the towns, the environmental detritus which characterised the landscape. It even turned the nature of work from an activity involving men to one which drew in at least as many women and children. And, such was the power of the technology, the phenomenal changes which had produced this cultural transformation had taken place within only a few decades.

Even the number of people experiencing the shock of the new culture had become inexplicably large. Fifty years before Peterloo, Lancashire towns did not contain sufficient inhabitants to fill St Peter's Field. The nature of this fresh force was one which was able to sustain human reproduction. Fifty years after Peterloo those towns could have filled the same Field ten times over.

The factory had set most of the important parameters by which millions of workers were made to organise the routines of a lifestyle for a lifetime. For substantial populations of civilians, it had created a discipline which was at least as regulated and demanding as that imposed by a military commander on his army of soldiers. The mills, still increasing not only in number, but in size, now housed thousands of workers in essentially institutionalised conditions. In addition, the country's laws were singularly restrictive and strictly enforced in a nation in which a division of its citizens by class had taken firm root.

Technology, then, was the overwhelming force determining the conditions of the working class in a rigid society. Within the factories, some of these conditions were shameful and even horrific – unacceptably long hours, pitifully low pay, short-time work and inhumane child labour. It was these conditions which fomented the militancy and strength of the early twentieth-century trades unions.

But it was far from the case that all life within the mills' walls was either unfair or inhuman. Dr Andrew Ure, one of many mid-nineteenth-century eulogists of the factory system, pointed out how it housed larger numbers of people, better clothed and fed than the mass of people had been in any previous century, how it provided protection against the weather never before experienced by generations of peasants and agricultural workers and, as each new piece of technology was added to the last, how it removed the back-breaking work which every task requiring the use of energy had once demanded from men and women alike, and substituted manual dexterity given muscle by the power of the machine.[4]

Factories, for all their shortcomings, to countless thousands of manufacturing workers, were communities to which they belonged, places which gave them an acceptable pattern of existence, fostered skills and developed pride in work. Had this not been the case, the fierce loyalties which developed in families of workers in the cotton and woollen mills of East Lancashire and West Yorkshire would never have persisted throughout the whole lifetimes of mills. These factories, along with the loyalty they inspired, were only to expire in the middle of the twentieth century when competition from Eastern countries with names not invented in 1819, over-whelmed them. Without loyalty of this kind, the position of the factory owners would not have been sustainable. The wicked capitalist mill-owner existed more frequently in Victorian novels than in real life. More commonly the founder or his descendant – boss and owner – though not a loved, was a respected, paternal figure: a pillar of the local community who disbursed good works as well as handed out wages.

The institutionalisation of the factory worker had many consequences. One of these, fostered by the growing socialist ethic of the trades unions, was that paternalism – either by the factory owner or by the State – was both desirable and neces-sary. The result was that the individual quickly learned to accept a situation in which decisions, which once could only have been made by himself, were made for him. This attitude crept into the culture as it had into the institutions. It would take more than a century and a half, when a successor to Lord Liverpool's Tory government was in power, to begin to question the desirability of the individual's expectation of being provided for from cradle to grave.

There is no easy answer to the question why, in 1789, the French peasantry sustained a bloody and epoch-making revolution while, only 30 years later, after the also bloody experience of Peterloo, the working classes of England most immediately affected by it, returned docilely to their factories. It is difficult to avoid the conclusion that technology had already created the institutionalised conditions to which they were able to turn, bathe their wounds and, both figuratively and literally, pick up the threads where they had left off.

Those looking for a new Jerusalem in Britain – as earlier was William Blake, who had never seen the inside of a cotton or woollen mill – were convinced that these were the dark places of Satan. Accordingly, they were astonished that such vast numbers of people would head for their reputedly appalling places of work, not so much with docility as with relief. The Protestant work ethic had been fostered in these northern manufacturing communities not by the Church of England but by the church far more closely linked to working-class radical reform: that of Methodism. Middle-class British social workers and central European sociologists alike have been forever perplexed by the paradox that these communities where the labour unions first came to life, were also those where workers adopted conservative attitudes, and developed bonds within and towards the factories which paid for their labour.

The vivid emblem of Peterloo was simply a marker. It pointed the division of England into a north and a south. The dominant culture of the north was, and was to continue to be, that of the manufacturing working class. Above this north–south divide were, broadly speaking, poorer people, living in poorer-quality houses and eating poorer food, with poorer opportunities to change these conditions, than those who lived below it. The demarcation was to last for at least the better part of two centuries.

The root of the dilemma of the manufacturing working class lay not in individual pieces of technology applied to particular industries but in the ungovernability of technology in general.[5]

Technology is irreversible. And such is the influence of certain pieces of successful invention that legislation is unable to control what has been wrought. In the nineteenth century, laws were formulated to control the finishing machines which motivated the Luddite Revolt. They failed totally. It took only a few years for the technology to dominate the woollen industry and displace thousands of finishing workers. In the twentieth century, legal methods to control the motor car in towns have merely served to demonstrate its singular ungovernability. By the mid-1980s, the streets of most major capital cities had been rendered impassable by the vehicle whose most desirable characteristic is its mobility. The aeroplane too, like the automobile, once its advantages became available to, and affordable by large numbers of people, in spite of its extraordinary technological success in carrying large numbers of passengers, soon demonstrated how vulnerable it made them. Governments have found no certain solution to protect them from the unpredictable actions of either striking air-traffic controllers or of terrorists. And one technological innovation at least, satellite communication, promises a multitude of problems for the twenty-first century which governments will be powerless to regulate.

Is there hope of progress? That depends on how technological progress is viewed, since these problems can only be
solved by technological means; there are no others. Within
only a few years the problem presented by cloth finishing
machines, which precipitated the Luddite Revolt, disappeared
when superior machines made their function unnecessary. It
took many more years for the wealth created by the Lancashire factories to be distributed so that the workers in these
factories were lifted above unacceptable levels of poverty.
This, when it came about, was the result of technology which
doubled, then tripled the output from adults using only half
the hours they had not long before been forced to work in
order to make a living. Outstanding twentieth- and twenty-
first-century technological problems, in their turn, will only
disappear as the result of technological solutions.

The nation which, in the late nineteenth and early twentieth centuries, enriched itself most spectacularly by seeking
out technological solutions, was the United States. As in the
case of Britain, the technology of cotton was a substantial
force shaping the nation.

Until 1794, the process of separating cotton from its seed
was very labour-intensive and controlled the speed of production of raw cotton wool. In that year, Eli Whitney,
a mechanically minded young graduate of Yale, patented a
gin – a hand-driven wooden cylinder covered with spikes –
which could turn out 50lb. of clean cotton lint in a day.

This technological advance had astonishing results. In
1784, England imported 20 million lb. of cotton, none of it
from the United States. By 1850, 1.5 billion lb. was being

imported, 82 per cent of which came from the southern United States.[6]

At the end of the Civil War, the cotton states were forced to abandon the slavery which had provided the power for Whitney's hand-driven gin. But within seven years, as a result of both the relative freedom of sharecropping and the rapid introduction of mechanisation, output of cotton reached its pre-war level. The industry now expanded fast along with other major technological industries.

In 1876, Thomas Henry Huxley, the British biologist and philosopher of science, went to the United States. He visited the Philadelphia International Exhibition built to celebrate the nation's centenary. There he looked with trepidation at the size of the machines which were the product of the burgeoning nation. 'I cannot say that I am the slightest degree impressed,' he said, 'by your bigness or your material resources, as such. Size is not grandeur, and territory does not make a nation. The great issue, about which hangs a true sublimity, and the terror of overhanging fate, is what are you going to do with all these things?'[7]

Huxley asked his question in the belief that the answer would reveal that nothing of what he had been shown could possibly enrich the spirit of mankind. He was never to see how these machines would soon be capable of spreading their products not just to the poor and the underprivileged of that country, but to the millions of others from Europe and elsewhere who, even then, were pouring into America.

Ungovernability is technology's frightening characteristic. Its desirability is for the wealth it creates. But its saving grace, its quintessence, is the democratisation it ultimately forces on civilisation.

The speed with which it imposes itself depends on the conditions in which it has to operate. Fifty years before Peterloo, the founding fathers of the United States enshrined their aspirations in the Declaration of Independence. But the lofty ideals expressed in that document only started to have real meaning for most citizens when the nation began to emerge as a powerful technological society.

The conditions under which this occurred were important. Henry Hobhouse, a twentieth-century descendant and namesake of Lord Sidmouth's Under Secretary, has pointed out how the dispossessed poor who flocked to the United States were not pauperised or forced by circumstances into towns and factories to form the proletariat, as they were in England.[8] America had space – cheap land – into which men and women could move to farm, to build, to set up business and apply the new technology. But equally important, it was not restrained by inflexible attitudes set in a rigid culture. The democratising seeds of technology had found some of their most promising soil.

It was not chance that the nation that eventually prided itself on being the world's greatest democracy had also become the world's greatest technocracy. Nor was it mere coincidence that the cries for democracy, first among the peoples of Soviet Russia and of China in the 1980s, should have come in the age of television and its communication across national frontiers by satellite.

On June 7th, 1819, at a meeting in Oldham, the

redoubtable old reformer, John Knight, chaired a meeting of workers at which several resolutions were passed. They were typical of the resolutions being adopted at meetings in many other districts of Manchester and, for that matter, many districts of Britain. In addition to the demand for the relief of the distress of manufacturing workers, they called for the reform of the House of Commons, universal suffrage, annual Parliaments, election by ballot and repeal of the Corn Laws.

Peterloo was to have no effect whatever on the speed at which these demands were met. But in due course, over many years, each one would be achieved (except annual Parliaments, a goal which eventually was seen to be disruptive of the process of government). It was neither political expediency, nor economic policy that made these great changes possible in such a peaceful fashion, but rather the force of technological change. During this time manufacturing and agricultural technique had created the wealth which supplied the basic needs of the burgeoning population. It also paid for the requirements of the Education Acts which contributed significantly to enfranchisement taking place in a fashion and at a speed acceptable to government and people alike. A further 50 per cent of the adult population, not envisaged by John Knight, was also to be enfranchised in the fulness of time. The technology of manufactured cloth had made it possible for women to produce what for centuries had been within the strength only of men. The appearance of women in the march to St Peter's Field, and on the hustings of Peterloo had been one of the earliest public manifestations of their claims for equality. This process of democratisation took a further century before it could break the political will opposing it. Only the social upheaval caused by the perfecting of the technology of the contraceptive pill finally created the conditions for truly practicable universal enfranchisement.

# 36

## The Good Men Do

The footsteps of the poor leave few traces. The path trodden by the young Bagguley, Drummond and Johnston is quickly covered by the dust of history. The snuffing of the workers' leadership was effective and enduring. The names of the three firebrands, like those hundreds who ran bleeding from Peterloo, can be found only among those records which enumerate the punished or the injured.

Only one workers' leader's life is fully charted: that of the weaver Samuel Bamford, who had acquired the skills to make the record for himself. When, in 1821, the time came for his prison's gates to open, precious as ever, Bamford thanked the magistrates for his release. He regarded it, he said, as 'becoming' of his class to submit to authority.[1] His exceptional literary talents soon helped him find work as correspondent for a London newspaper. It was not long before the warm embrace of the Establishment turned into a prolonged affair. He soon adopted at least some of the attitudes of those whom he had once bitterly condemned. When, in years to come, the Chartists rose to prominence, although the movement had the same aims which had sent Bamford to prison, he virulently denounced its leaders. He even submitted to becoming a special constable and carrying a truncheon. His apotheosis came on retirement, when he was appointed doorkeeper at Somerset House. Nevertheless, coloured as his memoirs are, they remain a unique record of early nineteenth-century working-class life, without which history would be the poorer.

Age is no respecter of classes. Just as with the working class, it readily manifests its tendency to move certain members to the political right, so it does in some members of the aristocracy. Sir Francis Burdett, mistakenly seen by a few workers as their eventual leader in a new republic, made this rightward journey at a steady pace. His enthusiasm for reform waned. By the time of the enactment of the Reform Bill 13 years after Peterloo, he was a Tory, dedicated to the idea of monarchy, but more particularly to the rights of the great English landowners, of which he was one.

However, Major John Cartwright – 79 at the time of Peterloo – had not shifted his ideals one iota. At 84, having completed yet another tract on the English Constitution, he sent a copy to the man who had retired from the presidency of the United States more than 30 years earlier, Thomas Jefferson. At 81, Jefferson replied, pointing out that their great ages assured them of a speedy meeting in the hereafter. He went on, 'We may then commune at leisure on the good and evil, which in the course of our long lives, we have both witnessed.'[2] Cartwright regarded the upsetting of the established order as evil. Like Burdett, he had as little wish to see the republican system of Jefferson's United States, as he had to be leader of an English working class.

Of their betters, the newcomer who, by virtue of his peculiar dynamism appeared to many workers of the manufacturing north to be their most likely potential leader, was Henry Hunt. However, this quite extraordinarily vain man, who did so much by his performances to publicise the cause of radical reform of the British Parliaments, had reached his apogee at Peterloo. But for his appearance there he would now be largely forgotten. And even there, as one of his biographers puts it, he was the wrong man in the wrong place at the right time.

His self-confessed love of the adoring crowd had turned him into a rabble-rouser whose indulgent displays repelled even those who admired his cause. By the time he reached Manchester, his intentions were as deeply suspicious to the authorities of law and order as were those of John Bagguley whose mantle he had inherited. His presence there was a substantial factor in exciting the intense hostility of the magistrates even before the crowds began to walk on to St Peter's Field.

Hunt, in truth, knew as little of the manufacturing population of northern England which faced him at Peterloo as they did of him. After his release from prison he attempted to recapture the mass support he so yearned for, but the response was considerably muted. Glimmerings of the old demagogue returned when he successfully campaigned for election in 1830 as Member of Parliament for Preston – only to be humiliatingly defeated in 1833 after Parliament had been reformed. But Hunt did not have a large sense of humour. The irony evaded him.

The other performer who, like Henry Hunt, saw life essentially as a drama and whose appearance was highly visible at the centre of Peterloo's stage, was Joseph Nadin. And whereas few, if any, of those who paraded as radicals on St Peter's Field, benefited from their performances, Nadin, as did several of the law-keepers involved, emerged in an even stronger position for self-enrichment.

Already, in the previous year, the attention of government had been drawn to Nadin's nefarious activities. In one scandal he was accused of planting stolen property on two boys. Nadin was subsequently cleared. Henry Hobhouse wrote to express the satisfaction with which this news was received at the Home Office. He said, 'It will afford Lord Sidmouth great pleasure to find that an officer, who has so long associated himself with reputation as Nadin has done, is able to exculpate himself completely from every charge which shall be proferred against him.'[3]

Not only had Nadin safely exculpated himself, he had made careful note of those who had tried to expose him. John Knight, James Moorhouse and John Thacker Saxton had collected evidence against him. All three, it will be recalled, were listed for arrest on the piece of paper Nadin carried on to St Peter's Field. Moorhouse was not even on the hustings. Nor did Nadin forget the attorney, George Teale, who had tried to bring the action. He subsequently sued Teale for malpractices in a case heard 16 years earlier. Nadin, acting as informer, won the suit, ruined Teale financially, and took an informer's reward.

Having made a fortune from his office, Nadin retired in 1821 and set himself up as a master cotton spinner. He died a rich man at 83.

The financial rewards after office were substantial for at least one magistrate – Nadin's employer, the Reverend Mr Hay. For his part in Peterloo, Hay was given the parish of Rochdale, one of the most valuable livings in England; it was worth £1,730 a year.

He spent his later years adding to his voluminous scrap-books, copying into them notes on, for example, horticulture, radicals, toasts and many near banal remarks of contem-poraries. These neat books give the impression of a man obsessed with order, lacking either the will or the ability to express original thought.

He quotes prominently, for his and for others' amusement, a witty exchange between a Mr Thelwall, accused of treason, writing to a friend: 'I shall plead my own cause,' writes Thelwall. The friend replies, 'You'll be hanged, if you do.' 'Then,' says Thelwall, 'I'll be hanged if I do.'

Hay took the friend's advice to heart. He wrote nothing whatever in his own cause to explain his action at Peterloo, but stuck in his scrapbooks thousands of the reported words of others defending the magistrates' action that day.

Hugh Hornby Birley, who had commanded the Manchester Yeomanry in their charge at Peterloo, claimed to the end that, during that action, he never lifted his sword from his shoul-der, except once – when near the hustings, he forced a passage for two women who were trying to escape the mayhem on the Field. He eventually became a magistrate and a deputy lieutenant of Lancashire. He played a prominent part in Sir Robert Peel's successful attempt to introduce Saturday half-holidays for workers.

The other commanding amateur cavalryman who, to his regret, was at the seaside rather than on St Peter's Field on August 16th, 1819, Sir John Leicester, received even more than simply the approval of the Home Secretary for the role played there by the Cheshire Yeomanry. A week after Peterloo, Lord Sidmouth, still believing the nation's stability to be in danger, confidentially suggested to Leicester that he should raise substantial numbers of infantry and attach them to his regiment of cavalry, thus making a powerful force permanently available in the Manchester district.

Leicester leaped at the suggestion. By September 29th, 1819, The Prince Regent's Cheshire Volunteer Legion was in being; £9,600 was raised in voluntary subscription to supplement Leicester's expenses in the venture. By the following January the Legion was 857 men strong.[4]

Still more honours were to be poured on him. In 1826 he was created Baron de Tabley. But Leicester's enthusiasms, in particular his simultaneous love of his personal, beautifully turned-out regiment, and of art, were by now beginning to stretch his resources. His position weakened when his offer to sell his eighteenth- and nineteenth-century paintings as the basis of a national collection of British art was rejected by Lord Liverpool's government. He nevertheless continued to buy pictures until the year of his death, when he was found to be insolvent. His executor was then forced to sell off 87 of the 115 great paintings in his collection.[5]

The professional soldier who also had been many miles distant from his troops when they moved into action on St Peter's Field, General Sir John Byng, like Leicester, received unreserved praise. His gentlemanly and liberal habits never deserted him. He was one of few senior generals to support the Reform Bill. He rose to the rank of Field-marshal, became a Member of Parliament, and was created the Earl of Strafford.

Nor did his love of racing nor of gambling diminish with the passing years. The Racing Calendar for many seasons after Peterloo is populated with his runners at York, Pontefract, Doncaster and Newmarket. At Doncaster, in September, 1822, he arranged a match over 1 mile of his filly Madelina against the Marquess of Queensberry's colt, Orator, for a prize of 100 guineas. Madelina, to Byng's delight, swept to victory. In four successive years, from 1824–7, he succeeded in having runners for the St Leger. But each horse he saddled was unplaced and, in spite of winners elsewhere, this classic prize to which he had devoted so many hours of his life and pounds of his military and farming income, evaded him to the end.

For several years following Peterloo, the officers of government responsible for the internal stability of the nation, in their cramped Home Office quarters in Whitehall, continued their rigid course neither dismayed nor deviated by what had occurred on August 16th, 1819. In years to come, however, their strength would be increased by an ironical addition. The young cornet of Hussars, William Jolliffe, whose first experience of bloody action had been his traumatic involvement at Peterloo, two years later inherited a baronetcy. Subsequently he became a Member of Parliament and Under Secretary of State for Home Affairs – thus taking the seat once occupied by Hiley Addington.

Hiley's brother, Henry, as long as he was Home Secretary, remained the iceberg against which any weakly navigated ships threatening the State risked floundering. His health continued to be poor. But his belief in the rigid application of the law, and in the established order of Britain – even if the price was the loss of individual freedom – was unshakeable. And the Establishment which mocked him recognised the value of his inflexibility as a buttress to its strength. In 1821 his attempts to retire caused dismay. The Prince Regent, now an uncertain King George IV, and members of government, persuaded Sidmouth to remain in the Cabinet, which he did for a further three years.

Throughout that time, the rigid attitudes he had adopted towards the misdemeanours of the lower classes remained as they had when he first took up his post in 1812. Seven months after Peterloo, Hobhouse recorded how Sidmouth had had an audience with his monarch. The new King, ill and depressed, was now faced, only weeks after his accession, with the Recorder's Report on prisoners under sentence of death in Newgate. Wishing to make one of his first acts a gesture of clemency, the King made plain that it was his wish that none of the prisoners should be executed.

Lord Sidmouth, however, had no sympathy with such a display of weakness at such a time. Some of these cases, 77 in all, according to Sidmouth, were, 'of so heinous a nature that it would be of very ill consequence that the offenders shod. be only transported.'[6]

The King, with the support of the Lord Chancellor and the Lord Chief Justice, persisted in trying to sway the Home Secretary. In the end Sidmouth compromised, but insisted that two utterers of forged notes, two servants who had robbed their masters, one horse stealer and one cattle-stealer should hang. It beggars belief to consider what trivial offences those whose sentences were commuted to a lifetime's transportation had committed.

Shortly after his retirement from the Home Office Sidmouth married a rich wife, 30 years his junior. Twenty-one years later, he died at the age of 86. The event went almost unnoticed in the country.

Henry Hobhouse, the lawyer who had understudied Sidmouth to remarkable effect, was highly valued by those he served: this in spite of the fact that he unquestionably overstepped himself at a crucial moment in history when trying to carry out what he believed might have been his master's wishes. Nevertheless, he left another mark for which historians, and others, have reason to be grateful. In 1826 he was awarded a sinecure: that of Keeper of the State Papers. His ordered mind was an ideal one to oversee a permanent system of arrangement of state documents. He thus prepared the ground for many generations which, in good time, would be able to examine in some detail the nuances of phraseology of the volumes of his, and of others' hand-written letters relating to Peterloo.

The third of the key trio of lawyers had equally little cause to regret his association with the events on St Peter's Field. With the help of Lord Sidmouth and of his friend Henry Hobhouse, the solicitor's clerk John S. Lloyd soon achieved his scarcely hidden ambition to become Prothonotary of Chester. His elevation was made following the third anniversary of the day on which he had ridden with the Cheshire Yeomanry at Peterloo.

There were many Stockport citizens who felt it was an unquestionably well-earned reward. The neglect of his own legal career in order to apply the policies of Whitehall had brought difficult financial problems for a man with expansive personal and family ambitions. Almost single-handedly on many dangerous occasions, Lloyd had kept the peace of the town. He used violent methods in violent times, and saw them triumph. Now in the prime legal position of his country, he would benefit accordingly.

Nevertheless, he was far from lacking compassion for the poor he policed. It was Lloyd who drew the attention of the Home Office to the miserable conditions of the weavers of Stockport during the years of slack trade preceding Peterloo. He set up soup kitchens for the hungry and berated those unscrupulous employers who tried to pay their workers with a system of truck. But his compassion was mediated by the requirement that the poor behave strictly according to the code he adopted for himself, in which the dual authorities of king and country were unquestionable. When his prosperity at last grew to the level that he believed it proper he should adopt a family crest, he encapsulated his creed in his motto '*non sibi sed regi et patria*'.

Not only prosperity, but social acceptance graced the remainder of Lloyd's life in Chester, where his offspring were soon to become pillars of the local community.

Lloyd's beloved elder son, John Horatio, who on more than one occasion, had walked alongside his father through threatening crowds of Stockport workers, moved confidently through life on a wave of achievement. He completed the Oxford education for which Henry Hobhouse had arranged finance, taking a Double First in Mathematics and Classics and becoming a Fellow of Queen's College then Brasenose College. He then set himself up in a highly successful legal practice.

But if J.S. Lloyd rejoiced in his son's academic triumphs, it is difficult to believe that he would have approved the paradox of his political conquest. For, when eventually the Reform Bill was enacted, John Horatio stood for Parliament and was elected Stockport's first Member of Parliament – as a Radical.

The funds which the Home Office had guided John Horatio's way eventually paid even more unusual dividends. As a most successful QC, he was able to keep a splendid house in London at 100, Lancaster Gate. There he made a home for his serene and beautiful granddaughter, Constance. It was to this house that she brought her intended husband, Oscar Wilde. John Horatio was attracted by the charm of the clever young man. However, after Wilde's intention of marrying her became clear, Lloyd thought it proper to ask certain questions. It was then that he discovered that, like the fictional character Wilde was to create, Oscar had only his debts to depend on. The rich and generous John Horatio Lloyd settled £5,000 in trust on the happy young couple and advanced a mortgage of £500 for their first marital home.

# NOTES

## Chapter 1  The Soldier's Return

1 *The Times*, June 4th, 1860.
2 Surveys, 1739–1873, Doncaster BC Archives Department, Balby.
3 Colvin, 1978, p. 189, quoting T.D. Whitaker.
4 *Country Life*, vol. cxxii, no. 3426, November 1st, 1962.
5 'The Building of Campsmount,' *Yorkshire Archaeological Journal*, 1975, *47*, p. 121.
6 Pellew, vol. 3, 1847, p. 194; Byng to Pellew, August 15th, 1846.

## Chapter 2  Manchester

1 Engels, 1969, p. 79.
2 Napier, 1857, pp. 56–7.
3 *The Times*, August 24th, 1819.
4 Kay, J. 1832, p. 24.
5 Ure, 1835, p. 17.

6 Clapham, J. H., 'Some Factory Statistics of 1815–1816,' *Economic Journal, xxv*, 1915, p. 477.
7 *The Times*, August 10th, 1819.
8 Gaskell, 1833, p. 133.
9 Kay, 1832, p. 58.
10 From Report on the Sanitary Conditions of the Labouring Population of Great Britain (1842), quoted in Briggs (1963, p. 98).
11 HO 40.3, Byng to Under Secretary of State, December 7th, 1819.

## Chapter 3 The Determinant of Change

1 Cooper, 1983, p. 61.
2 Defoe, 1742, 3rd edn.
3 Crabtree, 1923, p. 60.
4 Defoe, 1971, p. 544.
5 Baines, 1835, p. 360.
6 Baines, 1835.
7 Ure, 1835, pp. 106–7.
8 Hobhouse, 1985, p. 17.
9 Engels, 1969, p. 43.

## Chapter 4 Land of Liberty

1 Holland, 1854, vol. 2, p. 214.
2 *Imperial Calendar*, 1817.
3 Sidmouth mss., Bragge to Addington, November, 1787; quoted in Ziegler (1965, p. 50).
4 *The History of the Times*, 1935, p. 235.
5 HO 41.2, Addington to Ethelston, December 20th, 1816.

## Chapter 5  The Major

1  HO 42.123, Mellor to Eddie, November 29th, 1812.
2  HO 42.163, *A Political Catechism dedicated to Omar, Bashaw, Day & Governor*, 1816.
3  HO 40.3, Chippindale to Warren, December 4th, 1816.

## Chapter 6  Orators

1  *Manchester Political Register*, January 4th, 1817. HO 42.158, 'AB' to Chippindale, January 15th, 1817.
2  HO 42.162, Hay to Beckett, March 23rd, 1817.
3  HO 42.163, enclosures to letters from Boroughreeve and Constables of Manchester to Sidmouth, January 18th, 1817.
4  Pellew, 1847, vol. 3, p. 165; report of Nadin.
5  Dunckley, 1893, vol. 2, pp. 19–21.
6  *Annual Register*, 1817.
7  HO 42.158, deposition of Charles Burke.
8  *Ibid.*, HO to Lord Mayor of London, January 20th, 1817.

## Chapter 7  Local Law

1  *Manchester Observer*, January 9th, 1819.
2  Engels, 1969, p. 95.
3  HO 42.186, Ethelston to Sidmouth, April 24th, 1819.
4  HO 42.188, Ethelston to Sidmouth, June 30th, 1819.
5  Taylor, 1819, p. 32.
6  Prentice, 1851, p. 34.
7  *Manchester Observer*, March 7th, 1818.
8  HO 41.4, Addington to Fletcher, November 28th, 1816.

9 See Glen, 1984, for a valuable picture of the growth of Stockport industry during this period.

10 HO 41.1, Beckett to Lloyd, May 23rd, 1816.

11 HO 41.2, Addington to Lloyd, December 15th, 1816.

12 HO 40.3, Lloyd to Under Secretary of State, January 7th, 1817.

## Chapter 8  A Leader

1 HO 42.163, extracts from inclosures to Lord Sidmouth, January 25th, 1817.

2 HO 40.3, deposition of PC before Ethelston, January 28th, 1817.

3 HO 41.2, Addington to Byng, February 13th, 1817.

4 Sidmouth mss., address of W. D. Evans discharging prisoners apprehended on March 10th, 1817.

5 HO 40.5/4a, examination of John Livesey, March 11th, 1817.

6 HO 40.5/4b, I.M. to Fletcher, March 5th, 1817.

7 HO 423.164, examination of John Livesey, March 6th, 1817.

8 HO 40.5/40, examination of John Livesey, March 11th, 1817.

9 HO 42.161, Lloyd to Beckett, March 3rd and 5th, 1817.

10 *Ibid.*, Nadin to Hay, March 3rd, 1817.

11 *Ibid.*, Fletcher to Addington, March 5th, 1817.

12 HO 42.164, 'AB' to Fletcher, March, 1817.

13 HO 40.5/4b, examination of William Bunting, April 5th, 1817.

14 *Ibid.*, examination of George Bradley Torr, March 14th, 1817.

15 *Manchester Mercury*, April 1st, 1817.

16 HO 42.168, Evans to Sidmouth, March 6th, 1817.

17 HO 42.161, Byng to Beckett, March 9th, 1817.

## Chapter 9 Blanketeers

1  *The Times*, January 19th, 1817.
2  *Ibid.*, March 10th, 1817.
3  *Ibid.*, July 16th, 1816.
4  HO 40, 5/4a, Hay to Sidmouth, March 10th, 1817.
5  Heginbotham, 1892, vol. 1, p. 80; dispatch of Captain Newton.
6  Most historical accounts of the Blanketeers' meeting wrongly suggest far lower figures. These are probably the result of the well-publicised account given by Samuel Bamford who states a figure of 4,000–5,000. But Bamford was not at the meeting, and of his own admission despised its organisers, disagreed with its aims, tried to persuade Middleton people not to attend and attempted to diminish even the little it achieved. There is no reason to disbelieve either Mr Hay's figure of 12,000 marchers in the early morning streets or Cowdroy's of at least 40,000 in St Peter's Field at the peak time. Hanshall, in the *History of Cheshire*, put the figure at 70,000 (Heginbotham, 1892, vol 1, p. 79).
7  HO 42.161, Byng to Sidmouth, March 15th, 1817.
8  HO 42.164, deposition of John Livesey, March 3rd, 1817.
9  HO 40.5/4a, examination of John Livesey.
10  HO 42.164, deposition of B9.
11  HO 42.161, Byng to Sidmouth, March 15th, 1817.

## Chapter 10 A Neat Movement

1  HO 40.5/4a, memorandum of meeting at St Peter's Church, March 10th, 1817.
2  HO 42.162, examination of William Parrish, March 11th, 1817.
3  *Manchester Chronicle*, March 15th, 1817.
4  HO 42.164, Hay to Sidmouth, March 10th, 1817.

5  HO 42.161, Lloyd to Beckett, March 11th, 1817.
6  Heginbotham, 1892, vol. 1, p. 80.
7  HO 42.161, Greaves to Sidmouth, March 12th, 1817.
8  HO 79.3, Beckett to Lloyd, March 15th, 1817.
9  HO 42.162, examination of Benjamin Mellor.
10  HO 42.164.
11  HO 42.161, Byng to Sidmouth, March 15th, 1817.
12  *Ibid.*, Byng to Beckett, March 10th, 1817.
13  *Ibid.*, Byng to Sidmouth, March 15th, 1817.
14  *Ibid.*, Sidmouth to Byng, March 12th, 1817.
15  HO 41.2, Sidmouth to Byng, March 13th, 1817.
16  HO 42.165.

## Chapter 11  Moscow out of Manchester

1  HO 42.168, deposition of no. 1, April 3rd, 1817.
2  HO 40 5/4a, Hay to Sidmouth, March 29th, 1817.
3  Dunckley, 1893, vol. 2, pp. 73ff.
4  Prentice, 1851, p. 101.
5  Dunckley, 1893, vol. 2, pp. 97–8.
6  HO 40.5/4b, Hay to Sidmouth, April 4th, 1817.

## Chapter 12  Oliver

1  HO 79.3, Addington to Ethelston, April 14th, 1817.
2  HO 42.164, Knight to Hadwin, April 30th, 1817.
3  HO 42.166.
4  HO 42.165, Byng to Addington, May 24th, 1817.
5  HO 79.3, Addington to Byng, May 27th, 1817.
6  HO 42.165, Byng to Sidmouth, May 28th, 1817.

7  HO 42.166, statement of J. Dickenson, June 16th, 1817. Willans was a Quaker, would not give evidence on oath, and made only a verbal statement about the affair.

## Chapter 13 Scoop

1  HO 42.165, report of unnamed agent, May 23rd, 1817.
2  Sidmouth mss., Sidmouth to Byng, March 13th, 1818.
3  In 1932 in 'The Truth About Oliver the Spy' (*English Historical Review*, 47, pp. 601–16), A. R. Fremantle makes, in the face of the evidence available in the Home Office files, what seems to me to be an inadequate case that Oliver's primary object was to convey information to his superiors and not to influence events. My conclusions as to the role of Oliver coincide broadly with those in the admirable account given in 1919 by J. L. and Barbara Hammond in Chapter 12 of *The Skilled Labourer*.
4  Sidmouth mss., Byng to Sidmouth, March 9th, 1818.
5  Cowdroy's *Manchester Gazette*, November 8th, 1817.

## Chapter 14 Yeomanry Cavalrymen

1  HO 42.166, Liverpool to Sidmouth, June 7th, 1817.
2  Prentice, 1851, p. 122.
3  HO 42.172, December 28th, 1817.
4  Anglesey, 1973, p. 73.
5  Belfield, 1959, p. 122.
6  Jerdan, 1852, vol. 2, p. 258.
7  Anglesey, 1973, p. 78.
8  Leary, 1898, p. 30.
9  *Ibid.*, p. 79.

10  HO 42.161, Molyneux to Sidmouth, March 11th, 1817.
11  HO 42.164, Hay to Sidmouth, April 26th, 1817.

## Chapter 15  This Intelligent Person

1  HO 42. 175, Lloyd to Hobhouse, March 9th, 1818.
2  Sidmouth mss., Sidmouth to Prince Regent, April 22nd, 1818.
3  Ziegler, 1965, p. 368.
4  Pellew, 1847, vol. 2, p. 90; Sidmouth to Lord Chancellor, November 13th, 1812.
5  Hobhouse, 1927, p. 53.
6  HO 79.3, Hobhouse to Lloyd, July 15th, 1817.
7  HO 42. 174, Lloyd to Hobhouse, February 22nd, 1818.
8  *Ibid.*, Lloyd to Hobhouse, February 19th and 23rd, 1818.
9  HO 42.175, Lloyd to Hobhouse, March 12th, 1818.

## Chapter 16  Strike and Action

1  HO 42. 178, Chippindale to Fletcher, July 25th, 1818.
2  HO 42.179, Lloyd to Hobhouse, August 12th, 1818.
3  HO 42. 178, Stockport magistrates to Sidmouth, July 16th, 1818. HO 41.4, Hobhouse to Stockport magistrates, July 18th, 1818. *Ibid.*, Hobhouse to Lloyd.
4  *Manchester Observer*, July 23rd, 1818.
5  HO 79.3, Hobhouse to Norris, August 4th, 1818. *Ibid.*, Hobhouse to Lloyd, August 7th, 1818. HO 42.179, Lloyd to Hobhouse, August 8th, 1818.
6  HO 42. 179, report to J. Lloyd, August 10th, 1818. *Ibid.*, Norris to Hobhouse, August 11th, 1818.
7  *Ibid.*, Lloyd to Hobhouse, August 20th, 1818.
8  *Ibid.*, August 22nd, 1818.

9   *Ibid.*, and August 24th and 26th, 1818.

10  HO 79.3, Hobhouse to Byng, August 24th, 1818.

11  HO 42.179, Norris to Hobhouse, August 28th, 1818.

12  HO 42.180, deposition of John Livesey.

13  *Ibid.*, Norris to Clive, September 2nd, 1818.

14  HO 79.3, Clive to Norris, September 4th, 1818.

15  *Ibid.*, Clive to Lloyd, September 5th, 1818.

16  HO 42.180, Lloyd to Hobhouse, September 3rd, 1818.

17  *Ibid.*, Lloyd to Hobhouse, September 7th, 1818.

18  *Ibid.*, Bagguley to Harrison, September 26th, 1818.

19  HO 41.4, Clive to Lloyd, September 9th, 1818.

20  *Ibid.*, October 24th, 1818.

## Chapter 17   The Populist

1   Cowdroy's *Manchester Gazette*, September 5th, 1818.

2   Sidmouth mss., Gray to Irving, February 7th, 1819.

3   *Ibid.*, Douglas to Sidmouth, July 18th, 1819.

4   *Manchester Observer*, April 24th, 1819.

5   HO 42.183, Lloyd to Hobhouse, January 20th, 1819.

6   *Manchester Observer*, January 18th, 1819.

7   HO 42.183, 'B' to Fletcher, January 19th, 1819; *Manchester Observer*, January 23rd, 1819; Wheeler's *Manchester Chronicle*, January 23rd, 1819; HO 42.183, Attorney General and Solicitor General to HO, January 29th, 1819.

## Chapter 18   Grand Theatre

1   *Manchester Exchange Herald*, January 26th, 1819.

2   HO 42.183, Norris to Sidmouth, January 26th, 1819; *ibid.*, Thornhill to Byng, dated January 19th, 1819; Wheeler's

*Manchester Chronicle*, January 23rd, 1819; *Manchester Exchange Herald*, January 26th, 1819; *Manchester Mercury*, January 26th, 1819; *Manchester Observer*, January 30th, 1819.

3 HO 42.180, Lloyd to Byng, September 14th, 1818.

4 HO 42.184, Lloyd to Hobhouse, February 16th and 17th, 1819.

5 *Ibid.*, Maclean to Byng, February 16th, 1819.

6 *Ibid.*, Bagguley to Harrison, March 28th, 1819.

7 HO 42.186, Lloyd to Hobhouse, April 15th, 1819; HO 42.187, Lloyd to Hobhouse, May 13th, 1819; *Chester Chronicle*, April 23rd, 1819.

## Chapter 19  Sharpening Swords

1 HO 42.188, Lloyd to Hobhouse, June 17th, 1819.

2 *Ibid.*, Norris to Sidmouth, June 16th, 1819.

3 HO 79.3, Hobhouse to Norris, June 12th, 1819.

4 HO 42.188, Lloyd to Hobhouse, January 15th, 1819.

5 *Ibid.*, Prescot to Bulkeley, June 17th, 1819; *ibid.*, notice of weavers presenting a petition to Reverend Mr Prescot, June 28th, 1819; HO 41.4, Hobhouse to Prescot, June 25th, 1819.

6 HO 79.3, Hobhouse to Norris, June 18th, 1819.

7 HO 42.189, July 3rd, 1819.

8 HO 79.3, Hobhouse to Byng, July 5th and 8th, 1819.

9 HO 42.189, Johnson to Hunt, July 10th, 1819.

10 Hunt, 1820, vol. 3, p. 593; HO 42.190, Harrison to Bagguley, July 22nd, 1819; HO 42.4, Hobhouse to Byng, Fletcher and other magistrates, July 23rd, 1819.

11 *State Trials*, p. 464.

12 HO 42.189, Lloyd to Hobhouse, July 19th, 1819; HO 42.190, Harrison to Bagguley, July 22nd, 1819.

13 Hunt, 1820, vol. 3, p. 593–4.

14 HO 41.4, Hobhouse to Norris, July 17th, 1819.

15  HO 42.191, pamphlet, *To The Public*, August 6th, 1819.

16  HO 42.190, Lloyd to Hobhouse, July 24th, 1819.

17  HO 42.1, Lloyd to Hobhouse, July 26th, 1819.

18  HO 42.190, Lloyd to Hobhouse, July 24th, 1819.

19  HO 41.4, Hobhouse to Lloyd, July 25th, 1819.

20  Wheeler's *Manchester Chronicle*, July 24th, 1819.

21  HO 41.4, Sidmouth to Lords Lieutenant, July 7th, 1819.

22  Taylor, 1819, p. 164.

## Chapter 20  An Uncertain Meeting

1  HO 42.190, Hay to Hobhouse, July 28th, 1819.

2  HO 79.3, Hobhouse to Hay, July 30th, 1819.

3  HO 41.4, Hobhouse to Norris, July 17th, 1819.

4  HO 42.190, poster published July 31st, 1819.

5  Duckley, 1893, vol. 2, pp. 142–4.

6  HO 42.191, Norris to Sidmouth, August 8th, 1819.

7  HO 41.4, Hobhouse to Horton, July 27th, 1819.

8  *Ibid.*, Hobhouse to Norris, August 3rd, 1819, *ibid.*, Sidmouth to Attorney General, August 3rd, 1819.

9  *Ibid.*, Hobhouse to Norris, August 4th, 1819.

10  HO 79.3, Hobhouse to Byng, August 3rd, 1819.

11  *Ibid*, Hobhouse to Norris, August 6th, 1819.

## Chapter 21  Decisions of Propriety

1 *Manchester Observer*, August 7th, 1819.

2 Hunt, 1820, vol. 3, p. 603.

3 HO 42.191, Wright to Hobhouse, August 9th, 1819.

4 *Ibid.*, Norris to Sidmouth, August 9th, 1819.

5 *Ibid*.

6 *Ibid.*, August 11th, 1819.

7 Dunckley, 1893, vol. 2, p. 145.

8 HO 42.191, 'To the Inhabitants of Manchester', August 11th, 1819.

9 *The Times*, August 16th, 1819.

10 Hunt, 1820, vol. 3, p. 608.

11 HO 42.192, Norris to Sidmouth, August 14th, 1819.

12 HO 41.4, Hobhouse to Norris, August 13th, 1819.

## Chapter 22   A Conflict of Interests

1 HO 42.178, Byng to Hobhouse, July 26th, 1818.

2 HO 42.180, Byng to Sidmouth, September 5th, 1818.

3 See, for example, HO 79.3, Hobhouse to Byng, February 19th, 1818; HO 42. 179, Byng to Hobhouse, August 16th, 1818; HO 42.180, Byng to Sidmouth, September 6th, 1818; HO 42.191, Byng to Hobhouse, August 5th, 1819.

4 HO 42. 188, Byng to Hobhouse, June 7th, 1819.

5 Frenz St Leger, 1986, p. 66.

6 *York Herald*, July 31st, 1819.

7 HO 42. 191, Byng to Hobhouse, August 2nd, 1819.

8 *York Herald*, August 7th, 1819.

9 *Ibid.*, August 14th, 1819.

10 HO 42. 189, Byng to Hobhouse, July 16th, 1819.

11 Leary, 1898, p. 69; Byng to Leicester, July 15th, 1819.

12 HO 42.190, Leicester to Byng, July 22nd, 1819.

13 HO 41.4, Sidmouth to Leicester, July 26th, 1819.

14 HO 79.3, Hobhouse to Byng, July 17th 1819.

15 HO 41.4, Hobhouse to Norris, July 27th, 1819.

16 HO 42. 191, Byng to Hobhouse, August 2nd, 1819.

17 *Ibid.*, August 2nd, 1819.

18 *Ibid.*, Hay to Sidmouth, August 9th, 1819; *ibid.*, Byng to Hobhouse, August 10th, 1819.

19 English mss., 1/21, Byng to Hay, August 10th, 1819.
20 HO 42. 191, Byng to Hobhouse, August 11th, 1819.
21 English mss., 1/20, Hay to Byng, August 10th, 1819.
22 HO 42. 192, Byng to Hobhouse, August 15th, 1819.
23 Leary, 1898, p. 73.
24 HO 42.191.


## Chapter 23  White Moss

1 Rylands mss., 2/86; Huish, 1836, vol 2, p. 291.
2 HO 42. 192, Lloyd to Hobhouse, August 14th, 1819.
3 HO 42. 191, Norris to Sidmouth, 15th August, 1819.


## Chapter 24  The Road to Manchester

1 *State Trials*, p. 1187.
2 Pellew, 1847, p. 260; Captain Edward Smyth's footnotes to Jolliffe's account.
3 *State Trials*, pp. 1094–5.
4 Dunckley, 1893, vol. 2, pp. 149–60; Bamford's description of the events of August 16th.
5 *State Trials*, p. 339.
6 *Ibid.*, p. 219.
7 *Ibid.*, p. 366.
8 Dunckley, 1893, p. 153.


## Chapter 25  Strangers on the Streets

1 Huish, 1836, p. 305.
2 *State Trials*, pp. 228–9. Huish, 1836, p. 314.

3 Huish, 1836, p. 310.

4 *State Trials*, p. 1195.

5 English mss., 2/67, Hay to Sidmouth, October 7th, 1819.

6 *State Trials*, p. 1188.

7 Sidmouth pps., Jolliffe to Estcourt, April 11th, 1845. Jolliffe describes himself in this letter as a lieutenant. However, his memory after a quarter of a century, on this point at least, is at fault. The Army List for 1820 shows that Jolliffe was not promoted Lieutenant until the week after Peterloo.

8 HO 42. 192, Lloyd to Hobhouse, August 18th, 1819.

9 *Manchester Observer*, August 10th, 1822.

10 National Army Museum, handkerchief: *The Broad Sword Exercise*, 1798.

11 *State Trials*, p. 1190.

12 Taylor, 1819, p. 58.

## Chapter 26  To the Hustings

1 Dunckley, 1893, p. 154.

2 *State Trials*, p. 190.

3 Bruton, 1921, pp. 65–6.

4 Taylor, 1819, p. 57.

5 Bruton, 1921, pp. 50–1.

6 HO 42. 182, magistrate's account of the events of August 16th, 1819.

7 *State Trials*, p. 354.

8 Taylor, 1819, p. 58.

9 *State Trials*, p. 1164.

10 *The Times*, August 19th, 1819.

11 Bruton, 1921, p. 40.

12 Taylor, 1819, p. 133.

13 Dunckley, 1893, p. 155.

14 Baines, 1851, p. 104.

15 *The Times*, August 17th, 1819.

## Chapter 27  Magisterial Decision

1 *The Times*, August 19th, 1819.

2 HO 42. 182, magistrates' account of the events of August 16th, 1819.

3 *State Trials*, p. 1152.

4 *Ibid.*, p. 1179.

5 *Ibid.*, p. 1178.

6 Taylor, 1819, p. 166.

7 *Ibid.*, p. 165.

8 Rylands mss., 1/26.

9 *State Trials*, p. 1179.

10 *Ibid.*, p. 1152.

11 *The Times*, August 19th, 1819.

## Chapter 28  The Charge of the Yeomanry

1 *State Trials*, p. 1195.

2 *Ibid.*, p. 368.

3 *The Times*, August 19th, 1819.

4 *Ibid.*, August 19th, 1819.

5 *State Trials*, p. 256.

6 Longford, 1972, vol. 2, p. 61.

7 Bruton, 1921, pp. 51–2.

8 Sidmouth pps., Jolliffe to Estcourt, April 11th, 1845.

9 Taylor, 1819, p. 188.

10 *Ibid.*, p. 135.

11 *Ibid.*, p. 121.

## Chapter 29  This is Waterloo for You

1  *State Trials*, p. 1199.
2  Pellew, 1847, vol. 3, p. 258.
3  Sidmouth, pps., Jolliffe to Estcourt, April 11th, 1845.
4  Hunt, 1820, vol. 3, p. 618.
5  *State Trials*, p. 1112.
6  Taylor, 1819, p. 178.
7  *State Trials*, pp. 1102–3.
8  Taylor, 1819, p. 85.
9  *Ibid.*, p. 61.
10  Sidmouth pps., Jolliffe to Estcourt, April 11th, 1845.
11  Dunckley, 1893, vol. 2, p. 157.

## Chapter 30  A Degree of Peace

1  *The Times*, August 19th, 1819.
2  Longford, 1972, vol. 2, p. 61.
3  *History Today*, 1988, *38*, p. 26; Mutrie to Moore, 19th August, 1819.
4  HO 42.192, Ethelston to Sidmouth, August 16th, 1819.
5  Prentice, 1851, p. 163.
6  HO 42.192, Lloyd to Hobhouse, August 18th, 1819.
7  HO 41.4, Sidmouth to Hay, August 18th, 1819.
8  HO 42.192, Norris to Sidmouth, August 17th, 1819.
9  *Ibid.*, unsigned letter to HO, August 21st, 1819.

## Chapter 31  Relief

1  Rylands mss., 2/67, Hay to Sidmouth, October 7th, 1819.
2  *State Trials*, p. 1262.

3  HO 42.192, Hulton to Sidmouth, August 25th, 1819.
4  Rylands mss., 21/41. Pearson to Hay, August 31st, 1819.
5  Prentice, 1851, pp. 167–71.
6  English mss., 1/25a, summary of Casualties of Troops on 16th August, 1819.
7  HO 42.192, Lloyd to Hobhouse, August 18th, 1819.
8  *Ibid.*, Norris to Sidmouth, August 19th, 1819.
9  HO 41.4, Hobhouse to Norris, August 19th, 1819.
10  HO 79.30, Hobhouse to Byng, August 20th, 1819.
11  Sidmouth pps., Bloomfield to Sidmouth, August 19th, 1819.
12  HO 41.4, Hobhouse to Hulton, August 23rd, 1819.
13  Bruton, 1921, p. 70.
14  Prentice, 1851, p. 165.

## Chapter 32  Sustaining a Reputation

1  *State Trials*, pp. 10–12.
2  Sidmouth mss., Sidmouth to Liverpool, October 1st, 1819.

## Chapter 33  Great Expectations

1  Taylor, 1819, p. 124.
2  *Ibid.*, p. 64.
3  *The Times*, September 14th, 1819.
4  Taylor, 1819, p. 93.

## Chapter 34  Responsibility

1  HO 42.191, Hay to Hobhouse, August 1st, 1819.
2  HO 79.3, Hobhouse to Norris, July 26th, 1819.

3 HO 41.4, Hobhouse to Norris, August 4th, 1819.

4 HO 79.3, Hobhouse to Byng, August 3rd, 1819.

5 *Ibid.*, Hobhouse to Norris, August 6th, 1819.

6 HO 42.194, Byng to Hobhouse, September 5th, 1819.

7 *Ibid.*, Hobhouse to Byng, September 7th, 1819.

8 HO 42.192, L'Estrange to Byng, August 16th, 1819; HO 41.4, Sidmouth to Byng, August 18th, 1819.

9 Taylor, 1819, p. 185.

10 Sidmouth pps., Redesdale to Sidmouth, August 19th, 1819.

## Chapter 35 Technological Imperatives

1 Taylor, 1819, p. 49.

2 HO 42.194, Lloyd to Hobhouse, November 2nd, 1819.

3 Thompson, 1968, p. 748.

4 Ure, 1835, p. 17.

5 See Boorstin, 1978, p. 93.

6 Hobhouse, 1985, p. 157.

7 Quoted in Boorstin, 1978, p. 1.

8 Hobhouse, 1985, p. 156.

## Chapter 36 The Good Men Do

1 Dunckley, 1893, vol. 2, p. 329.

2 Quoted by Osborne, 1972, p. 152.

3 HO 41.4, Hobhouse to boroughreeve and constables, Manchester, February 5th, 1818.

4 Leary, 1898, p. 82.

5 *Country Life*, October 8th, 1987, pp. 104–7.

6 Aspinall, 1949, p. 17.

# BIBLIOGRAPHY

## Primary Sources and Contemporary Publications

*English Manuscripts* (John Rylands University Library of Manchester)

*Hay Papers* (Chetham's Library, Manchester)

*Home Office Departmental Papers* (Public Record Office)

*John Lloyd's Scrapbook* (Stockport Public Library)

*Lloyd Papers* (Chester Record Office)

*Relief List, Peterloo Relief Committee, Account Book* (John Rylands University Library of Manchester)

*Sidmouth Papers* (Devon Record Office)

*Surveys, 1739–1873* (Doncaster Borough Council Archives Dept.)

*An Impartial Narrative of the Late Melancholy Occurrences in Manchester* (Fisher, Liverpool, 1819)

*Annals of Sporting*

*Annual Register*

*Army List*

Aston, J., *Picture of Manchester* (Aston, Manchester, 1816)

Burdett, F., *Memoirs of the Life of Sir Francis Burdett* (Sherwood, Neely and Jones, London, 1810)

*Imperial Calendar*

[Philips, F.] *An Exposure of the Calumnies Circulated by the Enemies of Social Order, and Reiterated by their Abettors against the Magistrates and the Yeomanry Cavalry of Manchester and Salford* (2nd ed, London, 1819)

*Racing Calendar*

*Report of the Proceedings in the Cause Redford v. Birley and Others* (Wheeler, Manchester, 1822)

[Taylor, J.] *Peterloo Massacre, containing a Faithful Narrative of the Events which preceded, accompanied and followed the fatal Sixteenth of August, 1819, on the area near St. Peter's Church, Manchester, Including the Proceedings which took place at the Inquest at Oldham on the body of John Lees*, edited by An Observer (Manchester, 1819)

## Newspapers

London *Times*
London *Courier*
*Leeds Mercury*
*Manchester Chronicle*
*Manchester Exchange Herald*
*Manchester Gazette*
*Manchester Mercury*
*Manchester Observer*
*Manchester Political Register*
*York Chronicle and Advertiser*
*York Herald*

## Secondary Sources

Adams, A. (ed.), *A Memoir of Edmund Cartwright* (Adams and Dart, Bath, 1971)

Albrecht, J., *Major Hugh Hornby Birley* (Rawson, Manchester, 1925)

Angelsey, The Marquess of, *A History of the British Cavalry Vol. I, 1816–1850* (Leo Cooper, London, 1973)

Aspinall, A. (ed.), *The Diary of Henry Hobhouse* (Home and van Thal, London, 1947)

Aspinall, A., *Politics and the Press* (Home and van Thal, London, 1949a)

Aspinall, A., *The Early English Trade Unions* (Batchworth Press, London, 1949b)

Baines, E. (jun.), *History of the Cotton Manufacture in Great Britain* (Fisher, Fisher and Jackson, London, 1835)

Baines, E. (jun.), *The Life of Edward Baines* (Longman, Brown Green and Longmans, London 1851)

Baines, T. and Fairbairn, W., *Lancashire and Cheshire: Past and Present* (Mackenzie, London, 1869)

Belchem, J., *Orator Hunt* (Clarendon Press, Oxford, 1985)

Belfield, E., *Annals of the Addington Family* (Warren, Winchester, 1959)

Berg, M., *The Age of Manufactures (1700–1820)* (Fontana, London, 1985)

Black, R., *Horse-Racing in England* (Bentley, London, 1983)

*The British Turf* (Biographical Press, London, 1906)

Boorstin, D., *The Republic of Technology* (Harper and Row, New York, 1978)

Briggs, A., *Victorian Cities* (Odhams, London, 1963)

Bronowski, J., *William Blake and the Age of Revolution* (Routledge and Kegan Paul, London, 1972)

Bruton, F. (ed.), *Three Accounts of Peterloo* (Manchester University Press, Manchester, 1921)

Cartwright, F. (ed.), *The Life and Correspondence of Major Cartwright* (Henry Colburn, London, 1826)

Chapman, S., *The Lancashire Cotton Industry* (Manchester University Press, Manchester, 1904)

Clapham, J. H., 'Some Factory Statistics of 1815–16,' *Economic Journal, xxv*, 1915, pp. 475–7.

Clark Amor, A., *Mrs. Oscar Wilde* (Sidgwick and Jackson, London, 1983)

Codrington, G. R., 'Yeomanry Cavalry', *Journal of the Society of the Army Historical Research, ix*, 1930, p. 134.

Cole, G., *The Life of William Cobbett* (Collins, London, 1924)

Colvin, H., *Biographical Dictionary of British Architects* (John Murray, London, 1978)

Connor, T., 'The Building of Campsmount,' *The Yorkshire Archaeological Journal, 47*, 1975, pp. 121–32.

Cooper, B., *Transformation of a Valley, The Derbyshire Derwent* (Heinemann, London, 1983)

*Court Leet Records of the Manor of Manchester* (Manchester, Blacklock, 1889)

Crabtree, J., *Richard Arkwright* (Sheldon Press, London, 1923)

Darvall, F., *Popular Disturbances and Public Order in Regency England* (Oxford University Press, London, 1934)

Daumas, M., *A History of Technology and Invention* (John Murray, London, 1980)

Defoe, D., *A Tour Through the Whole Island of Great Britain* (Penguin Books, Harmondsworth, 1971)

Derry, T. and Williams, T., *A Short History of Technology* (Oxford University Press, 1960)

*Dictionary of National Biography*

Dunckley, H. (ed.), *Bamford's Passages in the Life of a Radical and Early Days* (2 vols) (Fisher Unwin, London, 1893)

Ellman, R., *Oscar Wilde* (Hamish Hamilton, London, 1987)

Engels, F., *The Condition of the Working-Class in England* (Panther, London, 1969)

Fitton, R. and Wadsworth, A., *The Strutts and the Arkwrights* (Manchester University Press, 1958)

Fletcher, J. S., *The History of the St. Leger Stakes, 1776–1901* (Hutchinson, London, 1902)

Fremantale, A. F., 'The Truth about Oliver the Spy,' *English Historical Review, xlvii*, 1932, p. 601

Frenz St Leger, M., *St. Leger, The Family and the Race* (Phillimore, Chichester, 1986)

Froude, J., *Thomas Carlyle: A History of His Life in London*, vol. I (Longmans Green, London, 1885)

Frow, R. and Frow, E., *Karl Marx in Manchester* (Working Class Movement Library, Manchester, 1984)

Galloway, J., *Recollections (1804–1894)* (Manchester Public Libraries)

Gash, N., *Lord Liverpool* (Weidenfeld and Nicolson, London, 1984)

Gaskell, P., *The Manufacturing Population of England* (Baldwin and Craddock, London, 1833)

Gibbon, E., *A History of the Decline and Fall of the Roman Empire* (Oddy, London, 1809)

Glen, R., The Working Classes of Stockport During the Industrial Revolution. Unpublished PhD thesis, University of California, Berkeley.

Glen, R., *Urban Workers in the Early Industrial Revolution* (Croom Helm, London, 1984)

Greville, C., *The Greville Memoirs* (3 vols) (London, 1874)

Hammond, J. L. and Hammond, B., *The Town Labourer, 1760–1832* (Longmans Green, London 1917)

Hammond, J. L. and Hammond, B., *The Town Labourer, 1760–1832* (Longmans Green, London 1919)

Hamshall, A., *The History of the Country Palatine of Chester* (Fletcher, Chester, 1823)

Heginbotham, H., *Stockport: Ancient and Modern* (2 vols) (Sampson Low, Marston, 1892)

Hills, R., *Richard Arkwright and Cotton Spinning* (Priory Press, London, 1973)

Hobhouse, H., *Hobhouse Memoirs* (Wessex Press, 1927)

Hobhouse, H., *Seeds of Change* (Harper and Row, New York, 1985)

Holland, Lord, *Memoirs of Whig Party during my Time* (2 vols) (Longman, London, 1852 and 1854)

355

Holland, Lord, *Further Memoirs of the Whig Party* (John Murray, London, 1905)

Huish, R., *The History of the Private and Political Life of the late Henry Hunt, Esq., M.P.* (John Saunders, London, 1836)

Hume, D., Smollett, T. and Farr, E., *The History of England* (George Virtue, London, nd)

Hunt, H., *Memoirs* (3 vols) (Dolby, London, 1820)

Hunter, J., *South Yorkshire*, (E.P. Publishing Ltd, East Ardsley, 1974)

Jerdan, W., *The Autobiography of William Jerdan* (4 vols) (Arthur Hall, London, 1852)

'John Horatio Lloyd', *Proceedings of the Institution of Civil Engineers*, 78, 1883/1884, p. 450.

Kay, J., *Moral and Physical Conditions of the Operatives employed in the Cotton Manufacture in Manchester* (J. Ridgeway, London, 1832)

Krieger, E., *Bygone Manchester* (Phillimore, London, 1984)

Lawson, P., 'Reassessing Peterloo,' *History Today*, 1988, 38, p. 26

Leary, F., *The Earl of Chester's Yeomanry Cavalry, 1797–1897* (Ballantyne Press, Edinburgh, 1898)

Longford, E., *Wellington* (Weidenfeld and Nicolson, London, 1972)

Marcus, S., *Engles, Manchester and the Working Class* (Weidenfeld and Nicolson, London, 1974)

Markham, F., *Napoleon* (Weidenfeld and Nicolson, London, 1963)

Marlow, J., *The Peterloo Massacre* (Rapp and Whiting, London, 1969)

Marshall, L. S., *The Development of Public Opinion in Manchester, 1780–1820* (Syracuse University Press, Syracuse, 1946)

Messinger, G., *Manchester in the Victorian Age* (Manchester University Press, Manchester, 1985)

Napier, W., *The Life and Opinions of General Sir Charles James Napier* (John Murray, London, 1857)

Osbourne, J., *John Cartwright* (Cambridge University Press, 1972)

Orton, J. *Turf Animals of York and Doncaster* (Southeran, York, 1841)

Parkinson, R., *On the Present Condition of the Labouring Poor in Manchester* (Simpkin, Marshall, London, 1841)

Patterson, M., *Sir Francis Burdett and his Times, 1770–1844* (Macmillan, London, 1931)

Pellew. G., *The Life and Correspondence of the Right Honourable Henry Addington, First Viscount Sidmouth* (3 vols) (John Murray, London, 1847)

Prentice, A., *Historical Sketches and Personal Recollections of Manchester Intended to Illustrate the Progress of Public Opinion from 1792 to 1832* (Charles Gilpin, London, 1851)

Read, D., *Peterloo, the 'Massacre' and its Background* (Manchester University Press, Manchester, 1958)

Redford, A., *The History of Local Government in Manchester* (3 vols) (Longmans Green, London, 1939)

*Reports of State Trials, Vol. I., 1820–1823* (HMSO, London, 1888)

Singer, C. *et al.*, *A History of Technology* (vols 1–5) (Clarendon Press, Oxford, 1958)

Slater, S., *Bury Folk at Peterloo* (Bury and District Local History Society, Bury, 1974)

Slugg, J., *Reminiscences of Manchester Fifty Years Ago* (Cornish, Manchester, 1881)

*The History of the Times*, ' "The Thunderer" in the making, 1785–1841' (London, 1935)

Thompson, E., *The Making of the English Working Class* (Pelican Books, Harmondsworth, 1968)

Ure, A., *The Philosophy of Manufacturers: Or an Exposition of the Scientific, Moral and Commercial Economy of the Factory System of Great Britain* (Charles Knight, London, 1835)

Walmsley, R., *Peterloo – The Case Reopened* (Manchester University Press, Manchester, 1969)

Ziegler, P., *Addington* (Collins, London, 1965)

# INDEX

# INDEX